John O'Farrell is a former comedy scriptwriter for such shows as *Spitting Image*, and *Smith And Jones*. He is the founder of the satirical website *NewsBiscuit* and can occasionally be spotted on such TV programmes as *Grumpy Old Men*, *Newsnight Review* and *Have I Got News For You*.

Apart from that he has published three novels, a memoir and two other collections of his Guardian column. His most recent book is *An Utterly Impartial History of Britain*, (or 2000 Years of Upper Class Idiots In Charge). His work has been translated into around twenty languages, although how the gags work in Norwegian is anyone's guess.

Acclaim for John O'Farrell:

Global Village Idiot

'His writing is entertaining and irreverent...refreshingly self-deprecating' *The List*

'The best of his humorous weekly columns for the *Guardian* over the past two years . . . O'Farrell writes the best topical gags in the business . . . this book is a lot of fun'
Big Issue in the North

'O'Farrell has a witty and engaging style and writes with warmth, passion and humanity. His best articles deal with the big issues of our time and our reactions to them: poverty, bigotry, religious intolerance and the move of *Match of the Day* to ITV . . . Measured and assured, O'Farrell's style does not obscure his arguments and the book is an effortless read'
Waterstones Books Quarterly

www.rbooks.co.uk

Things Can Only Get Better

'This book intrudes into private grief and my first instinct was to resist it. The 18 years of misery under the Conservatives was my own unique journey of suffering and how could anyone else understand it, least of all write about it? Alastair Campbell, Tony Blair's Press Secretary, had a similar initial reaction to Nick Hornby's *Fever Pitch*, a book that did for football what this book, in its way, will do for politics ... O'Farrell gently persuades us that what we felt is what he felt ... The book is very funny, constantly using a hard wit to puncture the pretensions of a Labour Party that was always about to win. And he positions himself adroitly as an outsider, approaching every political situation with a mixture of unease and clumsiness that always endears'
Philip Gould, *The Times*

'His quirky memoir transcends its subject matter, while pinpointing with self-deprecating honesty how it felt to be young, middle-class and left-wing under Thatcher. It's also very funny – he has Alan Bennett's eye for the hilarity lurking behind bourgeois pretence'   *Mail on Sunday*

'Excellent ... Whatever your politics *Things Can Only Get Better* will make you laugh out loud'   Angus Deayton

'With all the lunacy of Labour politics in the Eighties and early Nineties, it's a must-read for those who cast their first votes after 3 May 1979; twentysomethings may chuckle at the clever, funny absurdity of their near-elders. But in this post-ironic age, forty-plus-somethings might be forgiven for seeing not an apologia, but a *mea culpa* for the inanities of young, middle-class Labour supporters who delayed the jubilation of 1997 by nearly two decades'   *Observer*

'Very funny and much better than anything he ever wrote for me'   Griff Rhys Jones

'Very funny book ... about the pity and the misery and the sheer boredom of being a devoted Labour supporter'
Simon Hoggart, *Guardian*

'*Things Can Only Get Better* is really about growing up, but growing up in the Labour Party at a time when it was going through convulsive change. It is a hilarious read . . . a very funny account of O'Farrell's odyssey from left-wing innocence to a mature acceptance of New Labour'
The Mirror

'The whingeing memoirs of a snivelling leftie. The man should be shot'   Jack Dee

'The funniest book I have read for two and a half years'
Arthur Smith

May Contain Nuts

'O'Farrell is a consistently humorous writer with an acute ear for the absurdities of middle-class pretension. It's hard to fault his satire on competitive parenting or his conclusions regarding social inequalities'   *Mail on Sunday*

'O'Farrell is one of the best contemporary satirists in the business and he has middle-class pushy mothers down to a tee in this latest toe-curling, hackle-rising chronicle of hyper-parenting. The one-liners are sublime and the comedic situations utterly hilarious. Don't miss this'
Daily Record

'O'Farrell has scored a bullseye with this satirical salvo. Taps into Middle England's neuroses with terrific wit'
The Herald

This is Your Life

'Excellently done. O'Farrell gives an extra squirm to the traditional English comedy of embarrassment'
Sunday Times

'A splendid satire on our celebrity-hungry age'   *Daily Mail*

'Very funny'   *The Times*

The Best a Man Can Get

'Punchline fuelled, relentless humour . . . I don't think a woman is going to get much closer to the workings of a man's mind than this. Giggling several times a page with plenty of out-loud laughs is guaranteed. Is John O'Farrell funny? Very' *The Mirror*

'So funny because it rings true . . . Packed with painfully well-observed jokes' *The Times*

'This is SO good . . . so insightful about men, women, love and parenthood that you read every page with a wince of recognition. Fab, fab, fab' India Knight

'A hilarious confessional narrative. This wickedly observed page-turner lets bachelor-nostalgia joyride to its absurd conclusion . . . Piquant and irreverently sardonic' *Literary Review*

Also by John O'Farrell

Non-fiction
THINGS CAN ONLY GET BETTER
GLOBAL VILLAGE IDIOT
I BLAME THE SCAPEGOATS

Fiction
THE BEST A MAN CAN GET
THIS IS YOUR LIFE
MAY CONTAIN NUTS

and published by Black Swan

I Have a Bream

A HUNDRED FUNNY NEWSPAPER COLUMNS AND ONE THAT'S JUST STUPID

John O'Farrell

BLACK SWAN

TRANSWORLD PUBLISHERS
61–63 Uxbridge Road, London W5 5SA
A Random House Group Company
www.rbooks.co.uk

I HAVE A BREAM
A BLACK SWAN BOOK: 9780552773591

First published in Great Britain
in 2007 by Doubleday
a division of Transworld Publishers
Black Swan edition published 2007

Copyright © John O'Farrell 2007

John O'Farrell has asserted his right under the Copyright, Designs and Patents Act 1988 to be identified as the author of this work.

This book is a work of non-fiction.

A CIP catalogue record for this book
is available from the British Library.

Addresses for Random House Group Ltd companies outside the UK
can be found at: www.randomhouse.co.uk
The Random House Group Ltd Reg. No. 954009

The Random House Group Limited makes every effort to ensure that the
papers used in our books are made from trees that have been legally
sourced from well-managed and credibly certified forests. Our paper
procurement policy can be found on www.randomhouse.co.uk

Typeset in 11/16.25pt Giovanni Book by
Falcon Oast Graphic Art Ltd.

Printed and bound in Great Britain by
Cox & Wyman Ltd, Reading, Berkshire.

2 4 6 8 10 9 7 5 3 1

This book is printed on recyclable paper made from wood pulp bleached using non-toxic chemicals and sourced from trees grown in wholly sustainable forests. The little squirrels living in these trees were rehoused in another equally desirable part of the woods and were given lots of nuts and berries. The nuts and berries were GM-free and fell naturally from plants grown using wholly organic methods on land already set aside for non-intensive agricultural methods as laid down in the Woodland Charter. That agreement itself was printed on recyclable paper made from – oh fuck it, look we're all going to die anyway, so what's the point? I mean I've got a load of empty gin bottles clinking away in the back of the car that I still haven't taken down to the recycling centre especially after last time when I ran over a bloody badger and anyway it all gets shipped off to China to be incinerated, thus in fact adding to global warming so what can you do, I mean, have you seen the damage a badger can do to the front of a Renault Scenic? Oh and er, all the jokes are recycled as well.

Contents

I Have a Bream

Introduction

I just knew I'd get thrown out of the Optimism Society.
Everyone was saying, 'I wonder who's going to be made
Head Optimist' and I was like, 'Yeah, well, you can bet it's
not going to be me . . .' It's like I always know that the
toast is going to land butter side down. Though I suppose
I do put butter on both sides of my toast. Yet even if I'd
been the most wildly optimistic fantasist I would never
have dreamed that one day I'd be paid to write every week
for the *Guardian* about whatever subject took my fancy.
Back when I was nervously handing in inky scraps of comic
writing to my university magazine, the sum total of my
ambition was that (a) the editor might possibly publish
my satirical poem about the nuclear arms race being bad
and (b) someone would draw this damning invective to the

attention of Ronald Reagan, who'd then feel compelled to resign on the spot. Never once did I imagine myself having the privilege of writing a weekly column in a national newspaper – for a start it took me more than a week to type anything up.

But for five years I had my own slot in the paper I'd grown up with. Of course, when you finally get into such a position, you are supposed to affect an air of long-suffering martyrdom at the enormous responsibility and hard work involved. I remember once attending an event at the Edinburgh Festival featuring two leading sitcom writers discussing their lofty calling.

'Comedy writing,' opined one of them, rather pompously, 'is the hardest job in the world.' He paused for dramatic effect, but the moment was rather punctured by Arthur Smith, who was chairing the discussion.

'What about those divers who have to fix the legs of oil rigs into the bed of the North Sea?'

'What?'

'Well, that must be a pretty hard job. Is comedy writing harder than swimming down to the seabed and fixing oil platforms into position?'

'Well, that's hard in a different way – but you see comedy writing is incredibly difficult because—'

'What about a farmer in sub-Saharan Africa where there is no rain and your field might be full of old landmines – that must be quite hard?'

'Er, well, that's hard for logistical reasons. Whereas

comedy writing is incredibly arduous because of the ephemeral nature of—'

'Neurosurgeon? Bereavement counsellor? United Nations peacekeeper in the middle of war-torn Bosnia? Or just teacher? That's an incredibly hard job . . .'

Comedy writing is like any other creative medium – it looks difficult if you can't do it. I stare in wonderment at artists who can accurately sketch whatever they see before them; it's as if they've performed some sort of impossible magic trick. Or a sculptor who's carved a tender human form from a block of old stone. Or Tracey Emin's unmade bed . . . actually no, I think, 'Well, that's just rubbish; a child could have done that.' Of course there were times when it seemed impossible to conjure up some comic magic from the depressing string of grim news stories. Some protestors get through House of Commons security and throw purple flour all over the Prime Minister: 'Well,' you are left thinking, 'what could possibly be funny about that? The flour was packed inside condoms, you say? And they'd been given special seats *in front of* the security barrier? Hmm, there must be something funny about this story somewhere? What else have we got – Mark Thatcher involved with a Third World coup, the builders at the Athens Olympics aren't going to finish the swimming pool in time, God, are there no funny stories in the newspaper this week??'

To be honest I still can't believe what an incredible treat it was to sit down on a Friday morning and think, 'What shall I write about this week; what has happened in the

15

world that is funny, ridiculous or mad?' In fact thinking about it now I must have been insane to give the column up; I should ring them now and say I've changed my mind, that I'd like my old job back. (Hmmm, that's strange – there's an electronic voice saying that my number is automatically blocked.) Five years was a long time to write the same sort of column, in fact reading them back now I can see myself getting a little bit frustrated with the formula, and so during the last few months I began experimenting with a few different genres: police witness statements, exam papers, Home Office application forms, etc. I had wanted to call it a day immediately after the 2005 election, but the *Guardian* asked if I would stay on until July and consequently I wrote my final farewell piece once everyone was away on holiday. People still say to me how much they enjoy my column every week, which I suppose means that when people said that two years ago, they weren't reading it then either. When I left I did get a gratifying number of kind letters and not all of them shared the same postmark as my parents. But I must confess that I am still a little embarrassed at repackaging all these pieces that many people have read already. I only thought it worth doing because people have been so very complimentary about my previous two collections of columns: 'I keep them by the bed and when I can't get to sleep, I pick up your book and I find myself nodding off in no time . . .' or 'When I'm flying and worried about the plane crashing, I get out your book and the idea of plummeting to my death doesn't seem so bad anymore . . .' Even hip young street kids using the latest slang have described the books as really 'bad' and there can be no greater compliment than that. So it is with an eye on nostalgia, posterity and – perhaps more than anything – the money that I present this, the final collection of 'a hundred funny columns and one that's just stupid' (the Wiki-torial piece is the one I was thinking of). I hope you enjoy flicking through and reading the odd piece and failing to remember the news story to which it must have been referring. Please believe me when I say that the mad cow/Mrs Thatcher joke was incredibly original at the time. You also get a few other bits and pieces that you won't have read before and of course a free DVD of *Love Actually* (in participating stores only). It may be that you are still standing in the bookshop, reading this introduction trying to decide whether to splash out or not. All I can say is that if your dad really liked *Things Can Only Get Better* and you don't know what to buy him for his birthday, and you can't afford a big hardback about the Nazis and they've just called your plane on the Tannoy, well then, this is the book for you. An easy, dip-in-and-out collection that tackles the really big questions of our age such as 'Can the planet sustain indefinite economic growth?' (no, but if you buy petrol from the pump with a green handle apparently that makes everything all right) and 'Is the nation state irrelevant?' (only if it's Belgium), and most perplexing of all – how come a Blackberry isn't compatible with an Apple?

If on the other hand you have got this far and decided

not to buy this book then I quite understand, but can I ask that you place this copy somewhere prominent, perhaps on the tables in the politics section. Only please – don't put me on top of Ann Widdecombe. Really – once was more than enough.

J. O'F
February 2006

Losing my Maidenhead

A personal account of the best way to lose an election campaign

There are many different ways to have a mid-life crisis. Track down your ex-girlfriends and narrowly avoid getting arrested for stalking. Invent some incredibly successful career as a millionaire film producer to post on Friends Reunited. Or you could do what I did at the 2001 general election; go back to your home town to stand for Parliament and then be rejected en masse by the people you grew up with. In a perverse way there was something quite therapeutic about it.

I'd had a happy childhood growing up in Maidenhead. Summers would be spent playing by the banks of the Thames trying to catch minnows or hepatitis. More innocent childhood fun could be had beside the stream in the town centre; boys from my school developed a game similar to Poohsticks, except that instead of daintily dropping little twigs into the stream they chucked in supermarket trolleys. But by the time I was eighteen I was more than happy to leave this comfortable backwater of the M4 corridor, never, I thought, to return.

But twenty years later I wrote a book about Labour's eighteen miserable years of opposition; recounting how I had helped the Labour Party lose elections at every level, and I suddenly felt this masochistic urge to go back and add one final defeat to the tally. As I had recalled in the opening chapter of *Things Can Only Get Better*, I'd actually stood for Labour in Maidenhead once before, when I was the candidate at my school's mock election. In 1979 I had polled a total of thirty-five votes. I was hoping for at least double that this time. But to paraphrase an old gag, you only stand for election in Maidenhead twice. Once on the way up and once on the way down. It was great to be back.

The first hurdle was the local Labour Party's selection meeting. Out of all the contenders present I can honestly say that I looked the most like a Parliamentary candidate, delivered the best speech, gave the most informed answers and by the end I was quietly confident of winning the nomination – particularly since the other bloke hadn't actually turned up. The lack of competition for this seat confirmed my suspicions that the rest of the Labour movement did not consider this constituency to be the next major scalp on the governing party's hit-list. Someone told me that the seat was Labour target number

181. Considering there were only 162 Tory MPs I sensed that I wasn't going to be a priority.

My parents still lived in the Maidenhead constituency, in the once pretty village of Cookham, where the charming English scenes painted by Stanley Spencer were now obscured by rows of 4x4s blocking the view. On Bonfire Night the villagers at Cookham Dean hadn't put Guy Fawkes on their bonfire, they burnt effigies of Tony Blair instead. I marked them on the canvass cards as 'Probable Against'. The tanned Moschino-wearing inhabitants of this corner of Middle England somehow give the impression of having been nouveau riche for ten successive generations. My challenge was to knock on their doors and persuade them to vote for a minimum wage of £4.20. Lucky for them that their Croatian nannies couldn't understand a word of English.

The constituency also boasted a sprinkling of celebrities for me to canvass. Ulrika never seemed to be in, no matter how many times I volunteered to call on that address. Paul Daniels was magically absent. Timmy Mallet bashed me on the head with his 'Wacaday' inflatable hammer. How I laughed! But generally the message I got on the doorstep was 'No, sorry, we're not political', which my phrasebook translated as 'We're voting Conservative.' Occasionally I would meet with hostility. 'I'm not voting for the socialists!' said one angry man, though on reflection this could have been a statement of support for New Labour. At least I could rely on Jim, I thought, as I knocked on the door of an old school friend I hadn't seen for twenty years. 'No, John, I'm a Conservative now,' he said in a flat monotone. 'It's the tax regulations, you see.'

'Jim – what happened? You were always Labour at school.' Or was it really Jim? Maybe there was a body-shaped pod in the basement, where the Maidenhead Conservatives grew loyal supporters to replace the human beings that used to inhabit the town. Another name from school leapt out at me from the electoral roll as I canvassed the rougher side of the town. Oh no, not Hemmett! I hadn't seen him since I was fifteen when he punched me for 'being tall'. Nervously I inched up the front path of this council house. 'What if I can't answer his policy questions?' I fretted. 'He might give me a Chinese burn.' I rang the doorbell and his grown-up son opened the door to this disastrously scruffy flat clutching a can of Special Brew. It appeared that the Hemmetts had mastered the art of sleeping rough, *indoors*.

'Hello, is Kevin in?' I asked.

'No, he's in Reading.'

'Oh not to worry, maybe I'll catch him another time.'

'No he's in Reading jail. Six months. I'll tell him you was looking for him though,' he said, reading my name off the leaflet.

'Er, no, no – really, best not to worry him, forget all about it. Please, he can have my dinner money, I won't tell.'

Another council tenant said he would vote for me if I got him his free NHS glasses. I listened to his complex account of how some bureaucrat had said he was not entitled to free spectacles because he was on disability benefit as opposed to income support. All I could say was 'That doesn't sound right, I'll see what I can do', and conscious that I was unrealistically getting his hopes up I emphasized that I didn't have any actual power, I was only a candidate. 'Yeah, but when you get elected you'll be able to do something, won't you?' he said hopefully and I felt a pang of guilt that I would be letting down this supporter by failing to become his MP.

Because anyone who was familiar with the politics of the place knew that I couldn't win. Maidenhead had been Tory since the Bronze Age; the reason Stonehenge wasn't built at Littlewick Green was because they couldn't get planning permission unless the design included a conservatory. These were the terms under which I was standing; I was interested in being a candidate and in representing the Labour Party and if by some freak result I got elected I would do the job. But both the local party and I knew that I wasn't going to win and after years of desperately caring about the result of every campaign this was actually rather liberating. 'Remember, every vote *doesn't* count.' 'Vote for me, or not; whatever you think best.' 'May the best man come third.' Actually I was the only man, not counting the fringe candidates. I answered a question about women-only shortlists at a girls' sixth form, explaining why I thought we needed affirmative action to get more women into Parliament, and as I was speaking I could almost hear them thinking, 'But you're a *bloke*. Basically you're saying vote for one of the other two.'

Another few dozen voters lost; I was really getting into my stride now.

The local MP was Conservative front-bencher Theresa May, famous not so much for her vision of a new and fairer Britain as much as her Russell and Bromley footwear. Those were the shoes I was trying to step into. 'Get rid of May this May', I put on my pamphlet. And then they postponed the election a month because of the foot-and-mouth epidemic. 'Get rid of May this June', proclaimed my hasty rewrite. Hmm, it's not as if it was that strong first time round.

In the age of the Internet and emails, much of the election could be fought hiding behind a computer screen. For months before the election, I concocted press releases featuring photos of me doing something somewhere in the town, which I would send to the *Maidenhead Advertiser*. My hit rate was pretty high, though I discovered that the less overtly political the story, the more chance it had of being published; strangely there was little interest in my exciting and I felt rather surprising exclusive entitled 'Labour candidate criticizes Conservatives'. After Budget Day, for example, I spent many hours researching exactly how much extra cash each local school was getting from the Chancellor, the precise amounts going to Maidenhead's health centre, Thames Valley Police, the local hospitals; all there alongside a digital photo of me chatting away with Gordon Brown. It took me a couple of days to get the precise figures together from various Treasury and Labour Party websites and all right, so the photo was a couple of years old, but I felt it was my finest work to date. When I got the *Advertiser* on Friday, I flicked through in search of my *magnum opus*. Page 3: 'They're cycling to Sicily!' Fair enough, big charity story, they couldn't leave that out. Page 7: 'What's on in Maidenhead', always a busy quarter-page or so. Page 9: 'Planning permission for shed refused' – and then three hundred pages of overpriced houses. I couldn't believe it – not even a couple of lines! But that's just the way these things work. If your story happens to occur at the same time as a major world drama – the death of Diana, 9/11 or 'Planning permission for shed refused' – then you're always going to get knocked off the news pages.

But over the months leading up to the campaign my investment in a primitive digital camera had definitely given me the edge – nothing makes a story easier to print than having the picture already provided. On one occasion I organized an instant demo with half a dozen party members and a hastily drawn placard saying 'Save the Town Hall'. The local Liberal Democrats had spent weeks on this campaign, petitioning and leafleting, and now they were furious that just because I'd supplied a photo, I was the candidate who got his face in the local paper. But that was the trouble with the Liberals in Maidenhead: they were all substance and no spin. The only other local media seemed to be BBC Radio Berkshire, which featured local traffic news and agony aunts who helped distressed callers from Ascot talk through their domestic traumas such as 'Ocado have delivered non-organic avocados again'. I was invited on to take part in a local election phone-in, and confided to my parents that I was a little nervous about all the callers being hostile. But I dutifully sat on the panel, with the Liberal candidate on one side and Theresa May on the other, and did my best to defend the government's record on issues about which I knew very little. And then a voice came on the line that I recognized as my mother. My mum had phoned up to say that she agreed with John O'Farrell. 'Sorry, caller, we didn't catch your name,' said the host.

'It's Mrs O'F— it's Joy; Joy from Maidenhead.'

'And on which issue did you say you agree with John O'Farrell?'

'On all of them. Every issue,' she confirmed, managing to restrain herself from asking what time I'd be home for tea. An hour later I was standing in my parents' kitchen saying, 'Mum! I'm thirty-nine, I can manage!'

'But the others were all against you, dear.'

'Mum, they are the other candidates; they're supposed to be against me! When Gordon Brown is doing *Election Call* on the five economic tests for Euro-convergence, he didn't have his mum ringing up and saying, "Och, I agree with Gordon!"'

But my parents were very supportive during the campaign, even having a go on the Tannoy bolted to the top of my brother's Mondeo on election day. 'Vote for my son!' my mum said proudly. She passed the peculiarly shaped microphone to my dad who seemed momentarily confused by the technology as he held the long handset to his ear and said, 'Hello?' And then the voters of Maidenhead were treated to the image of a rusty old Mondeo plastered with Labour stickers driving along booming out the message 'No, darling, it's not a telephone – you speak into it – tell them to vote for John!' Looking back it's hard to believe that we failed to take the seat.

Election day itself involved calling on all the doors of the Labour voters who had promised to vote for me. That was a busy hour or so. Back in the lonely committee rooms the polling numbers of electors who'd already voted were methodically read out, only to be endlessly greeted by the word 'against' from the person checking our records. Eventually the system detected a vote that had been cast by a supporter and I felt a rare flush of pride. 'Oh yes . . .' she said, 'number 21a, the Johnsons; they're very good, they always come out for us.'

'What?' I exclaimed. 'So you actually know every Labour voter by name, do you?'

It might seem pointlessly quixotic to throw your energies into the Labour Party in a place such as Maidenhead. But local politics was only part of the picture for the inspirational band of party members who worked so hard during the campaign. Being people who cared and wanted to make a difference, they were also busy with all the other things that helped the local community to function: some were school governors or helped at youth clubs, many worked for local charities, fundraising for Mencap or answering the phone for the Samaritans.

(Although, in Maidenhead, working for the Samaritans is probably the best way to keep in contact with your fellow Labour activists during election time.)

A few hours later I found myself standing on the platform in the historic setting of the Magnet Leisure Centre. The result had been obvious since the 3-D bar chart of counted ballot papers showed me lagging well behind the other two parties, and even though this had been what I expected to happen, as I listened to the official figures I couldn't help but be disappointed that I hadn't done better. The whole experience confirmed to me that despite being something of a political anorak, I was never really cut out to be a politician. For one thing I really don't fancy working that hard, but I was also useless at remaining on message; if I disagreed with a Labour policy I couldn't help saying so. When the returning officer showed all the candidates the spoilt ballot papers, one of them bore the scribbled message 'No-one is left wing enough.' Theresa May burst out laughing and said, 'I don't think they can have met John O'Farrell', which I took as an unintended compliment.

I got a measly 15 per cent of the vote, but I was still flattered that 6,577 people were prepared to put their trust in me. In a way we were all winners that night. Actually no, Theresa May was the winner; I was definitely the loser. But something had happened earlier in the evening which had dented my affected indifference. In the final hours I had been knocking on doors in the area where our support was least abysmal when I found myself face to face with the disabled voter who had shown such faith in my ability to help him. 'Oh it's you,' he said. 'Remember I said I'd only vote for you if you got me my free glasses.'

'Yeah, look, I'm sorry, but like I said, I'm only a candidate, I'm not even on the council or anything but I sent off a letter about it, I did, really.'

'I know you did and look, I've got them!' And triumphantly he held his free reading glasses aloft.

'What? You mean, it worked?'

'Yeah. They'd made a mistake and your letter made them check.' And he demonstratively put his new bi-focals on to re-read me the correspondence. In a split second I saw what it was all about. Being an MP wasn't about going on *Newsnight* to defend a bad set of figures or pretending to support a policy you disagreed with. It wasn't about constantly knocking the other parties or asking syco-phantic questions in the House of Commons. It was about winning little victories for ordinary people every day of the week. Battling away on a thousand fronts for unglamorous causes that would never appear in the paper or get you promoted. It was a couple of hours before I would be defeated at the count and suddenly I under-stood the purpose of being elected.

And ever since I lost my Maidenhead I have had a far greater respect for politicians and the work they do on our behalf, for the ludicrously long hours they work for little or no thanks. I was exhausted after weeks of campaigning and I hadn't even been trying my hardest to win. But immediately after a gruelling campaign all the elected politicians would be straight back to the House of Commons, to slog away for endless hours in Westminster before dashing back to their constituencies to give up their weekends as well, finding what time they could to squeeze in their families in between. And for this are they are relatively poorly paid, held in contempt and mocked by smug outsiders like me. After years of getting easy laughs at their expense writing for *Spitting Image* and *Have I Got News for You*, I couldn't help but feel a pang of guilt at my own contribution to the electorate's lazy cynicism. I drove away from the Thames Valley with a sense of optimism and a renewed faith in politics and our system of government. That one voter's free glasses had made me see it all so clearly. Despite all its faults our democracy really does work; we should respect and treasure it. From now on, I'm going to stop making facile disparaging gags, I decided. That's it; no more scorn or cynicism. Why do we have this terrible blame culture, I wonder? I blame the politicians.

Not *that* Madonna picture, stupid

25 July 2003

I don't know much about art. I don't even know what I like. Obviously I have heard of Raphael, I'm not that un-cultured. He was one of them Teenage Mutant Ninja Turtles, wasn't he? And don't even ask what I thought when I heard they'd paid millions for a picture of Madonna.

This week the Heritage Lottery Fund paid eleven million pounds towards the purchase of Raphael's *Madonna of the Pinks*, prompting a fierce debate about art, heritage and money. 'What a waste of lottery cash,' said Nicholas Soames. 'That money could have been far better spent on Winston Churchill's notes to the milkman.' Meanwhile the lucky vendor, the Duke of Northumberland, has promised to put the cheque on public display so people can come and admire it. 'It's a wonderful figure, isn't it? Look at the way all those noughts seem to just go on and on . . .' Lottery ticket buyers will be delighted that their money has been put to such good use. 'My biggest hope was that the lottery fund secured that little Raphael painting for the National Gallery. Oh, and maybe that I won the rollover jackpot, but that was a secondary consideration, obviously.'

The purchasing committee did their best to defend their decision to spend eleven million pounds on a painting only eleven inches tall but the truth is that they were just as surprised as anyone else when it arrived. That's the trouble with buying things on the Internet. The box of cornflakes is much too big and the Renaissance painting turns out to be tiny. 'Well of course I didn't look at the bloody measurements, did I? I just saw it on eBay and somehow imagined it a lot bigger. Now let's draw lots for who's going on *Newsnight*.' Despite all the criticism, I'm not sure we really want to start determining the relative merits of paintings according to their size. By that logic the Tate Modern would be full of huge murals of UDF gunmen in balaclavas firing volleys over the Shankill Road, as William of Orange waved a flag saying 'No Surrender'.

The problem with the visual arts is that it only takes a second to look at a picture, so everyone feels qualified to offer some sort of instant judgement. You can't offer an on-the-spot analysis on the merits of a classic novel, because it takes much longer to watch the BBC adaptation. But before an opinion is offered on a great painting it should be studied at length, it should be seen in its original form – we should stand there in the gallery staring at it for ages, trying to pretend to know what we're looking for. 'Hmmmm – wonderful light,' says the man next to you, and just in time you stop yourself saying, 'Yes, and positioned so perfectly above the picture.' Eventually of course an American tourist will come and stand right in front of you, which is your chance to slip off to the gift shop to buy a couple of Monet fridge magnets to show everyone you made the effort to do something vaguely cultural.

Everyone would agree that it is important to preserve paintings. Hundreds of works have been lost down the years; for example, one of Reubens's models kept tearing up his pictures in tears, saying, 'Why do you have to make me look so fat, fat, fat?' And with both California and London vying for this painting I don't think that was a particularly helpful compromise suggestion from the Deputy Prime Minister that we snip the painting down the middle and have half each.

But was it so important to keep this painting in the United Kingdom? Most people seem to think it was a waste of money, but then public opinion will always say spend the money on something else. Democracy isn't just about going along with what most people think when stopped by pollsters in the high street. There has to be debate and informed discussion and that is what took place on the Heritage Lottery Fund; that is why we delegate these decisions to them. Perhaps we should revert to choosing which paintings hang in the National Gallery according to a straightforward popularity test. The prerecorded talks on those little handsets would be rather different. 'This famous work is of course far from naturalistic – it is not normal for dogs to play poker or smoke cigars. Observe the bulldog with the whisky bottle secretly passing the ace of spades under the table, while the boxer sweats anxiously at the way the betting chips are piling up. Now moving on to our next classic acquisition, notice how the lady tennis player is not actually wearing any knickers . . .'

You too can have an ego like mine

1 August 2003

Sacramento, California, 2004. An attempt to rectify the budget crisis hits a new stalemate as Democrats declare themselves unable to vote for cuts to key welfare programmes ensuring that the new budget will fail to secure the two-thirds majority required under state law. Suddenly the Governor hits upon a solution. From within his enormous bionic forearm springs a robotic rocket launcher which blows the abstaining liberals out of the plate-glass window and into the burning oil refinery below. 'This politics business is easy,' says Governor Arnie as all other motions are passed unanimously by his Republican mutant droids who now control the Senate.

At some subconscious level this is what the supporters of Arnold Schwarzenegger believed would have happened if he had become Governor of California. That he would have solved the problems of real life just as easily as the battles he wins in his films. *Terminator 3* is released today, with Arnie still promising, 'I'll be back', although *Terminator 4* might be a little different if Arnie decides to go into local politics.

'Help, there's been a terrible disaster, Governor!'

'Vot is it?'

'There aren't enough canapés for your "Women in Business" state luncheon.'

'OK – vith my incredible robotic powers I vill, er, ring up some more caterers.'

Of course, you have to admire the sheer physical hard work and single-mindedness of a world-class bodybuilder like Arnie Schwarzenegger. It takes an incredible amount of effort to get your ego up to that size. You have to constantly push yourself to the front and pump up your own importance. Tantalizing us with talk about a foray into politics was just another exercise in Arnie's ego workout. Strange that the announcement of his decision not to run should coincide with the film's release date.*

The prospect of the Terminator gaining genuine political power might seem like some terrifying joke if we hadn't already passed that point a couple of decades ago. Since Ronald Reagan became President there have been all sorts of show business stars standing for office across

* Schwarzenegger of course subsequently reversed this decision and successfully ran for the governorship of California. Fortunately he could not run for the presidency since he was not born in the United States, but was created by a crazed scientist out of indestructible metal at some point in the distant future.

America. Sonny Bono split from Cher and hooked up with the US Congress, Clint Eastwood rode into Carmel and had the mayor's badge pinned on his chest, and World Wrestling Federation star Jesse Ventura won the governorship of Minnesota by two falls and a submission.

As a result things have rather changed at New York's famous High School for the Performing Arts. The bright-eyed hopefuls skip across the polished floor in their leotards and leg-warmers and sing, 'Fame! I want to live for ever! Fame! I want to get to grips with the federal budget deficit!' Instead of learning Shylock's plea from *The Merchant of Venice*, they perform Bill Clinton's denial of sexual impropriety or Richard Nixon saying 'There must be no whitewash at the White House.' Hard to im-agine even the finest thespian making those speeches sound convincing.

The truth is that you always had to be a good actor to be an effective politician, convincing others that you fervently believed some murky half-developed solution to an impossibly complex problem. 'I'm voting for Stanley Baldwin! He moved me to tears with his impassioned speech about the problem of the Gold Standard.'

Perhaps the popularity of showbiz candidates stems from the death of community; voters feel more comfort-able with the familiar personalities from their TV screens than some unknown wannabe from their own neighbour-hood. But if we are worried about people becoming disengaged from the democratic process then surely it is a good thing that as many famous role models as possible think politics is a career worth pursuing. If the Terminator is really not going to run in California, maybe some other Hollywood hero should step into the breach. 'Governor Buzz Lightyear' has a ring to it.

And with all these stars fighting it out in the debating chambers of the United States they'll need someone special to keep them all in order. This is why Jerry Springer is considering running for the Senate. That would wipe the smile off Arnie's face, the moment when the American public were confronted with a few disturbing truths about him on live TV.

'And now on *Jerry Springer* – "My dad was a Nazi stormtrooper and I invited Kurt Waldheim to my wedding."'

'Vot is dis, Jerry?'

'And also, Arnie, we have several women here who accuse you of serial groping and drug use. Do you deny all this?'

It would be fun to watch the ugly on-screen mêlée as the studio guards rushed to break it up: three burly security officers suddenly spotting they were up against a former Mr Universe and all simultaneously thinking, 'Er, maybe we'll just leave this one to Jerry . . .'

iMac-ulate conception

22 August 2003

This week the world's first Internet sperm bank baby was born to the proud mother and her partner, an Apple Power Mac G4. Mum was reported as being delighted with her healthy little boy, although apparently her computer had been rather hoping for a little palmtop. This iMac-ulate conception was made possible thanks to a British website called ManNotIncluded.com (although you can apparently get much cheaper sperm on eBay). The historic nativity marks another milestone in the startling advancements in embryology which merits serious reflection and it is certainly not at all just an excuse to do a load of smutty jokes. The donors earn £40 for their semen, so for a teenage boy it must seem like a more attractive prospect than doing a paper round. The donor is guaranteed anonymity, but that hasn't stopped countless women getting themselves pregnant and then crying to their friends, saying, 'He doesn't ring, he doesn't email . . .' In fact the dawn of the Internet sperm bank has fuelled the notion that men are now officially surplus to requirements. Women can become pregnant without a partner, raise the children, earn the money and run the home. Yeah, but who's going to shoo that enormous hornet out of the holiday villa then?

Of course, the Internet has been associated with sperm production for some time, though usually by men on their own. Now, as I understand it, people can actually get sperm down the Internet, though I imagine you'd have to have broadband.* Of course, receiving sperm via a modem is not as straightforward as it sounds; sometimes the computer crashes and then a message pops up on the screen saying, 'Sorry, this has never happened to me before.' Furthermore ManNotIncluded.com cannot guarantee that all their customers will definitely get pregnant. The fertility of many of the women involved is falling off sharply, and if they are still using Windows 95 then it's even more of a long shot. Critics fear that if the idea of the Internet sperm bank really takes off it could precipitate the death of the traditional high street sperm bank, where the tellers knew your name and valued your custom.

* This must be the greatest breakthrough since the Corby Trouser Fax, which allowed you to send off your crumpled trousers to the dry cleaners and get them faxed straight back to the office washed and ironed.

People are scared of this latest development because it involves the word 'Internet'. But the idea of women deliberately getting pregnant by men they don't know is nothing new; this development just saves the mother-to-be enduring a whole evening pretending to be impressed by his golfing anecdotes. The history of parenting is a chronicle of accidents, unwanted babies and unsuitable parents but we talk about carefully planned IVF as if it was crossing some new moral frontier. Imagine if Henry VIII had had access to all the human fertilization options that are available today. He would not have had to divorce Catherine of Aragon and split from Rome, and England would still be a Catholic country and then, er, well we wouldn't have all the human fertilization options we have today.

I'm sure that before the mother of the world's first Internet sperm bank baby went ahead with this controversial procedure there must have been much soul searching and many sleepless nights. But finally she plucked up courage and announced, 'I'm going to do it. I'm going to type my credit card details onto the Internet.' Rather predictably the religious right have opposed this latest development. 'The whole procedure is horrible,' said a spokesman for Life. 'Children are far too important to be the result of sperm bought by email.'

No-one is saying that children are not important; the point is that everyone should have the right to have them. If new technology makes it easier for lesbian couples and single women to become pregnant, then surely it is better that they have sperm that is screened for AIDS and hepatitis and a few computer viruses as well. The alternative for single women who desperately want children is to get pregnant by some complete stranger they just met at the speed-dating party, or, perhaps even more difficult, to ask a male friend to be the anonymous father to their child. How many women could trust a man this much? A bloke I once knew was asked to do this by a female colleague; to sleep with her 'as an act of friendship'. All summer they had countless 'acts of friendships', in the office stationery cupboard in the morning, in the park at lunchtime. For months and months this man said that he had willingly given up his time and energy 'as an act of friendship'. He never told her he'd had a vasectomy. He said it didn't seem that important.

On the road to ruin

29 August 2003

This week Wykeham Street in Scarborough was named as the worst rat run in Britain. Estate agents are already adjusting their details: 'House for sale in award-winning street'. The council had tried putting in a pedestrian crossing, but when the little green man came up, it showed him desperately dodging lots of little speeding cars. There is also a little old lady with a lollipop sign to take children across when there is a gap in the traffic. (No luck yet and it turns out that when she started waiting she was only twenty-seven.)

A 'rat run' sounds like some sort of charity jog by rodents keen to improve their image, but it is of course a side street that suffers from being heavily used by through-traffic as a short-cut. You may have seen people indulging in this anti-social practice when you were cutting down a side street as a short-cut. Apparently the problem has got worse since local authorities spent millions of pounds deterring traffic from using the main roads in the town centre. Who could have possibly foreseen that all the cars would just cut down all the back streets instead? It makes you want to go into those traffic planners' offices to complain, except you can't go straight into their offices any more; you have to go up two flights of stairs, along the corridor, back down the fire escape and in through the side door.

Local authorities have tried all sorts of traffic calming measures over the past couple of decades, most notably the infamous road hump that was brought in mainly just to annoy Jeremy Clarkson. These were introduced after intensive lobbying from Kwik-Fit Replacement Exhausts, though the companies that repair dented bodywork thought that those narrow metal pillars were a much better way of slowing down traffic. Speed humps spread very rapidly in many urban areas and they say the Monaco Grand Prix will never be the same again. In the past, successive governments have also been very effective at slowing down speeding motorists by introducing another concept known as 'the traffic jam'. This enormously popular method of slowing cars soon spread to all major roads, and after a ten-year pilot scheme on the M25 is now used on all of Britain's motorways as well. Statistics show that if you laid all the cars in Britain end to end, then, well, things wouldn't be any different.

Yet the adverts always show the latest new car speeding up some sweeping mountain road, as if this was the typical driving experience of the British motorist. Why is everybody going up that mountain; is there an Arndale Centre at the top of it? Car adverts should have to have quickly spoken disclaimers underneath the exciting footage: 'Warning; being stuck in the Hangar Lane gyratory system may not be as stimulating.'

Now the 'four wheels good, two legs bad' lobby have a new ally in the shape of the shadow minister for transport. Tim Collins is the Tories' own Toad of Toad Hall, though not as good-looking. He is so anti-pedestrian that I wouldn't put it past him to go up behind blind people at pelican crossings and go 'Beep-beep-beep-beep!' This summer he unveiled the Tories' new approach to transport and declared that the next Conservative government will raise the speed limit on motorways and scrap speed cameras. They are not going to take them down, they just expect them to be demolished by all the speeding hot hatches careering off the road out of control. Road humps will also be purged. It's worth noting that road humps are also opposed by undertakers, presumably because they take away business.

Thousands of people are killed on Britain's roads every year and yet this barely registers on the national news agenda. If some mystery new illness from the Far East had killed over 3,000 people last year, the country would be in a state of total panic. But we are so used to road death statistics that there is an airbag inside our heads protecting us from the shock. Any backlash against the anti-car movement should be resisted; we have to stop ourselves using cars for unnecessary journeys. Don't drive to the gym to use the stairmaster. Walk the kids to school next week, it'll be much better for their health to get some exercise and breathe in all that fresh carbon monoxide. Only use your car if you are totally convinced it can be justified on environmental grounds; so one trip a month to the bottle bank is all you're allowed. We have to get out of our cars and onto public transport. After all, what is the point of sitting in a car for hours and going nowhere? Isn't that what trains are for?

Hey, let's call in the UN!

5 September 2003

Lord Hutton was at a dinner party the other evening and somebody said, 'So have you been following all this Hutton Inquiry stuff?' And Hutton replied, 'Well, I started to read it when it began, but I can't be bothered with it all any more.'

'I know what you mean, there's just so much of it, isn't there? Pages and pages in the bloody newspaper – we're bored to tears with it all.'

'Somebody mentioned it at work the other day but everyone was so uninterested that we ended up chatting about the cricket instead.'

'What work was that?'

'Oh, you know, the Hutton Inquiry.'

The reason why the deliberations at Courtroom 73 are even less thrilling than ITV's *Rosemary and Thyme, The Gardener Detectives* is because it's all a complete sideshow. The real issue is 'Did America and Britain have a legal right to go to war without the backing of the United Nations?' An inquiry into that would be a short one: it doesn't take long to say, 'Nope.'

Yet strangely, this week has seen a U-turn in George Bush's attitude to the United Nations. At last he has seen the error of his ways and is now keen to see UN troops deployed in Iraq as soon as possible. How wonderful it is to have an American President committed to international law and global democracy. French fries are back on the menu! Thank God, says Mrs Bush, no more Californian champagne!

Of course some sceptics out there will probably say that Bush only wants an international force involved now because he's realized that lots of American soldiers are still being killed and this is damaging his popularity rating in the run-up to next year's Presidential election. Honestly, the cynicism of some people never ceases to amaze me! As it happens, he was prepared to put American soldiers in the most dangerous parts of Iraq, but this plan was abandoned when he was told that there was no way of ensuring that these troops would be Democrat voters from Florida. George Bush is being very magnanimous by bringing in the UN at this most dangerous time. Indeed, his concern for international co-operation is such that he is prepared to hand over all sorts of other jobs of great importance to non-Americans. 'Say, guys, NASA are a bit worried that the Challenger might blow up again, so we think it would be a wonderful gesture to have some United Nations astronauts on board for the test run. Oh, and we need someone to go into the gangland of downtown Los Angeles and take all the guns and the flick-knives off the Crips and the Bloods – as a gesture of goodwill we would like to hand this job over to the United Nations as well. Oh, and the jury in that big Mafia trial have all had death threats – I think what the global community needs now is UN jurors for Mafia trials.'

Having not been involved in the decision that created the lethal chaos in Iraq, it's hardly surprising that the UN are unenthusiastic about being brought in to clear up the mess. It's the same argument as before with the positions completely reversed. George Bush is saying, 'We cannot simply bypass the United Nations on Iraq', and Kofi Annan is insisting, 'No, please, the UN has failed to fulfil its historic purpose, so I really feel this job must fall to America.'

In fact many other countries have already been persuaded to deploy troops, including Lithuania, Honduras and Mongolia. Even the Albanian army are now in Iraq. Ha! What chance do the enemy stand now? The Albanians have promised to bring in their army's mobile unit as soon as they get her back from the donkey sanctuary. Oh, and the Lithuanian army has promised to bring his friend. But the response has been less positive from more-developed countries where the national leaders have answerphones. In a few months' time they'll bump into Bush and say, 'Oh George hi, apparently you left some sort of message about us sending troops to Iraq or something? You know what, I think the message must have been wiped off, because we would have been there like a shot if we'd known. Such a shame, remind me to switch to voicemail . . .'

If the United Nations really wants to do something for the world they should leave George Bush to clear up the mess he created in Iraq and let him suffer the electoral consequences at the polls next year. This is a win–win situation: don't deploy any troops and help bring about regime change in the rogue state of America. 'Oh, they won't get rid of me that easily,' says Dubya. 'I'm too clever for that. I'm George W. Bush. The "W" stands for "smart".'

Arms fairs – good or bad?

12 September 2003

There are times in politics when you have to take a personal stand on a point of principle, even if what you believe may alienate many friends and allies. Well, in the week that Europe's largest arms fair has been held in London I am prepared to really stick my neck out and and say, 'Arms fair? Booo! People who sell cluster bombs? Bad!' This controversial position has been adopted after a good deal of rigorous analysis so that I could be totally confident that my opposition was logical and intellectually watertight.

'Is it likely that Britain is going to completely abolish all its armed forces?'

'Well, no . . .'

'So should those troops have the right equipment to allow them to carry out their duties effectively?'

'Er, well, up to a point, I suppose . . .'

'So is it not reasonable for Britain and other countries who seek to defend themselves to have an arms fair at which they can see the range of equipment on offer?'

'Um, well . . . BOOOO! DOWN WITH THE ARMS FAIR!'

Geoff Hoon opened this four-day event on Tuesday and amazingly was still clinging on as Defence Secretary when it ended. Back at Downing Street he asked the Prime Minister why the fair was staged at this particular time. 'Oh, no particular reason,' said Tony. 'So you didn't demonstrate the new British-made bulletproof vest like I suggested?'

Other defenders of the event say that they are responding to every country's right to self-defence. You just have to read the visitors' book from previous years to see how many satisfied customers have bought these defensive weapons to help make the world a safer place. Mr S. Hussein of Baghdad wrote, 'What a great event! I bought dozens of missiles on sale or return. You sell them and then with my brand-new missile launcher I return them back to you.'

Mr M. Sukarnoputri of Indonesia writes, 'I have spent billions here, even though the weapons are sold on the understanding that I will not use them to attack less-powerful neighbours or oppress my own people. That's okay because I was only ever intending to use my new helicopter gun ship as a novelty paperweight.'

Most shoppers need a bit of advice to help them decide what to buy; they can be spotted hovering nervously next to a piece of military hardware trying to catch the eye of the assistant.

'Excuse me, I've just been put in charge of my country's army and I need a "troop carrier" apparently.'

'Well, how about this one, sir? This is the Piranha III armoured fighting vehicle featuring a BAE Systems AMS II turret.'

'Right, is that a good one?'

'Well, it's got a 120mm mortar.'

The minister tries to nod as if this sounds impressive but can't help feeling hopelessly out of his depth. 'Okay, well there's a few others I want to look at, so I may come back.'

The range of goods on offer is quite extensive. There's a Challenger 2 battle tank which costs a million pounds (plus another thirty-five quid for the number plates). There are British-made assault weapons on sale, although if you notice your enemies placing an order for these then you can always buy the secret weapon guaranteed to jam these rifles known as 'a grain of sand'. The chief buyer for the Swiss army was particularly excited about the little penknife with the bottle opener and magnifying glass. You can even buy a warship if you can face pushing it past the till and then finding you have to get it off the trolley so they can swipe the bar code annoyingly placed right underneath. Basically you can buy anything you want as long as you've got an Uncle Sam loyalty card.

Outside, demonstrators tried to make their voices heard as best they could considering they'd clearly spent a lot less money when they went to their own Peace Protestors Fair. 'This Tannoy can issue a stinging rebuke from behind a police barrier. It has a little button here for extra distort; completely inaudible at fifty yards.'

Britain is one of the world's biggest exporters of arms (second only to either the United States or Western Samoa; I can't remember which it was now, definitely one of those two). The apologists for this sorry state of affairs say that hundreds of thousands of British jobs are dependent on this industry. Well, thousands of people make a living out of burglary and mugging but you don't get ministers giving the opening speech at the crowbar and flick-knife fair. 'Britain's criminals lead the way with – oi, come back with that microphone.' The more an economy is dependent upon the sale of arms, the less that country will be inclined to see that peace prevails around the world. Instead of opening the event last Tuesday, Geoff Hoon should have declared the arms fair closed and then fallen on his sword. Except, of course, if it was a British-made sword, it probably would have snapped in two.

I have a bream

19 September 2003

It is time for a new literary prize in Britain: to be awarded to the author not nominated for the Booker Prize who has written the most transparent article criticizing the type of books shortlisted for the Booker Prize. 'Where oh where are the historical novels?' writes a famous author of historical novels. 'Why oh why have the judges completely overlooked Computer Manuals?' declares the author of *Windows X-P for Beginners*. 'Surely the time has come to acknowledge novels that explore subjects like Martin Luther King's pet fish,' writes the author of *I Have a Bream*. Why can't these authors write what they really think when they see the Booker shortlist? It would make a refreshing change to read an eight-hundred-word piece that just said 'Bastards! Bastards! Bastards! Bastards!'

Literary prizes are like beautiful baby competitions: everyone is convinced that their own offspring is quite obviously the most deserving winner. Writers are particularly egocentric creatures. If some poor woman is interviewed weeping on the news about how her husband's been kidnapped by Colombian bandits, any normal person would watch with sympathy and listen to what she is saying. But an author would be feverishly scanning the spines on the bookcase behind her thinking 'Typical! Not one of my books on her shelves! Look, she's got bloody Mandela's *Long Walk to Freedom* all right, but where is my hilarious account of the problems of having a second home in Gloucestershire?'

This year's Booker shortlist has been criticized for being too obscure, too international and too highbrow. It is certainly true that major bestsellers are unlikely to get onto the list, but the rules are quite clear on this: 'No pink covers with a scratchy drawing of a scatty girl carrying too much shopping while talking on a mobile phone, no authors' names in embossed gold lettering and no moving deaths from cancer of a secondary character halfway through.' Populist books already have a great prize of their own – it's called the bestseller lists. If your book gets to number one then that information will be plastered across the cover of your next book. And if you failed to get to number one, then not to worry because your publishers will choose a cover which is strikingly similar to a book that did. The point about having a highbrow book prize is that it encourages people to buy more literary works. All right, so they won't ever get around to reading any of them, but you can't have everything. The books that are for sale in the supermarkets don't need any more help; but the Booker Prize has the chance to bring some other books that are worth reading to our attention. We are still a long way from the day that we ask the teenage shelf stacker in Sainsbury's where we might find Gabriel García Márquez. 'Er. . . Magical Realists . . . aisle seven, next to tinned fruit. Do you want a hand carrying that Vikram Seth to the car?'

Or perhaps the real reason why bestsellers are rarely nominated is that none of the Booker judges have the courage to admit that they couldn't finish any of the difficult books either. 'I thought the opening paragraph was very interesting.'

'Yes, I was about to quote from chapter one as well.'

'Very literary, I thought. I liked the way he put lots of describing words in front of his doing words.'

Maybe they should get us interested earlier in our lives by having the Pre-school Booker Prize.

'I was very impressed with the elliptical narrative of the Biff and Chip story.'

'Indeed, the almost Proustian irony of Floppy the dog getting all muddy again straight after his bath. Such ineluctable bathos!'

All awards in the arts are by their nature bogus because they only reflect the opinion of one small group of judges (except the Sony bronze award given for third-best radio comedy in 1996; that was entirely valid). But they are still worthwhile and necessary if they bring more people to books. People who knock the Booker Prize underestimate what a great love of literary fiction we have in this country. Whether it is Jane Austen's *Sense and Sensibility* starring Emma Thompson and Kate Winslet or more modern literature like *High Fidelity* starring John Cusack, millions of Britons like nothing more than curling up and watching a video adapted from great literature. Speaking personally I'd always hope to create a great work of fiction rather than some half-arsed attempt to second-guess the market and hope the novel gets made into a movie. A theme I explore in my next book, *Bridget Potter of the Rings*.

Living in a box

26 September 2003

Imagine the excitement when Channel 4's Head of Entertainment burst into the boardroom earlier this year.

'Guess what! I've just signed a massive deal to secure the rights for a new one-man show starring David Blaine!'

'David Blaine the famous magician and illusionist?'

'The very same!'

'What a coup, we'll make this the highlight of our autumn schedule,' exclaimed the controller reaching for the champagne. 'So what's the idea of the show?'

'Well, I haven't had time to read the proposal properly yet . . . um, let's have a look: "David will sit in a glass box for six weeks . . ." '

'And?'

'Er . . . I think there must be a sheet of paper - missing . . .'

As entertainment spectaculars go, the sight of David Blaine doing nothing is right up there with the week when all the badgers failed to turn up for *Badger Watch Live*. Basically it's a bloke who looks like he needs a shave sitting down wrapped in a blanket. You can see that beside thousands of cash machines in any major city in Britain. But the difference here is that David Blaine is an attention-beggar – a sign has gone up near Tower Bridge: 'Attention-beggars are known to be operating in this area. Please do not give them any attention as this only encourages them. If you wish to give attention to someone, why don't you read a book to your kids or ring your mum up?'

Of course, it's not all just sitting there in silence for forty-four days. Now and then Blaine might scratch his head or have a drink of water; these are the sort of gripping highlights that you'll have missed if you haven't paid a fiver to watch it live on the Channel 4 webcam. The endurance part of the stunt is that David is doing all of this without food. Just when every TV show is full of people preparing and tucking into delicious nosh, Channel 4 and Sky have discovered that showing people not eating is even less interesting. We are now halfway through his marathon fast and something has to be done to liven things up a bit. Maybe they could cover the box, relocate it and pull the sheets off to show David that he was now being dangled over downtown Baghdad. That might make him jump about a bit more.

But despite the dullness of the performance, the stunt has turned out to be the source of a great deal of entertainment. Because in the face of all the hype and the multimillion-pound deals, the British people have responded with a heart-warming refusal to be impressed. The real entertainment has come from ordinary people on the ground. First prize goes to the person who attached a Big Mac and fries under his remote control helicopter and then manoeuvred it to hover outside where the starving Blaine was trying not to think about food. The other day I got a pizza leaflet saying 'We deliver anywhere'. Perhaps now is the time to put them to the test.

Blaine's organization were unprepared for the level of antipathy that their man has provoked. Part of the problem is that he completely lacks any humour or humility, but the other thing he fails to understand about Britain is that you're only allowed to do this sort of thing if it is for char-idy. If he was starving himself to raise money for famine relief we'd cheer him all the way and send all our milk bottle tops to *Blue Peter* on his behalf. But frankly this is just showing off and so young David has to be taught a lesson. When he comes out we should organize an enormous audience to be present but crucially we'll pretend we've all turned up to watch another man performing ten yards away. To the amazement of the crowd, this entertainer will be able to throw a peanut in the air and occasionally catch one in his mouth. Plus he can do a shadow puppet of a dog and then a rabbit. And amid the gasps and cheers one audience member should notice the emaciated David finally staggering exhausted from his glass box and nonchalantly say, 'Oh hi, David, you're just in time. Have you seen this bloke? He's incredible.'

Because it's all very well being buried alive, or standing on a tall column for a day and a half or being encased in ice, but if Blaine really wants to impress us, how about some endurance tests that Britons can relate to? 'Witness every second live on the web as David Blaine attempts to watch a game of cricket. Then gasp in amazement as Blaine reads to the end of *Memoirs* by Douglas Hurd.' Or 'Watch David try and get served at the returns desk at Ikea'. Plus 'Can he stay in bed during "Thought for the Day"?' Or the very ultimate test of endurance: 'Live on Sky One and before your very eyes, David Blaine will attempt to follow proceedings at the Hutton Inquiry.' Nah, it could never be done, could it?

Privatized Labour Conference

1 October 2003

The first gathering of the Labour Representation Committee was now over a hundred years ago, when the party itself first came into being. Back in 1900 the conference was not that much different to today's. Security was as tight as ever of course – police checked everyone entering the conference centre to make sure they had a big moustache and a hat. Keir Hardie gave a powerful speech, and during the standing ovation Mrs Hardie came up onto the stage and to the shock of delegates they engaged in an intimate handshake. But sadly the whole event was knocked off the front page of *The Times* by lots of small advertisements for snuff and domestic servants. The Labour Party was created *that* Tuesday at two o'clock. And at five past the first person resigned because the party had moved too far to the right.

A lot of people I know have resigned from the Labour Party in the past twelve months over issues of principle such as the Iraq war, foundation hospitals or Roger Moore getting a knighthood. Others have chosen to remain, while a third group have sent off their angry letters of resignation but then forgotten to cancel their direct debits.

But there were still enough independently minded Labour members left in the party to force a vote on foundation hospitals and a debate on Iraq at this year's conference, so now things are going to change. This was the last-ever Labour conference that will have been organized and run by – the Labour Party. An internal document which has come to my attention reveals that Downing Street is planning a new PFI that will see a private company taking over the Labour Party conferences of the future. Next year a new public–private partnership will see debates being chosen by business sponsors – so look out for a composite motion 27c: 'This conference believes that "There's a difference at McDonald's you'll enjoy." '

The people's party is doing away with the slogan 'For the many not the few' and Cabinet ministers will take to the podium to repeat the soundbite 'I'd rather have a bowl of coco pops' to standing ovations from the remaining faithful. And instead of conference ending with the traditional singing of 'The Red Flag', this commercial sponsorship will mean that Labour members and ministers will link arms to sing a moving rendition of 'Do the shake and vac and put the freshness back'. Party activists wishing to purchase their conference seats will have to ring Ticketmaster, but only after all the corporate customers have got all the best places in the executive boxes. If other members wish to follow events in the conference hall, negotiations are currently under way to sell the TV rights to the new Sky Conference Channel Extra. Obviously the broadcaster will not have any influence or input into the conference agenda, there was *always* going to be a debate chaired by Tara Palmer-Tomkinson entitled 'TV's worst conference bloopers from hell'.

Security will of course remain an issue, because this year, *despite* extensive precautions and checks, George Galloway still managed to get into the building. Labour Party members will no longer need to bring their membership cards, because all that sort of information will be stored on the Home Office's new super-smart ID cards. One swipe through the machine should get you through the checkpoint, although certain Labour members taking part in a pilot scheme have complained that their cards seemed to set off alarms and cause burly security officers to bundle them off the premises.

Finally, as part of this new public–private Labour Party, or the Barclaycard Labour Party as it will now be known, there are plans to allow the more successful individual party members to opt out. The first of these so-called 'foundation ministers' will be Tony Blair. With this new autonomy he will be allowed to act independently of

Labour Party policy and will not be stifled by petty bureaucratic restraints such as listening to majority opinion in the Cabinet or indeed taking any notice of the Labour Party Conference. So at least some things will be the same as they've always been . . .

Bobbies off the beat

2 October 2003

There were embarrassing scenes in the headquarters of Kent County Constabulary this week. A 44-year-old black man was apprehended inside the office of the Chief Constable. Two keen young officers were quick to pin the suspect to the ground as they handcuffed him and shouted questions into his ear.

'Right I'm going to ask you again, sunshine – what are you doing in the Chief Constable's office?'

'I'm the new Chief Constable, ow, get off! You're breaking my arm!'

'Right, we've got him for impersonating a police officer as well. Chuck him in the cells with that Boateng bloke who claimed he was Chief Secretary to the Treasury.'

The appointment of the country's first black chief constable came in a month of good news for Britain's police. There are more bobbies on the beat than ever before, crime continues to fall and Sky One are asking officers to send in their tapes for a new series of the *World's Scariest Police Chases*. 'This country now has more policemen than ever before,' the Home Secretary announced to the Labour Party Conference this week. Some cynics say that 'sleeping policemen' should not be included in this total, that this is another attempt to massage the figures, but that is just typical of the people who criticize this government whatever they do.

There are now 136,386 police officers in the UK, although judging by the Met's ability to estimate crowd numbers at demonstrations, this is probably about half a million out. Thousands of new officers are already on duty, including several who aren't in the masons. When quizzed about the influence of the masons in Britain's police forces, one chief constable made clear his determination to stamp it out: 'It's a tough job, but we're just going to have to roll up our trouser legs and get on with it.' It has taken a while to get the figure up to the government's target because, of course, it takes time to train a new recruit to the force. A police horse for example cannot just sign up for the Met and start its duties the very next day. It takes a long time to teach a police horse to crap right outside the main entrance to the football ground. Urinating at the exact moment that the Queen is walking past takes months of training. Meanwhile, for the human recruits who drive into the Hendon police training college, the lessons start almost immediately. 'No, no, drive in again, but this time go much too fast, mount the pavement, and park in the middle of the street even though there are plenty of spaces on either side.'

With more officers and fewer crimes, David Blunkett is right when he says that we have to work to reduce the fear of crime. The new recruits to the force can help with this. Home beat officers should be visiting pensioners, looking at the flimsy locks on their front doors and saying, 'Nah, that's fine, you're not very likely to get burgled anyway.' Or 'If I were you I'd keep all your cash in a jar in the front window – that's as safe as anywhere.'

The important thing is to make the police officers we have as effective as possible. Like 'the weathermen always get it wrong' or 'there are too many repeats on the BBC', the need for 'more bobbies on the beat' is one of those lazy clichés that everyone agrees with even though the opposite is actually true. It has become so embedded in the national psyche that it would be almost sacrilegious to suggest that having policemen walking up and down Acacia Avenue all day might actually be a bit of a waste of their time. In most residential streets in Britain *nothing happens all day* except the regular delivery of several tonnes of pizza leaflets. Even if there was a crime, what use is a policeman on the beat?

'Help! I've just been burgled! Look, they're driving off in that van, quick after them!'

'I'm not going to catch a bloody two-litre Sherpa, am I,

madam? I'm on foot, I thought that's what you wanted.'

'What we meant was that we wanted a policeman hovering on every doorstep. But with an armed response unit parked just around the corner.'

And the Prime Minister says, 'Isn't that what we all have at the moment?'

Down to the last viewer

10 October 2003

The bigwigs at Granada had been lobbying hard for their proposed merger with Carlton. *Coronation Street* viewers may have noticed a slight difference in the everyday chit-chat in the Rovers Return.

'What's the matter, Deirdre. Why are you crying, luv?'

'I'm just so worried that the government might block the proposed merger between Britain's two major independent broadcasters, Hayley.'

'There, there, pet, don't fret, I'm sure the Trade and Industry Secretary knows that shareholders would greatly benefit from an amalgamation as long as she doesn't force them to flog off their advertising sales departments . . .'

'Aye, I mean it's not as if it's going to affect the programmes . . .'

Well, this was the week when ITV finally became one company. Gone are the days of all those different logos and musical stings that came to feel like part of the actual programmes: Thames led into *Magpie*, ATV preceded *Crossroads* and *Sale of the Century* was made even more glamorous with those spine-tingling words 'And now from Norwich . . .' as the statuette of a knight on horseback went round and round on a little podium. (During an earlier round of takeovers that little figurine was valued at £12.50, thereby doubling the value of Anglia TV at a stroke.)

Now there will be one ITV company, one broadcaster and, pretty soon, only one viewer. The problem for ITV is that the audience it originally poached from the BBC (the social class which advertisers scientifically categorize as the 'working-class oiks') are switching to Sky One to watch such sophisticated entertainment as *When Ibiza Reps in the Nude Crash Their Cars on the Holidays from Hell.**

Critics of the deal fear that one side-effect might be the end of local TV reporting. How will we cope? No more interviews with the lady whose golden retriever was sent a final demand for the council tax. No more reports from Exmoor about the mystery big cat that disappeared just

---

* To be fair, some of the cable channels are doing their best to up the intellectual content of their output. They don't have *Topless Darts* any more. They have *Topless University Challenge*.

before the cameras got there. 'And now on local news, some stories that were not important enough to be on the main news that you just watched three minutes ago. Or if they were, here are those stories all over again.' More importantly what are we going to do without the essential local weather forecast that comes immediately after the national weather? Because I don't know about you, but when they show that UK weather map I never look at the bit where I live, oh no, my eye goes straight to Rockall every time.

The government permitted the merger to help ITV compete against the BBC and Rupert Murdoch's BSkyB. Anything that can be done to help fight off the complete takeover of the British media by Rupert Murdoch has to be worth it. But hope that ITV might become a major player in the cut-throat world of global broadcasting is as misplaced as the belt on Simon Cowell's trousers. ITV has been fattened up and will now be sold to an American corporation. One of the favourites is Viacom, who own Blockbuster video. So every film on ITV will be preceded by twenty minutes of fast-forwarded trailers. Maybe they could even get Blockbuster staff to co-host GMTV. 'So, Kevin, what's on the show today?' And Kevin will stare at Lorraine blankly before finally mumbling, 'Dunno.'

The Disney corporation is also a likely bidder, which might liven the schedule up a bit. All the animals in *Emmerdale* would have big cartoon bodies, and would keep bursting into song. The CCTV footage on *Police! Camera! Action!* would feature an open-topped carriage trundling down the A1(M) with two cartoon mice sitting in the back smiling and waving at everyone.

Whoever takes advantage of the government's recent decision to lift the ban on non-EU ownership of ITV, there will be nothing independent about Independent Television. Just when we thought *Blind Date* had been axed, it returns for a one-off special in a brand-new format. The head of ITV will sit there on the stool nervously seeking reassurances from these prospective partners, while on the other side of the screen the three predators will be all sweet talk and promises even though they're obviously only interested in one thing. Except of course in this version it's the viewer who gets screwed.

My big hope is that ITV be purchased by Hallmark. Not only are they interested but they could easily raise the billions required by selling several birthday cards. Every night Trevor MacDonald will do a damning report into the evil drugs gangs stalking jungle Britain, which will end with this lovely thought: 'On this special day when we are one, I hope it's filled with birthday fun. For looking back at all we've done, I know our love has just begun. Goodnight.'

Leaves on the phone line

17 October 2003

Over the past few years the job of giving out the details of train journeys has been enormously simplified. There's just a desk with an answerphone relaying the message: 'The trains are all buggered. You're better off sitting in a traffic jam.' Of course, there is always the option of getting travel details online but that presumes that their computers don't crash as often as their trains do. But now it has been revealed that there is a new plan: callers wanting to know how to get from London Waterloo to Chessington South will soon have to go via Bangalore Junction, changing at New Delhi Parkway. Train operators are planning to shift Britain's telephone rail enquiries service to India. It's not that network rail's call centres have been unreliable, apart from the occasional unforeseen delay caused by leaves on the phone line. But by paying Third World wages to the people informing us about our Third World transport system, they are hoping to save up to £10 million, or roughly the price of an open return from London to Edinburgh.

The first step will be to coach the Indian operators to behave just like the traditional British rail employees who have always gone out of their way to be as informative and helpful as possible. So when the phone rings on their desk in Bangalore, the keen new staff have been told to sit there and watch it ring for ten minutes. Fighting all their instincts to be cheerful and polite the trainee will finally answer it with a grumpy indifferent 'Yeah?'

'Oh, hello, yes, I wonder if you can tell me the times of trains from London King's Cross to Luton Airport?'

'Nah, mate.'

'I'm sorry?'

'No trains from King's Cross to there, mate. It's St Pancras for Luton Airport, isn't it? That's bleedin' obvious.'

An exchange like this would earn the Indian full marks for sounding convincingly British, although there'd then be an extra bonus if he gave out the times without mentioning that the trains were not running today because of engineering works.

The proponents of transferring this service to the Indian sub-continent claim that they can actually provide a better quality of staff, employing graduates to do a job which rarely comes top of British kids' lists of 'what I want to do when I grow up'. They insist that the people at the other end always speak excellent English (unlike that NHS pilot scheme when they tried handing over the job of answering 999 calls to a call centre in Korea). But for the rail companies, moving their enquiries office to Bangalore does have its downside of course. When the locals have to give out information about the state of Britain's network they're going to have to stop themselves giggling down the phone. And the risk assessment of this project also mentioned the possibility of all-out nuclear war between India and Pakistan, which might perhaps make it harder for callers to get through. At which point all the English people would tut and say, 'Honestly! What excuse will they come up with next?'

In fact there are already thousands of call centre employees in India dealing with our insurance claims, flight enquiries and telephone banking. This seemingly unstoppable trend is all part of the post-imperial cultural exchange. We took the Koh-i-noor diamond but we're giving back telephone call centres, so it's almost quits. The operators are taught to give the impression that they are also English but every so often the mask slips and they make some give-away remark such as 'Didn't we do well at the cricket!' And to make the atmosphere as realistically British as possible the canteen does not serve any Indian food until they have had at least ten pints of lager.

Meanwhile, back in Britain thousands of call centre employees face being thrown out of work, even though many of these traditional jobs date right back to the late 1990s. There is talk of some of them getting work as tour guides in the proposed Call Centre Heritage Museum, but that will surely be a minority. These redundancies are part of a trend which began with the decline of British manufacturing and is now reaching the service sectors. All sorts of jobs that were traditionally done in the UK are now done thousands of miles away. Our parents' shoes were made in Nottingham but our kids' trainers say 'Made in Indonesia'. Toy cars are made in China, while our own vehicles are made in Japan. And now even the job of deciding British foreign policy has been farmed out to a little office in the United States. It did use to be done by a British bloke apparently, but just like the old British rail phone line, no-one could ever get through to him.

There is less to him than meets the eye

22 October 2003

The journalist Michael Crick recently unearthed some fairly astonishing secret information. Following a thorough investigation he discovered that for the last two years Iain Duncan Smith has been working as Leader of the Opposition. What's more, IDS had actually been paid public money to occupy this position, even though there is very little evidence that he's actually done anything. The Tory leader immediately held a press conference angrily denying that he was unimpressive and ineffective, while the assembled journalists chatted amongst themselves or played snake on their mobile phones. Now the crisis around IDS has reached fever pitch, with so many senior Conservatives insisting that their leader's position is secure that he's realizing he can't have much longer left. The last Tory leader never to fight a general election was Neville Chamberlain. Apparently he had a few problems over European unification as well. Perhaps his wife was in charge of his private office too.

'What's in my diary today, darling?'

'Oh sorry, I forgot to mention – you were supposed to ring Adolf Hitler and tell him not to annexe the Sudetenland.'

'Oh dear, too late, never mind. Well, I don't suppose anything will come of it . . .'

It was the accusations about Betsy Duncan Smith which precipitated the current crisis. The charge is that the taxpayer paid for his wife to work in his office, though she barely did enough to warrant her salary. Behind every mediocre man is a woman being paid to do nothing. IDS can hardly be blamed for this because attempting to boss your spouse around is always difficult.

'Right, I've gotta dash, Betsy, could you type up those letters, ring back those journalists and send out those press releases?'

Betsy stares back at her husband in fuming silence. 'All right, but you've got to do something for me,' she finally snaps.

'What?'

'Well, it's all about you, you, you, isn't it? I'll do all that for you, Iain, if you promise to start picking up your pants. And you stop mixing your peas into your mashed potato, and you remember to ask how my flower arranging evening class went . . .'

Betsy was in charge of his diary but apparently did very little. Well, give it a month or two and that will be a perfect arrangement because his appointments diary will be completely empty.

'Right what have we got this week . . . Monday, let's see, hmmm . . . Waitangi Day, New Zealand. Um . . . Tuesday . . . full moon. Wednesday . . . it's the vernal equinox . . . how am I going to fit all this in?'

The latest blow to his fragile grasp on the Tory leadership was on Wednesday, when a major donor to the party said IDS should step down. This could be the straw that breaks the camel's back, though when you consider that there have only been about two or three straws in total you realize that we are talking about a pretty crappy camel here. Duncan Smith has decided not to follow John Major's tactic of saying 'Back me or sack me', because everyone would immediately reply, 'Okay, you're sacked.' So he is opting to limp on from crisis to crisis and see if he can stretch this tactic out right up until the next general election.

Oh joy, oh joy! Let us not forget that this is the Conservative Party that seemed to be in power for ever, that wrecked the social fabric of this country, the party of Thatcher, Tebbit and Michael Howard. Every blow that they suffer is another step away from them ever returning and should be celebrated like the day that Maggie was deposed. But while the current situation is just about perfect, we can't have things getting any worse for them. Much as we enjoyed the last Tory putsch in 1990, it brought the (well-founded) anxiety that a fresh leader might appeal enough to the voters to bring victory at the polls. So we should only be in favour of deposing Iain Duncan Smith if they're going to get a leader with even less public appeal. Osama Bin Laden would be my choice. By opting for a Muslim it would show the Tories to be modern and inclusive, and although Osama has been in hiding for the past couple of years, his profile is still higher than their current leader. This week William Hill ceased to take bets on whether IDS will still be leader at the next election. This was the final blow for the Tories, because with all the big donors pulling out, it was their last chance of raising enough money to carry on.

'So before you resign, Iain, don't forget to pop into the bookies and put everything we've got on IDS stepping down.'

'But shouldn't we give that job to someone who won't be recognized?'

'Um . . . I don't think there'll be a problem.'

IDS was of course deposed as Tory leader later that month. Who can forget the iconic image of that huge bronze statue of the Tory leader crashing to the ground? No, hang on . . .

Wrong end of the stick insect

31 October 2003

In this week's papers there was another big scare story about the danger of Britain being over-run by visitors from overseas. It was the usual tale – the ports unable to stop them, the government doing too little too late, the dangers to Britain's economy – and the question has to be asked: has Britain become a soft touch for insects? Because according to a report from the National Audit Office all sorts of agricultural pests and diseases are now pouring into this country, many of them without work permits or valid passports.

Of course, the right-wing press immediately went on the attack. 'Labour put Colorado beetles in luxury hotel!' screamed the *Daily Mail*. 'Potato Brown Rot may have al-Qaida connections,' warned the *Daily Telegraph*. 'Bloody aphids – they come over here and drink our sap!' ranted the *Daily Star*. Before long, Tory MPs who obviously had nothing else to worry about this week were spotting another chance to attack foreign parasites. 'Increasing trade and travel make it much more likely that new pests and diseases will spread here from other countries and do enormous economic damage,' said Edward Leigh MP. Not a word about how the insects might have suffered in the journey here on EasyJet economy class or about the humiliation felt by a giant spider found hiding in a bunch of grapes and then forced to be the novelty closing feature on local news extra. 'Now is not the time for complacency,' he added, clutching the press release about the dangers of the Western Flower Thrip. Heaven forbid that any of us should ever be complacent about the Western Flower Thrip. Most of us have worried about little else for the past five years.

Apparently, one of the biggest new fears is a fungus known as Sudden Oak Death. This species feels it has got a very bad deal from the British press. 'Look just because I'm called Sudden Oak Death, the media always focuses on the "instantly fatal to Britain's best-loved tree" angle. I do plenty of other things, you know, it's not all just killing oak trees very quickly, but do they ever want to talk about that? No of course they don't . . .' At this point the interview was suddenly curtailed because the tree from which the fungus was speaking came crashing to the ground.

The other new threats are Mushroom Virus X, which

used to be called Mushroom Virus Little but changed its surname as a political statement, and Tobacco whitefly, which is a danger to over sixty species, including tomatoes and cucumbers; in fact they are starting to regret the day they persuaded it to give up the tobacco. All that effort with those tiny nicotine patches and this is how the Tobacco whitefly thanks us.

Of course, it is possible that someone at the National Audit Office has just made all these species up. They were given the sack last week so to get their own back on their last day they sent out a press release warning of the dangers of a potato ring rot and a soil-based pest called Rhizomania. Apparently this disease broke out in Bury St Edmunds in the 1980s and devastated the sugar beet crop. Yeah right, who can forget the great Bury St Edmunds sugar beet crisis of '87?

Made up or not, you're a lot more likely to encounter these problems in the paper than you are to suffer them in real life. But the same is true with human immigrants to these shores. Prejudice and hostility are based upon what people have read and heard, rarely connected with any direct personal negative experience. When I was knocking on doors at the last general election, voters frequently cited asylum seekers as an issue, repeating tabloid myths or downright lies about refugees, how easy it was for them to get into the country, how they got priority treatment on the NHS and didn't have to queue for the Professor Burp's Bubble Works at Chessington World of Adventure. And then I would ask them, 'So have you ever met an asylum seeker?' and they would stammer, 'Well, no, not in person but you read about it all the time.' Immigrants don't wipe out potato crops, they just pick the potatoes for appalling wages, thereby keeping the prices down for the rest of us. And yet the same language is used to describe people fleeing torture and persecution that was used to describe this week's warning about scary creepy crawlies and invisible viruses that also apparently threaten these shores. The howls of outrage that greeted the government's decision to grant an amnesty to 50,000 asylum seekers could not have been greater if the refugees had their pockets stuffed with Colorado beetles infected with rabies. 'Britain is being overrun!' they scream. 'Influx will cripple our economy', and 'Asylum seekers infect turnip crop' (all right I made that last one up).

The traditional way to kill an insect is to hit it with a rolled-up newspaper. Asylum seekers just get whacked by the whole of Fleet Street.

This is your captain slurring

14 November 2003

There is an increasing tendency for people to use the ready availability of air travel as an excuse to fly off to some European capital with the sole intention of getting smashed out of their heads before making complete idiots of themselves during the flight home. But it must be time to call a halt to this when the worst offenders are the pilots supposed to be flying the plane.

This week the captain of British Airways flight BA761 from Oslo was arrested along with his first officer and the purser for apparently being drunk as they turned up for duty. 'This was more than just having a few glasses of wine,' reported an onlooker. They'd hoped that no one would notice them going out boozing, but they took so long reversing the jet out of the pub car park that it was bound to raise suspicions. By the time they were competing to do handbrake turns on the runway, passengers were getting a little nervous about getting on board.

It makes you worry about the airline's priorities. You spend half an hour queuing at security while they make sure you don't have any nail clippers in your hand luggage as the pilot staggers straight past clutching a bottle of tequila singing Abba hits. Because this is not an isolated incident. A few years back, Channel 4's *Dispatches* exposed a rampant drinking culture among air crews which resulted in fourteen British Airways staff being suspended. And this week a BA insider said, 'Risks are still being taken because many believe that they won't get caught.' No matter how much the plane is swerving from cloud to cloud, the chances of the pilot spotting the flashing blue light of a police patrol plane in his rearview mirror remain pretty slim.

It can be a little unsettling for the nervous flyer to look down onto the jagged peaks below, knowing that your life is in the hands of the man flying the plane. And then his slurring voice comes over the Tannoy: 'This ish your captain speaking. I really love you. No I'm not just saying that, I really, really, no shut up listen right, I love all you passengers right, because you're really like, you know . . . lovely.' You reassure your anxious partner that modern aircraft are pretty well flown by computer these days when the first officer comes on the Tannoy. 'We are currently flying at 30,000 feet, oops nope, 25,000 feet, hang on,

30,000 feet, oooh I feel all sick now.' And then he breaks off because the air hostess has just wheeled the drinks trolley through the doors into the cockpit before the plane makes an unscheduled stop-off at Dublin airport to stock up on more duty-free.

It's not so bad during the elated, joyful period of intoxication. It's when the drunken pilots start to come down, when they get all depressed, that the real worry sets in. 'I'm worthless, I'm nothing – I should end it all now.'

'No no,' says the stewardess, filling up his cup of coffee. 'Don't end it all now. Why don't you see how you feel in the morning; then by all means, when the plane is on the ground, then you can kill yourself.'

In PR terms this latest scandal is another disaster for BA. In a recent survey of frequent fliers, a sizeable majority expressed a preference for pilots who were 'sober'. Of those who responded to the question regarding the preferred physical state of their air crew, very few people ticked the box marked 'completely rat-arsed'. 'British Aleways!' screamed the front page of the *Sun* as tabloid journalists expressed their horror of anyone drinking during working hours.

Maybe the drinking culture has spread right through the company. That would explain how the baggage handlers bust your brand suitcase with the little wheels on. They were trying to skateboard on it. And we all thought those colourful paintings on the tail fins were wonderfully ethnic and abstract, but there's a far simpler explanation. The artist was pissed. Perhaps the company directors have been turning up to board meetings at the end of a six-hour pub crawl. That must be when they decided it would be a great idea for us to book and pay for a ticket and then be told that the flight is deliberately overbooked and our seats are not available. It would explain why BA was fined for bullying travel agents or sued for dirty tricks against Virgin. 'Thatsh a good plan . . . lishten, we try and poach their passengers by impershonating Virgin shtaff! Brilliant, I can't believe we didn't think of that before the pubs opened.' Until you realize that the reality is a lot scarier. That all these policies were decided upon when BA's management was stone-cold sober.

What the Queen saw in the *Mirror*

21 November 2003

It was the sneakiest piece of subterfuge undertaken by a British newspaper for some time. This week the *Daily Mirror*, claiming to have a bona fide piece of journalism about breaches in royal security and the risk from terrorists, managed to smuggle a load of gossip, tittle-tattle and *Hello!*-type photo shoots into their paper without anyone noticing. 'Look at these photos of Sophie's bra chucked across a chair – a terrorist could have hidden a couple of grenades in there! And just look at these astonishing photos of the Queen's corgis in her private apartment! A member of al-Qaida could have easily hidden a bomb inside one of them! Thank God this paper has exposed this terrible breach in security as we selflessly do our bit in the war against terrorism. More pictures of the Queen's toilet on pages 2–17 . . .' Apparently none of the royal family ever suspected that this ordinary footman was an undercover *Mirror* hack. Until one of them asked for a newspaper and he brought them the *Daily Mirror*.

The bogus footman in question was Ryan Parry, who apparently applied for the job in the royal household by downloading a form off the internet and then giving in a forged reference. The security checks were every bit as vigorous as you would expect. 'Right Mr Parry, you say you are attracted to the job by its generous take-home salary of £9,000 a year, which certainly has me convinced. And you definitely look like the man in the photo on that press pass pinned to your lapel.' But just to show that they were no mugs, while he was sitting there they rang the phone number scribbled beside his referee (a 'Mr Made-up-name of Droitwich') but then got distracted because Parry's mobile went off in his pocket.

Ryan Parry worked inside Buckingham Palace and Windsor Castle for a couple of months, fetching and carrying at the whim of his masters while they shouted and swore at him. So not much change from working for a tabloid newspaper really. Many papers feature photographs of him in his footman's uniform riding on the back of the Queen's carriage with a great big white circle around his head. You'd have thought that this might have drawn attention to him, wouldn't you? The Home Office were horrified by the story printed in the *Mirror*:

'We have a royal family that has cuddly toys in their bedrooms??' We learn that whoever opens Prince Andrew's curtains in the morning is told to 'Fuck off!', which is probably why his mum doesn't do it any more. Parry claims that Princess Anne also uttered the dreaded 'f' word inside the palace (no, not 'Fergie') and that the Queen insists on having the *Racing Post* on the top of her pile of newspapers every morning, probably because it is the only paper not full of embarrassing revelations about the royal family. It's also revealed that the Queen owns a number of Tupperware containers. That was the last time she went to one of Norma Major's parties.

This embarrassment comes only months after Aaron Barschak managed to gatecrash Prince William's twenty-first birthday party by ringing on the doorbell and mumbling, 'Er . . . I'm a mate of, um – Dave's?', and holding up a four-pack of lager.* Now there are calls for far tighter security from the same papers that have been calling for the royal family not to be so aloof and distant from their subjects.

With this security scandal in the open, steps were taken to tighten procedures immediately. Everyone's credentials were double-checked to ensure that they really were who they said they were, which is when the real scandal of the week was uncovered. The very next day a shifty-looking man called George W. Bush attempted to get into

---

* Since the London bombings of July 2005 and the erroneous gunning down of a suspected terrorist, Aaron Barschak has seemed reluctant to repeat his stunt of dressing up as the head of al-Qaida and rushing past armed police towards members of the royal family.

Buckingham Palace claiming that he was the President of the United States. A few checks and legal enquiries quickly revealed that this man, who has a history of unstable and dangerous behaviour, is not the rightful president at all but an impostor who lied and cheated his way into the job. It turns out that he's actually been working under-cover at the White House on behalf of a number of oil corporations but had got away with it until now. He had access to America's nuclear codes and had already made full use of US and British military forces. An immediate inquiry has been ordered by the relevant security forces. 'Sod the royal family,' said a spokesman, 'it's the safety of the rest of us I'm worried about.'

A great British tradition: men in wigs and tights

28 November 2003

There were tense scenes in Buckingham Palace on Wednesday as the Queen tried to choose her outfit for this year's State Opening of Parliament. With the carriage driver tooting his horn outside the front door, Philip dashed into the bedroom to hurry her along.

'What's wrong with that ermine robe thing? You look nice in that, dear.'

'No, no, I wore that last year! And it's so 1720s. Now what about this crown? Be honest, it's not too flashy, is it?'

'Well, it is the Crown Jewels of England, darling, it's supposed to be a little bit flashy.'

Meanwhile, at Black Rod's house another argument was going on.

'Darling, I asked you weeks ago, you promised you'd get off work early to pick the kids up.'

'I didn't realize that was today, I've got a very important job on this afternoon. I have to, um, you know, bang on the door with a stick.'

'Well, anyone can do that, can't they? Get Brian or someone to cover for you.'

The annual State Opening of Parliament is the day when the government of Britain is briefly transformed into a vaguely kinky Regency costume drama. The origin of all this pomp and pageantry dates all the way back to the long-forgotten Friday afternoon when it was dreamed up by a Victorian PR agency. 'Let's make up some really stupid titles like "Rouge Croix Pursuivant of Arms" and make them wear wigs and stockings,' they said, never imagining they'd get away with it.

Few people have any idea what these arcane jobs actually involve. There was an awkward moment during last year's Cabinet reshuffle when Peter Hain was summoned by the Prime Minister to be told his new post.

'Peter – I am giving you the job of Lord Privy Seal.'

'Golly. Right, um, excellent.'

'You do know what the Lord Privy Seal does, don't you?'

'Um, of course I do, he, er . . . well, it's a vital role . . .'

'Which areas do you think you'll most want to concentrate on?'

'Well, um, all of them, all of them,' stutters Hain, desperately racking his brain for what job a 'seal' might do, suspecting that balancing a ball on your nose at the circus can't be right. 'But basically I'd want to, um, to um . . . you know, lord it around the privy dressed as a seal.'

'Exactly, go and get started then.'

Surely it is no coincidence that this time of year brings two similar traditions: the State Opening of Parliament and the beginning of the panto season. While the British people still flock to see the one set of minor celebrities in stupid costumes, the pomp and pageantry of the Palace of Westminster are criticized for appearing irrelevant and in desperate need of reform. Perhaps the solution is to mix them up a bit. The fawning commentary from the BBC's heritage correspondent wouldn't sound all that different. 'And now here comes Her Majesty in the traditional giant pumpkin carriage, with her royal footmen dressed as white mice. And as the procession enters Prince Charming's palace, we can see the Lord Chancellor exchanging a few words with Dick Whittington's cow there. Many of these titles of course date back centuries, a living link with our glorious past. There's Puss in Boots, followed by Widow Twankey, a post which is currently held by John Prescott and how very dignified he looks in that wobbly wig with those balloons stuffed up his dress. Later he will be taking his place on the front bench of the Commons for the traditional 'Oh yes I am' and 'Oh no you're not' section of the pantomime.

People defend all this splendour and tradition on the grounds that it attracts tourists. 'There's a German lady who comes every year.' 'Yeah, well, she is the Queen.' But the important differentiation to make is between outmoded symbolism which doesn't really harm anyone and traditions which have involved the old Conservative establishment clinging on to genuine political power. So this week the government rather rudely took the opportunity of their annual visit to the House of Lords to tell them that they were going to take away their supreme legal powers and abolish ninety-two of them. There was also an extra paragraph written in at the last minute in red crayon that stated that any lords convicted of a criminal offence would be stripped of their peerage, 'especially', continued the Queen, 'if they are called Jeffrey and write crappy novels'. The government is right to modernize the House of Lords by abolishing the hereditary peers and creating a supreme court. But unless the Prime Minister goes on to make our second chamber genuinely democratic he will simply be replacing one pantomime with another. Except this time no-one will be shouting, 'They're behind you!'

Mickey Mouse economics

5 December 2003

The boardroom battles at the Disney corporation were always more heated than most. Donald Duck would always lose his temper and then get even madder when nobody could understand what he was saying. Minnie would stick up for her husband when he was accused of having a Mickey Mouse job. Then Baloo the Bear would start going on about the Robin Hood film again and how Little John had ripped off his act, and finally Bambi would pop his head round the door and there'd be an embarrassed silence when he said, 'You haven't seen my mum anywhere, have you?'

But this week saw a milestone in the history of the world's best-known entertainment group. The last remaining member of the Disney family has resigned from the board and launched a bitter attack on the corporation's chief executive. The final straw had been the meeting when they were going to talk about EuroDisney. He'd queued for thirty minutes to get a seat, but loads of French teenagers kept pushing in ahead of him.

It's going to be tough for Roy Disney to get a job anywhere else.

'So you've been at the Disney corporation for thirty-seven years, Mr Disney. What made you decide you'd like to work here at Warner Bros?'

'Well, I've always sort of personally identified with the whole Warner Brothers brand.'

With Disney now controlled by chief executive Michael Eisner, the revamped Eisnerworld theme parks are going to see a few changes. As your boat enters the magical cave you will gasp in excitement as you hear the model executive announce the rotation of committee and chairmanship assignments among independent directors! Tell your six-year-old daughter to cover her eyes as you pass the merging of the Executive Performance Subcommittee with the Compensation Committee!

In his bitter resignation letter Walt's nephew, Roy Disney, accuses the current management of 'always looking for a quick buck'. But it was always the aggressive marketing and ruthless corporate drive rather than the erratic quality of the product that made Disney the economic powerhouse it became. From its earliest days Disney was accused of dubious labour practices. At the time of its first full-length feature, critics pointed to the blatant exploitation of dwarf workers living in cramped conditions in a remote cottage in the woods. Despite digging out truck-loads of diamonds every day, the dwarves were forced to share one small bedroom between all seven of them. Disney aggressively refuted accusations of ripping off its workers, denying rumours that they'd negotiated the price for the diamonds with Dopey before all the other dwarves got back. But even if property prices were particularly high in Disneyland, you'd have thought that with all those huge diamonds coming out of the ground every day they might have been able to afford a spare bedroom for Snow White and maybe a proper door to stop the animals coming in all the time.

Little has changed and today those Pocahontas dresses that cost six months' pocket money in the Disney Store are stitched together for a few cents in Third World sweatshops with appalling working conditions. When Mowgli tried so hard to get back to the man-village nobody told him he'd be spending the rest of his childhood assembling Mickey Mouse lunchboxes. Disney executives say that labour practices in Haiti or wherever are not their responsibility since these workers are not Disney employees. By this logic, Cruella de Ville could deny any connection with the killing and skinning of any Dalmatian puppies. 'How those raw materials are obtained is not my responsibility, darling. I simply purchase animal by-products from independent sub-contractors called Jasper and Horace.'

It is the extreme contrast between the magical world

that Disney tries to sell us and the grim reality of their corporate practice that is particularly galling. Why can't they be honest about their values and beliefs? Why can't the prince in *Sleeping Beauty* slay the dragon because it attempted to unionize the workforce? Why can't the crocodile chase Captain Hook over the horizon because he tried to broadcast anti-Disney news stories on the Disney-owned ABC channel? Since they are currently expanding their theme parks into the Far East, why not push their exploitation one more step and have a Disneyland Bangkok where you could hire prostitutes in the character of Disney heroines? Western sex tourists could keep Cinderella out after midnight, sleep with Sleeping Beauty and be a beast with Belle while the Little Mermaid wondered why nobody ever picked her. But of course Disney would never let the magical mask slip. They know that we still somehow imagine that the fairy-tale land they present us with is the world we buy into when we eagerly hand over our cash. And we thought Bambi was naïve . . .

My, how you've grown – outwards

12 December 2003

They're making a few changes to Enid Blyton's *Famous Five* stories so that modern children can relate to them.

'Well, it's the summer holidays at last!' said Julian. 'And we've got weeks ahead of us sitting in the basement with the curtains drawn, playing computer games.'

Suddenly the door burst open. 'Listen everyone!' exclaimed Anne. 'Timmy just spotted some smugglers sailing out to the island! Let's go and investigate.'

'Shut up, Anne, and get out of the way of the screen. And tell Mum to put some more pizzas in the microwave, I'm on level 7 of *Washington Sniper 2002*.'

This week the British Medical Association issued a terrifying report on the health of today's teenagers. They are eating too much junk food, they smoke, they have sexually transmitted diseases and they drink too much alcohol. And the problem is that if they're doing all this in their teens, what possible motivation is there for them to go to university? No wonder they're all depressed; all they need now is the prospect of a big debt around their necks to really finish them off. The report reveals our adolescents to be the most obese generation of Britons ever, so in an attempt to cheer them up a bit the government proposed giving them the vote at sixteen, but then spoilt it by adding, 'That's if you can fit inside the polling booths, you big fat lardy-pants.'

Obesity is becoming so normal that kids are being teased in the playground for not being fat. Now visiting aunties say, 'Aah, hasn't he grown? I remember him when he was only *this* wide.' Obviously, fizzy drinks and fatty junk food are a major factor in this trend; when asked what was their last meal many kids admitted they'd just had a Big Mac, double fries and a large Coke and were planning to have the same again at lunchtime. Coca-Cola insist that they do not target children under twelve in their advertising, no, they just sponsored the charts because *Top of the Pops* is very popular with the over-sixties. (Apparently the *Antiques Roadshow* was already sponsored by Pepsi Max.) Why can't they find a drink more suitable for young children, like the sponsor they have for the Carling Cup?

If the foods that are making our children overweight are going to be allowed to advertise, they should at least be a bit more honest about it. The Burger King advert could change its strapline to 'Heart disease? You got it!' Then a chronically overweight man could roll around on the ground unable to get up, with a cheery voiceover chortling, 'You know when you've been Tango-ed!'

The other problem for today's young people is lack of physical activity. They need healthy sporting role models who are fit and active, like that Gary Lineker from the Walkers crisps adverts. Sport is now something to be watched on cable, unless it's on channel 117, when frankly it's just too much effort to press three buttons on the remote control. When we were children we got a lot more exercise getting up off the sofa and walking across the room to change channels. And there was no children's TV all through the school holidays, so we sat there staring blankly at *Pebble Mill at One* instead. Occasionally we might have gone off and played on our own outside, but now in Tony Blair's nanny state we are not allowed to play in the street any more apparently, just because it's the A412(M).

Parents are driving their children to obesity, because they are driving them to school and to piano lessons and to games workshops. Parents need to be encouraged to let their children run off and play on their own for a bit. And obviously the best way to do this is for the newspapers to spend weeks obsessing over every grisly detail of the Ian Huntley trial.

The part of the BMA's report with which I have a problem is the confident assertion that today's adolescents are the most depressed young people ever. More unhappy than a generation that lost fathers and brothers in the trenches? Or a generation that was evacuated or bombed? Yup, today's teenagers are suffering from far greater depression because McDonald's have started doing salads. The fact that the fast-food giants are suddenly on the defensive shows that attitudes to healthy eating may be changing. There's been talk of the government forcing fatty foods to carry health warnings, and perhaps the time is right for this. Nothing too alarmist, just something like 'Eat this burger and die, yer fat walrus!' or 'Warning, these heart-attack-inducing hot dogs are made from mashed up old donkey bollocks.'

Kids would run a mile. Or rather, their parents would drive them.

Ulster says maybe

19 December 2003

One of the perks of being Prime Minister is that you get to have all sorts of famous personalities round to your house on a regular basis. This week, for example, lucky old Tony got to have Rev. Ian Paisley round for a good old heart-to-heart.

'So would you like tea or coffee, Ian?'

'NO!'

'Suddenly turned a bit chilly, hasn't it?'

'NO!'

'So, how do you see the Northern Ireland assembly shaping up?'

'NO!'

Matters weren't helped when Cherie popped her head round the door.

'Tony, darling, can you just sign this Christmas card to our priest? You know, Father Patrick O'Flaherty at St Mary the Virgin and Loads of Other Catholic-type Saints.'

The veins were near to bursting on Paisley's head as she continued: 'Yes, it was such a lovely mass on Sunday, when we said that prayer for the poor Pope . . .'

The glass shattered in Paisley's hand as Tony whispered to his wife to change the subject. 'Sorry, of course. So, Ian, how are Rangers doing at the moment? Dumped out of Europe and eight points behind Celtic last time I looked . . .'

The Prime Minister has invited representatives from all sides to Downing Street. He was supposed to be talking to Martin McGuinness but apparently there was a bit of a hold-up at the little security kiosk. Every time the police scanned his details through the computer all sorts of sirens and flashing lights suddenly went off.

'Sorry about this, Mr McGuinness, our anti-terrorist software seems to be playing up. Dave, what does it mean when the words "No! No! Don't let him in!" flash up on the screen?'

'I dunno, just press "delete" and open the gate manually.'

As if there haven't been enough delays to the peace process already. Imagine if Martin McGuinness finally decided to go to confession; we could be kept waiting another year or so.

This week's talks are a result of the recent elections in the province, in which the DUP and Sinn Féin became the two largest parties. The peace process had been coming under increasing pressure as both communities began to realize what the details really involved. For example, Orangemen are still permitted to march, but halfway down the Garvachy Road they have to agree to swap their bowler hats for black berets and sunglasses. Nationalist songs will have an extra verse admitting that it's much cheaper to pop over the border to fill your car up. And in future the two communities may only have street murals that acknowledge the other side's point of view. End-of-terrace houses will have to feature giant paintings of William of Orange at the battle of the Boyne, carrying a flag saying 'Not so much surrender as a sort of negotiated compromise for building tolerance and inclusivity'. And beside King Billy will be a couple of republican terrorists in balaclavas giving his horse a friendly pat and a sugar cube. In fact, to celebrate the diverse culture of Ulster, a major new art prize has just been inaugurated for 'Best Sectarian Mural'. Brian Sewell was on hand to cast his critical eye over the finalists, in which various terrorist gunmen were depicted firing their ArmaLite rifles into the air.

'This is the most vulgar and clichéd painting I have ever seen,' he told the artist, the local brigade commander of the UVF, who began to eye the baseball bat leaning in his doorway. 'Appalling brushwork, no awareness of light or form . . .' continued Sewell as his agent was frantically waving to him to shut up. 'The depiction is almost child-like in its naïve incompetence . . .'

'Brian, I'm taking you home now . . . He's not been well, he doesn't know what he's saying . . .'

Another possible step forward is that Britain will rule the six counties, but it won't always be the same ones. There will be a rota, so that next year it might be Wexford, Clare, Cork, Laois, Galway and Roscommon. Then the following year we might do it the other way round, with Dublin ruling Avon, Norfolk, Surrey and the rest of the Home Counties. That would be no less logical than the situation that has survived since 1921.

This week Ian Paisley* restated that he would not talk with politicians tied up with violence. To which Tony Blair said, 'Oh come on, Iraq was months ago.' The idea of Paisley presiding at Stormont with Gerry Adams as his deputy sent a shiver down the spine of everyone hoping that moderation and compromise might prevail. What the province needs is an outsider with experience in government who is less extreme than either of Ulster's two main parties. 'Hmm, actually there is someone who's suddenly become available . . .' said Tony '. . . and Belfast might feel just like home after six months in an Iraqi cellar . . .'

---

* To give credit to Ian Paisley, he has at least tried to move with the times. He now wears a charity wristband with the inscription 'Make Popery History'.

Public convenience for sale. No chain

2 January 2004

'One chocolate assortment gift box – only orange crèmes left. Value 85 pence . . .'

'Excuse me, what are you doing in my kitchen?'

'One Bosch electric egg boiler still in packaging. Obvious unwanted Christmas present. Retail price £14.75 but completely pointless, so actual value, zero.'

For months now, auditors from the Office of National Statistics have been going all over the country working out how much we are all worth. They've been adding up the value of everything in the British Isles: every building, every field, every road, every car, every house and all their contents and worked out that these islands and everything in them are worth £4,983,000,000,000. Then they remembered to include the cashew nuts from all the hotel mini-bars so that bumped it up a bit.

The survey took ages. At the end of the first morning, the auditor and his friend were still going through the loft at Sea View Cottage, Land's End, when they realized that this might be a much bigger job than they'd anticipated. Soon the project was scaled up a bit. Important-looking officials would stride from county to county, pointing flashy laser measuring devices around the place, while an anxious Tony Blair scurried behind them trying to talk up various aspects of the property.

'Ah yes, this is Kent, we call it "the garden of England": could look quite nice with a bit of decking from B&Q maybe? Oh and um, down at the bottom there, we put in a little tunnel for getting next door to France.'

'Hmm – what are the neighbours like?'

'Oh, very nice. Mr Chirac – we've never had any disagreements with him, have we, darling?'

'Ooh no, certainly not. Ah, I see you've spotted Dungeness Nuclear Power Station . . .'

'Oh dear, I've been meaning to mend that leak for ages . . .'

Of course, it was our French landlords who first introduced the idea of this national audit back in 1087. Norman bureaucrats went from village to village, outraging the Saxons by telling them they were Council Tax band D. Back then the Domesday Book estimated the total value of England to be £37,000, although this may have been a deliberate underestimate because William I wanted to keep down his insurance premiums with Friends Provident. The total value of Rotherham, for example, was only £100. Today it is nearly twice that. Even as recently as 1994, the total worth of Great Britain plc was estimated at only £2.8 trillion, with the subsequent massive rise being attributed to spiralling property values and the creative pricing of printer cartridges.

But at the beginning of 2004 we are apparently richer than ever. And we can secretly feel pretty smug as we sit around at dinner parties talking about how ridiculous property prices have got these days.

'Five trillion pounds, the agents said, and it needs loads of work doing on the railways and everything . . .'

'Yes, and if we redecorated Scotland we could get even more . . .'

But there is a basic flaw in all of this. Although there may well be around five trillion pounds' worth of assets in Britain, we don't actually own the Toyota factories or the McDonald's restaurants or the Warner cinemas. The notion that everything in Britain belongs to us is as quaint as the idea that we own our own homes (which make up over half of the estimated £5 trillion but are of course heavily mortgaged to HSBC or whoever).

The apparent purpose of this modern-day valuation is to help estimate economic growth, but it is difficult not to suspect some other motive. The estate agent's details for Britain have now been printed on two sides of A4 with a slightly blurred photo of the sea view. 'Historic detached property in slight need of renovation, attractively laid to lawn with many interesting features. Much potential for improvement. Ample parking (on M25).' And the un-real estate of Great Britain will soon be appearing in the global executive edition of *Country Life*, before you get to the boring articles about dry stone walls and the photo of some posh deb who's off to Exeter University. A surprising number of unique opportunities have just come on the market. Canada is described as having a 'large garden', Luxembourg as 'bijou pied à terre'. Western Sahara is 'guaranteed damp-free'. Up till now they've only attempted selling off bits of these countries, the railways or the power stations, but this was just nibbling around the edges. Far better to flog the whole lot off in one big go and cash in now before the multinational corporations realize that they already own everything. They tell us that five trillion divided between all of us would leave us with £80,000 each.

There's going to be a hell of a rush to buy Albania.

Diana was murdered; it said so on the Internet

9 January 2004

'Hello and what do you do?' asks Prince Charles politely.

'Shut it, scum! We've dragged you in here on a murder rap and you're gonna rot in a cell for the rest of your life.'

'How fascinating, and you work in this little basement interview room, do you?'

'Listen, you wife-murdering bastard, either you sign this confession now or we beat you to a pulp and you sign it later.'

'Jolly good, splendid, keep up the good work,' smiles the heir to the throne, turning to another policeman who's taking off his jacket and getting out his truncheon. 'And what do you do?'

Mind you, given the royal family's recent record of failing to spot undercover journalists, they can't be sure who they might be talking to during the inquest to Diana's death that was opened and adjourned this week.

'So, Your Majesty, would you say your super soar-away *Daily Mirror* was Britain's best-loved newspaper?'

'Er, you are definitely the official coroner, aren't you?'

''Course I am, Your Maj. Now can we just have a picture of you reading the *Mirror* and giving the camera a big thumbs-up?'

Charles has suddenly found himself at the centre of all the conspiracy theories after the *Mirror* published extracts from a letter by Diana in which she apparently wrote, 'My husband is planning "an accident" in my car, brake failure and serious head injury . . .' You'd think she'd have worn her seat-belt really, wouldn't you?

Apparently this paranoid premonition proves that His Majesty took the ceremonial silver wire-cutters off the velvet cushion, snipped through the brake cables and said, 'I now declare this Mercedes lethal' as assembled dignitaries broke into light applause. You might have seen the reconstruction on *Crimewatch UK*: Nick Ross saying, 'Did you see a man in plus-fours with big ears, tampering with a car outside the Paris Ritz? Do you recognize this artist's impression, which we borrowed from the National Portrait Gallery?'

But just imagine that the secret services had planned to murder Diana: would this really have been the best way to go about it? For months, we are asked to believe, top agents at M16 racked their brains for a foolproof plan to dispose of the most photographed woman in the world.

'How about crushing a bottle of sleeping pills in her bed-time drink and forging a suicide note?'

'Nah, that would never work!'

'Plant a bomb under her car and claim it was the IRA?'

'No, get real! We need something that is totally within our control and easy to execute.'

'I know, we get her in a car followed by dozens of journalists and persuade the driver to commit suicide by crashing into a pillar at a hundred miles an hour.'

'Yup, that should be easy to arrange.'

'Oh, and we do it in Paris, because if we're looking for someone to co-operate in a British cover-up, who better than the French authorities?'

We know the British secret services are incompetent, but they're not that incompetent.

If they had really wanted Diana out of the way there could have been dozens of easier ways to get her killed. Wait till Prince Philip was out shooting and tell him she was an endangered species. Ask Diana to take Princess Anne's dog for a walk.* But there is an immutable law of modern celebrity which states that the more famous you are, the less willing people are prepared to believe that your premature death was caused by the rather dis-appointingly mundane reasons given. Modern celebrities are the stars in a real life soap opera, and so when reality

* Princess Anne's bull terriers had recently developed a habit of attacking people. Not con-tent with killing one of the Queen's corgis and biting a royal maid, they actually landed Anne a court appearance after they attacked two children. But the judge wouldn't criticize the royal dogs because they can't answer back.

comes crashing in and pointlessly kills them off, there is a desperate search for some sort of deeper meaning. No decent film or novel would just kill off the heroine in a random accident at the end; the traditions of narrative fiction demand a murderer or a conspiracy which is then exposed for the story to really satisfy.

By conceding to demands for an inquest, the royal coroner has caved in to the fantasists who've been demanding a rewrite to the end of the Princess Diana fairy tale. Now there might as well be no holding back. The inquest should be broadcast in place of *Brookside*, with every dramatic twist and turn that the scriptwriters can come up with to satisfy the Internet nutters. 'Yes, all right, I murdered Diana,' Charles will suddenly weep in court, 'because she was going to tell everyone the truth about how the CIA killed Elvis and Marilyn Monroe. But then aliens from the Roswell incident kidnapped her demanding we confess that the moon landings were all filmed in Nevada and that's why Bush had to destroy the twin towers so no-one would find out . . .'

'At last,' they will say, 'a story we can actually believe in . . .'

2020 vision

16 January 2004

This week the first colour photos came back from Mars. NASA scientists sat at their computers for ages waiting for the digital photos to download and wishing they'd paid the extra to get broadband. But when the first images of the Red Planet confirmed that it was indeed sort of reddish, they were beside themselves with excitement. 'The surfaces of the rocks are remarkably smooth and the shapes are quite varied,' enthused lead scientist Dr Steven Squyres, 'some of them quite rounded and some of them quite angular.' It doesn't get much more thrilling than this. 'Right, so no actual green men then?' asked the journalist in the front row. 'Or Klingons in flying saucers maybe?' added another optimistically as the next twenty photos of smooth rocks were proudly described.

But having seen these postcards from another planet, George Bush decided that we really have to see this place for ourselves and on Wednesday announced a massive expansion of the United States space programme that will see a manned flight to Mars within the next couple of decades. Take-off is planned for the year 2020, or later if they let Dubya do the final countdown from ten to lift-off. Tony Blair was straight on the phone offering technical help from Britain's own Martian space programme.

'You see, our chaps have been kicking their heels a bit since they lost their Beagle probe, so anything they can do to help . . .'

'Er, that's really kind, Tony, but I think we're going to be okay,' replied George, as his advisers frantically shook their heads and mouthed 'No!' as emphatically as possible.

'No, really, we helped you in Iraq, perhaps we can use all the British know-how from the failed Beagle mission to make this a sort of joint US–UK mission to Mars. Hello? Hello? Oh, we must have been cut off.'

The flight to Mars will take six months, so one of the biggest challenges will be organizing the in-flight entertainment. Astronauts will spend the first few weeks flicking between the channels showing *Mr Bean* or non-stop Motown classics. It's either that or take off the little headphones and listen to the bloke in the next seat moaning about the fact that you have to pay extra for them. And when the little trays of food come round he will complain that he definitely pre-ordered the vegetarian option in an obvious ploy to get everyone else's cheese triangle, and then he'll wait until the entire row have their tray tables spread out before announcing he needs to go to the toilet.

Finally the pioneers will step down on to the surface of Mars, only to discover that their baggage has been flown to Mercury. 'This is one small step for man, one giant leap for the drilling rights of Exxon.'

Another part of George Bush's exciting vision is the idea of an occupied lunar base. 'Man to live on the Moon' screamed one of the front pages, though disappointingly it won't be David Dickinson from *Bargain Hunt*. Research scientists will be sent to live in the lunar pod for extended sabbaticals to study sun spots or whatever, although of course the real reason will be because they kept nicking the Head of NASA's parking space. Quite how they are going to get the builders out to the Moon to build this accommodation has not been explained, though NASA are currently developing a space suit which hangs down at the back to reveal the builder's bottom crack. Having a second home on the Moon will be a terrible worry in the winter months when it's just sitting there empty, but NASA are hoping they'll be able to find a nice lady from the local village to pop in and water the plants and put the heating on before they arrive.

Fifteen years later, after his father promised a mission to Mars that never materialized, Dubya has set out his own 2020 vision, this time missing out the detail of how it will be paid for. Apparently much of the cost could be met by internal savings at NASA; rinsing out and reusing the paper cups at the water cooler, that sort of thing. Cynics have been quick to point out that the President has made these bold and exciting announcements at the beginning of an election year, but there is a good practical reason for this. NASA will spend months desperately searching for volunteers to risk their lives spending months cooped up flying to a lifeless desert, but no-one will be mad enough to want to do it. Then in November Bush will be re-elected to a second term and suddenly millions of people will rush forward screaming, 'Get me to Mars, the Moon, whatever. Just get me off this planet as quickly as possible . . .'

Drugs war: it's peace, man

23 January 2004

The war on drugs has taken a dramatic new turn. Yesterday, before the world's media, a peace treaty was signed between the British government and cannabis. Hardliners had insisted that there should have been no talks with cannabis supporters until all joints were put beyond use, until they laid down their bongs and stopped giggling. But secret negotiations had been under way for some time. The government said they would downgrade the drug from class B to class C and discourage police officers from automatically arresting for possession, while for their part the cannabis delegation said that the carpet was so red, it was like really, really red.

There have been some concessions from drug takers. They have promised not to sit in the corner at parties taking far too long to roll a joint while they bore everyone about how Microsoft are in the pay of the Pentagon. They have undertaken to stop ripping up the mini-cab cards that were pinned up by the telephone. And they have finally admitted that T-shirts featuring a marijuana leaf under a sign saying 'Keep Off the Grass' are not really all that funny.

Users of cannabis have been complaining for some time that they were being pointlessly targeted and also that it was much harder to roll joints on CD cases than album covers. But a more lenient approach to the drug has been gradually emerging over the last decade. The House of Commons is now populated with a generation of politicians who can't credibly deny that they've ever smoked cannabis and so they all anxiously rehearse casual admissions that contain the words 'dabbled' and 'university'.

This liberalization comes at the same time that stricter limits are being placed on the smoking of tobacco in public places. Soon you will overhear people on trains saying, 'Excuse me would you put that cigarette out, please!'

'It's not a cigarette, it's a joint.'

'Oh, terribly sorry, do carry on.'

Restaurants will be divided into 'Smoking', 'Non-smoking' and 'Hey, squat down and, like, skin-up'. Now cannabis will be placed on the same level as prescription drugs, with the reaction that hundreds of people will rush to their doctor's surgery saying, 'I'm going to the Glastonbury Festival at the weekend and I wondered if you could prescribe me something to help me relax?' Maybe Rizla could even begin making king-size cigarette papers specifically for rolling joints. No, that would be too obvious, no one would go that far just yet.

Until recently, 90 per cent of all arrests for possession of drugs were for cannabis. At last our bobbies will have more time to get on with more important tasks, such as using their highly sophisticated methods for searching out drug dealers by pulling over any black man who's got a nicer car than them. The idea of freeing up the police from the front line of the drugs war is being extended. Rave venues have recently been fitted with 'speed cameras' to take photos of anyone out of their heads on speed. The dancers may have thought that was a strobe light but it was in fact the double-flash of the police camera that recorded them dancing suspiciously quickly.

It is the more pernicious drugs that the police should be concentrating on. I don't mean heroin or cocaine or ecstasy, I mean the real social menace: echinacea and arnica and all the herbal remedies that are sold at great expense and don't do anything whatsoever. All over Britain traumatized children are being forced to take fish oil while the callous drug pushers in the health food shop buy another gold-studded collar for their Rottweilers and laugh at the gullibility of the liberal middle classes. 'Wanna score some more St John's wort, man? It'll cost you, brother, this is good shit, brother, I ain't cutting in no low-grade marigold.' Suddenly, armed police burst in. 'This is a raid! Hand over your royal jelly!'

But everyone agrees that cannabis was overdue for downgrading. Everyone, that is, except Michael Howard. The Leader of the Opposition couldn't make himself look any more out of touch if he called it 'pot'. A previous Conservative attempt to appear to be tough on cannabis backfired when half a dozen members of the Shadow Cabinet admitted to having smoked it (though not presumably all at the same Tory cheese and wine do). Michael Howard refuses to answer this particular question, because once you start answering these sorts of enquiries, next they ask if you have ever tried the blood of a Transylvanian virgin and he can't be expected to remember every detail of his wayward youth. The Leader of the Opposition has actually announced that his Conservative government will reverse this measure. So he actually thinks he's going to be Prime Minister, does he? I don't know what Michael Howard has been smoking, but it must be pretty powerful stuff.

(The government later reversed the decision to downgrade cannabis after a number of scientists said the drug could affect long-term memory. Cabinet ministers were heard to comment, 'Did we downgrade it? I don't remember that. Etc. etc.')

Nuclear warheads – buy one get one free

13 February 2004

Every year there's a different craze, a new gadget on the market that everybody has simply got to have. First it was mobile phones, then it was digital cameras and now this year's big fashion is for nuclear warheads. Suddenly they've become so easy to buy that street traders have them piled up at the covered market on Saturday mornings.

'I don't want a nuclear weapon, I want an iPod,' says the teenage boy doing his birthday shopping with Mum.

'You can't have an iPod, they're too expensive. What's wrong with some enriched uranium and the technology to develop an atomic bomb? Kevin's got one – he got sent home from school, remember?'

Now George Bush has said that the illegal trade in

nuclear technology has to be stopped. The turning point was the recent confession by Pakistan's top nuclear scientist that he had flogged nuclear secrets to North Korea, Libya and Iran through the black market.

'Oh spiffing. Anything else?' asked Donald Rumsfeld. 'I mean, perhaps he'd like to get Bin Laden some nerve gas for his birthday?'

'What's this guy's name?' asked the concerned President.

'Abdul Qadeer Khan.'

Bush was immediately able to process this information and somehow deduce that he must be one of the bad guys. Apparently Dubya has some sort of secret code; when he hears a name like 'Abdul Qadeer Khan' he just immediately knows which side of the fence to place him on. Indeed, his first rule for policing the spread of atomic weapons is 'No nuclear technology for anyone with the letters "Qa" in their name.' It is amazing that it has taken America this long to wake up to the rapid spread of enriched uranium to regimes less stable than a Russian reactor. A couple of years back Bush clearly stated, 'We have to cessate the proliferization of atomical capacibility' but his advisers just smiled and nodded at him. Now the transformation of Bush into a campaigner against nuclear weapons has caught his advisers off guard. Last week he finished his face-painting workshop and went straight off to join Rumsfeld at the peace camp outside Pakistan's nuclear reprocessing plant. 'You can't kill the spirit!' they sang. '. . . Although carpet bombing from B-52s can get pretty close . . .' They've kept themselves busy tying ribbons and peace messages to the wire fence, you know the sort of thing: drawings by children saying 'I want to grow up, not blow up' or White House communiqués saying 'Tell us what you're up to or we nuke the entire Middle East.'

His government is extremely concerned about the development of this so-called 'Nuclear supermarket'. Apparently there are lines of fundamentalist terrorists queuing at the extra-wide checkout loaded up with plutonium rods labelled 'Buy One, Get One Free' while the bored girl behind the till presses the bell and shouts, 'How much are the fissile isotopes?' So the call has gone out to all members of the nuclear club to stop the spread of nuclear technology going any further. Many in the Republican Party will be very disappointed at this interference with the natural laws of free enterprise. 'Isn't it always the way? Something new comes on the market and the meddling bureaucrats from federal government start fettering our freedom to trade with their endless petty rules and regulations like 'No H bombs for crazed suicidal terrorists' or whatever the latest bit of red tape decrees.'

But this episode has proved what the anti-nuclear lobby has argued all along, that there is an inextricable link between the increased development of nuclear power and the spread of nuclear weapons. Western governments have been taken in by their own propaganda, believing that it is possible to export the know-how for 'peaceful' nuclear power programmes without having to worry about

129

dangerous by-products or hidden agendas. 'Oooh, so what shall we do with all this left-over nuclear material?' they imagined Third World leaders saying to one another. 'Shall we pop it in the recycling skips in the council car park, or shall we sell it at vast profit to that dodgy-looking bloke with the forged passport?'

Unless things change pretty soon we are going to reach the stage where every terrorist and mad dictator will have stockpiles of nuclear weapons, and eventually all-out global atomic warfare will become inevitable. Still, it's not the end of the world.

I think; therefore iPod

20 February 2004

This week the world's most advanced human-shaped robot has been performing to amazed audiences at the Science Museum. The gig was booked after weeks of haggling with his agent. 'I'm sorry but my boy is not sharing a dressing room with the dalek. He gets star room number one with a whole crate of WD40 and top billing above the animatronic Gollum.'

The new Japanese robot is called Asimo, short for 'Advanced Step in Innovative Mobility' (and it was also his grandfather's middle name). He really does possess an incredibly advanced range of human skills. He can walk up and down. He can shake hands. He can wave. Apparently the royal family are worried he might make them completely redundant. Asimo will even stride towards you and offer an outstretched hand as a greeting, except for the teenage version which barely looks round and just grunts from the sofa. All week crowds at the Science Museum have gasped as the robot has followed orders to walk up steps, walk down steps, turn around and come back. While the security guard stood there silently thinking, 'Well I can do that! Walking up steps, that's easy. But does anybody ever ask me? Oh no, I'll just stand here being ignored while they applaud that stupid robot.' There are fears that Asimo's new-found celebrity status may be getting out of hand. He's already been photographed in the 'Party People' section of the colour supplements, chatting with weathergirl Suzanne Charlton and the drummer from The Darkness saying, 'Of course I love performing; but what I really want to do is direct.'

This robot has been developed by Honda, so if he's anything like that Honda I used to have, when the weather's cold you'll have to push him along and jump on him to get him started. Asimo is small, only one metre twenty, and looks like an extra from a science fiction film. He is connected to the Internet, so that he can provide all sorts of useful information to his owner like how to get your android a penis enlargement. He can recognize different voices, walk in different directions and in a decade's time they're hoping he might even be able to fetch sticks. A lot is being made of his highly developed ability to walk down stairs, with no apparent credit being given to his British forerunner, the Slinky. The Japanese may well make the cleverest little robots, but we can still pride ourselves that we make the hardest. In a straightforward fight, Asimo wouldn't stand a chance against one of those destructive monsters from *Robot Wars*. We can feel a surge of patriotic pride as we imagine Asimo being sliced in two by Mr Psycho's rotating blade while a strange man in an anorak impassively wiggles his remote control behind the screen.

The long-term plan must be that these sorts of automatons will eventually do all sorts of jobs currently undertaken by humans. But the question that everyone's asking is what is there to stop all these foreign robots coming over here and signing on the dole? I mean, once you let them in, they'll take advantage of our generous benefits system and bring in all their robot relations and we'll just be swamped. And all the British robots in our car plants are now seriously worried about their jobs.

I'm sure there are other good reasons for developing computerized androids, if only to inspire hundreds of would-be screenwriters into depicting a nightmarish future in which the robots rebel and turn on their masters. Of course, it's all very well having a robot around the house, but you'll never be able to find the right charger. 'No, that's not for the robot, that's for the digital camera. Or is it the mobile, I'm not sure now.' Maybe that's why they are finally developing an electronic domestic robot. Because someone has to learn how to work all the other electrical equipment lying unused all around the house.

Pink is the new pinko

27 February 2004

First the enemy was the mighty Soviet Union, the 'evil empire' with its massive nuclear arsenal and plans for world domination. Then came crazed fundamentalist terrorists backed by rogue dictators hiding weapons of mass destruction. But now America faces an even greater threat to its very survival – yes, it's Simon and Julian, the couple who run 'Shampoodle – the Pet Pamper Parlor'.

For this week George Bush has put gay weddings at the top of the political agenda, proposing the radical step of an amendment to the American constitution. The crisis began on Monday when spy satellite photos clearly showed Simon and Julian choosing a wedding cake with two little men on top. Surveillance teams at the Pentagon reported increased present buying in the soft furnishing department of Bloomingdale's by other suspected local gays and their allies (single women in their forties). Meanwhile chemical experts reported that Simon and Julian were believed to be secret-stockpiling spumante and cassis, which could be made into pink champagne within forty-five minutes. A gay wedding might occur at any time; America is now in a state of pink alert.

This is clearly such a major political issue that it urgently requires a change in the American Constitution. Now the famous document will read 'All men are created equal . . . but when we say "men" we mean real men who like a beer and a ball game and leering at cheerleaders, not the effeminate faggoty types who jog through Central Park in tiny silver shorts, not that I was looking at their butts, obviously.' It will be the first constitutional amendment to be scrawled in green ink.

Meanwhile the British Conservative Party is suddenly heading in the other direction. This week the Tories announced that they were organizing a gay summit in Westminster. Michael Howard recognizes that there is a lot of ground to make up for a party in which 'safe sex' means making absolutely sure your wife can't find out. The Tories' understanding of gay culture may be a little outmoded, but they'll be doing their best based on their memories of boarding school.

'We're having my old Greek master giving descriptions of the male athletes running naked in the Olympic Games.'

'Yes, and I'll be explaining that being a homosexual doesn't automatically mean that you went to Cambridge in the 1930s and then spied for the Russians.'

But the conference is a step in the right direction. Unlike the American Right, the Conservatives are embracing the gay community because they have finally realized that there is nothing lower than trying to use fear and prejudice for narrow party advantage. So don't vote Tory 'cos they're obviously a big bunch of poofs.

But thanks largely to their militant Christian wing, the American Right is stuck in the political Stone Age. By making a constitutional issue out of gay marriages, Bush is hoping to make his enemies become associated with homosexuality. He is relishing the moment when Democrat senators find themselves having to raise their hands to vote to defend the rights of gays, but trying to do so in the most macho manner possible. As the TV cameras swing around the room seeking a raised arm that displays any sign of a slightly limp wrist, the senators will all be chewing gum, while some will have their shirt sleeves rolled up to reveal a tattoo of a naked lady that they've hastily drawn on their arm in biro during the debate.

'Hey, I really like cars and motorbikes and stuff like that, don't you?'

'Oh yeah, definitely, and beer and swearing and football.'

'Yeah, when all those big muscly guys all pile on top of one another – damn, damn, I didn't say that!'

George Bush has finally come out of the closet about

his homophobia. He sat his parents down and said, 'Mom, Dad, there's something I have to tell you. I think I may be homophobic.'

'Are you sure, son . . .' stammered his mother. 'I mean, it might just be a phase . . .'

I know in these days of political correctness one is supposed to be tolerant and broad-minded but I'm sorry, I just think it's disgusting. I mean these Christian Republicans – I don't mind them having these views in private, but why do they have to flaunt them so openly? What they say to each other about gays behind locked doors is their own business, but now you get them ostentatiously parading their anti-gay views, and boasting about it on the television, I mean, what if children were to hear? Bush knows that there is no real chance of a constitutional change this side of the presidential election, he is just seeking to boost his poll rating by stirring up hatred against a completely harmless minority. The issue is a complete Aunt Sally. Or should that be Uncle Sally?

Lord Chancellor abolished – Sky News clears the schedules

5 March 2004

At school, the crucial democratic concept of the separation of powers was patiently explained to us with a Venn diagram on the blackboard. A big circle for the legislature, another circle for the judiciary with a slight overlap containing the law lords. However, more complex legal and constitutional issues were lost amid giggling that the first two circles of the Venn diagram looked a bit like a pair of bosoms.

'Yes, boys, I know it might seem amusing that Britain does not have a total separation of powers,' said the teacher, slightly surprised that he'd managed to engage with the class quite so well. 'Now these dots in the middle of each circle represent . . .' But now the boys were doubled up and weeping with laughter, apparently at the anomalous position of various Cabinet members.

So it is with attempts to excite the public about plans for a supreme court and the abolition of the post of Lord Chancellor. The editor of the *Daily Star* must have really fretted about what angle to take with Lord Woolf's criticism of plans for a supreme court this week. 'Hmmm, we could either have a two-page article explaining that he has raised some interesting constitutional points, even though the reform itself is surely long overdue. Or we could just put, "Phoney Tony's Crony is a Sloaney Moany".'

Opposition to a proposed British supreme court has become increasingly vociferous. Judges are finally waking up to what last summer's announcement will mean (so a slightly shorter nap than normal, then). The decision to abolish the historic post of Lord Chancellor was rather absent-mindedly mentioned as part of a Cabinet re-shuffle, when such a major constitutional change should have been properly discussed alongside reform of the House of Lords, with detailed plans of what powers a supreme court would wield, who would sit in it, where it would be based and how many tens of millions the build-ing would go over budget. I'm not saying that this is a policy written on the back of a fag packet, but when he read out his big new idea, Tony Blair said, 'We are abolishing the Lord Chancellor UK duty paid.'

And yet the idea itself is a sound one in principle. The trouble with a country that has not had any major social upheaval since 1066 is that you keep discovering these historic posts that nobody ever got round to abolishing. In fact, when Tony Blair came to power, the civil service tried to slow him down a bit by inventing a few fictional constitutional sinecures for him to worry about.

'Prime Minister, have you given any thought to appointing the new Keeper of the Crown's Goats Inordinary?'

'Er, what does the Keeper of the Crown's Goats Inordinary do?'

'Well, he presents you the shortlist for the post of, um, Lord High Rod of Steward.'

'Of course, yes I knew that.'

Defenders of the current system fall back on the argument of tradition: 'But it is custom and practice that the law lords are privately educated white men from Oxbridge . . .'

Although some of these traditions are older than the judges themselves, many conventions seem pretty random. For example, why should it be that judges wear red robes and horsehair wigs because that particular outfit happened to be fashionable three hundred years ago? What about all the other periods of our history; why are they not represented?

In the new supreme court, judges should wear a variety of costumes: the lord chief justice will be dressed as a Viking, with a special big-horned helmet for state occasions. Other appeal judges will come clanking into the court dressed in suits of armour, following Second World War ARP wardens, teddy boys with quiffs and sideburns, dandy Elizabethans in doublet and hose, mods and rockers, and finally one embarrassed judge representing that brief period in the sixties when naturism was all the rage.

Historically, the Lord Chancellor has always sat on the woolsack, the wool representing the main industry in Britain hundreds of years ago. This too needs updating; the new Speaker of the Lords should sit on a pile of home delivery boxes from Domino's Pizza with a couple of nicked car stereos underneath for good measure.

Bit by bit this government has been dragging the British constitution out of the seventeenth century. But it needs to be done properly or not at all. Instead of half-heartedly tinkering to bring our system of government into line with the European convention of human rights, Tony Blair should be boasting about the extent of his reforms.

'I am proud to announce that I've definitely settled on a total separation of the legislature from the judiciary.'

'Right, so no more barristers in the House of Commons then, Prime Minister?'

'Ah, um, look, this may need a little more thought than I realized . . .'

Drugs are for losers (but we've managed without them)
12 March 2004

There was a great moment for British tennis this week, when Greg Rusedski, one of this country's greatest national sportsmen, was cleared of taking drugs. This followed a disturbing eight months, during which the Canadian also-ran Rusedski had brought shame on his native North America. But his exoneration means that the British star known as 'our Greg' can hold his head high once more.

However, concern about British tennis does not end there. Evidence is emerging that both Rusedski and Tim Henman, along with dozens of other British players, may have failed a random 'tennis test'. This rigorous testing regime scientifically analyses the number of sets accumulated by a tennis player in relation to their opponent, and the leaked results make shameful reading for the British game. 'This is nothing to do with me,' wept one British player. 'I don't know how that big net got there. This is the first I have heard of it.'

Drugs in sport have been a serious problem ever since the 1960s, when competitors in the Olympic high jump took an hour and a half to come down again. And who can forget the scandal of that seven-foot, bearded East German weightlifter? What was she called? Anna something? When the Olympic committee asked her if she'd had anabolics she said no, it was just the shorts she was wearing. Then there was the disgrace of Ben Johnson, who was stripped of his Olympic gold medal when his urine was discovered to contain more chemicals than a bottle of Sunny Delight.

The subsequent clampdown on the 'drug cheats' was severe and uncompromising. Life bans were imposed, records revoked and medals taken away; at which the drug-taking athletes giggled slightly and said, 'Yeah, whatever.' Since the use of drugs has become so widespread, perhaps the way forward is to incorporate drugs into the spectacle of modern sport. After the tests, a panel of judges could hold up their marks to reveal the amount of illegal substances found in the bloodstream. 'Oh, excellent scores. This Russian gymnast has scored straight 6.0s right across the board, as he brushes the white powder off his hands and then sniffs up what's left of it.'

We could do away with the old-fashioned baton, and competitors in the relay race could pass on a big fat joint to the next runner. 'Oh, and a fantastic performance by the British team in the urine test! They got it in the bottle every time!' The IOC symbol could be redesigned so that the Olympic flame had a little spoon of white powder just above it. It might improve Afghanistan's chances of hosting the Olympics, which, frankly, were looking like a bit of a long shot.

Although there is obviously a difference between recreational and performance-enhancing substances, there are breathtaking double standards regarding the purity expected of our sporting heroes, compared to other influential pillars of our society. Imagine random drugs tests on City brokers. 'There was shock in the City of London today when a top trader, having just won a £1m bonus, tested positive for cocaine, speed and mochachino. He is to be stripped of his loud tie, and faces a two-year ban on shouting across a room while holding three telephones.' The only reason that the City is opposed to completely replacing banknotes with plastic is because you can't snort cocaine through a rolled-up credit card.

Advertising is another industry in which drug use is rife. What other explanation could there be for a load of dancing cows singing in close harmony about a packet of butter? Campaign managers are making key decisions while completely out of their heads: 'Let's get hedgehogs to advise kids on crossing the road. I mean, who has a better record on it than them?'

Rock stars are, arguably, even greater idols for the young than athletes. But for the past forty years they have been almost expected to fill their body up with illegal chemicals. 'There was shock and disappointment today, following a random drugs test, when rock star Keith Richards was discovered not to have been taking random drugs. A spokesman said he denied rumours that his blood test had shown traces of blood and hoped that these upsetting allegations of clean living could be resolved in the next couple of months, or as soon as he wakes up.'

Meanwhile, poor Cliff Richard is considered uncool because the only time he was discovered slumped unconscious surrounded by drugs is when he fell asleep in the chemist while waiting for his prescription. But then Cliff would claim that he gets a big enough natural high from going along to watch Henman and Rusedski and hoping to see a British world tennis champion. Talk about being out of your head . . .

It's the economy, stupid

19 March 2004

The Left are traditionally not that good at managing money. Many of us still haven't got around to cancelling that direct debit to the Anti-Apartheid Movement. So previous Labour chancellors approached budget day like a paranoid lefty late with his tax return, desperately searching for old receipts and scraps of paper that had fallen down behind the desk and terrified that they'd go to prison for fraud for having written in the square marked 'Do Not Write in This Box'.

'Help! There's four blank stubs in the old cheque book; what could they have been for?'

'Er, was that the extra three billion you gave the DHSS?'

'I dunno. Maybe it was that two billion that went to the MoD?'

'Oh, just write something illegible and make up an amount . . .'

So it has been a bit of a shock to have a Labour Chancellor who understands economics. Of course, there are still those in the Cabinet who think all this finance stuff is boring and heave a big sigh when it comes to 'Item 5: Treasurer's Report'. While Gordon is talking about the public sector borrowing requirement they sit there colouring in all the letter 'o's on their agendas, waiting to read out their motion of support for Tibet. Actually many of them are secretly a little jealous that the Chancellor is the only minister who seems to get his own special day once a year. 'Why isn't there a big media frenzy about my big decisions?' sulks the Minister for Defence Procurement. 'Where are the big newspaper spreads saying "How will the navy's switch to US radars systems affect you?" Well, frankly, it won't.'

For the growing section of the Left that is automatically hostile to any Cabinet member, this week's budget seemed like it might throw up an issue around which they could unite.

'Right, the Blair government have really done it this time! They've just announced thousands of public sector workers are to be sacked.'

'That's terrible! Who is it, the nurses? The teachers?'

'No, the er . . . tax collectors.'

A slight pause while this sinks in.

'Right, yes, well, they are still workers, comrades, and we must defend their jobs and their right to, er, collect our taxes.'

'Yup, so who's coming on Sunday's march in support of these sacked tax collectors then?'

'Oh it's on Sunday, is it? Oh no, I'm doing, um, stuff, and oh dear, that's such a shame, I so wanted to come . . .'

Meanwhile, over at strike HQ, Inland Revenue workers are preparing themselves for the fight ahead, writing signs with catchy slogans like 'Hands Off the Inland Revenue Now or within 30 Days from the Date Given in Section One of This Placard'. As industrial action spreads, the union does its best to provide for the workers.

'Right, here's my application for strike pay.'

'Oh no, this is the wrong form. For Class 4 strike pay, you should have filled out form CF359, and sent it to the other office. Unless of course you have already submitted form IR341 for additional personal allowance strike pay before 5 April last year.'

Supportive members of the public throwing their spare change into the bucket being shaken outside the building are tersely reminded not to give cash, but to enclose cheques or postal orders with their tax reference number clearly written on the back. Somehow it seems this struggle is failing to capture the public's imagination.

Radical activists may not be that excited by Inland Revenue reform or budget forecasts and spending reviews, but the biggest lesson for the Left over the past decade has been that single inescapable truth: 'It's the economy, stupid.' All the new schools that are being built, the new and refurbished hospitals, the working families tax credit, the minimum wage, and the record rises in child benefit and the other achievements that have made a tangible difference to people's lives – these have all been possible because of a victory in that one unglamorous political cause: a sound and growing economy.

This budget has served to remind us how totally Labour has succeeded in replacing the Conservatives as the party of economic competence. But now Labour faces an even greater challenge, making the electorate feel that the state of the national finances is the sexiest of political issues. We need demonstrators holding all-night vigils demanding that the lifetime limit for retirement savings be lowered. We need British celebrities at the Oscars controversially speaking out against the freezing of insurance premium tax. We need balaclava-clad militants storming on to the set of the *Six O'Clock News* and angrily screaming, 'We demand an earlier assessment of the five economic tests for joining the Euro!'

We have to care more about the economy. If the meek are to inherit the earth, we're going to need the accountants to organize it. Anyway, must dash, we're spending the whole weekend organizing a Labour Party jumble sale. We raised £37.50 last time.

Stairlift to heaven

26 March 2004

Every so often we're presented with a horrific vision of a
nightmarish future: alien invaders enslaving mankind or
global power blocs in a state of permanent nuclear warfare. But this week came the most terrifying prediction of
all: by 2050 the majority of the world's population will be
pensioners. An entire planet just like Eastbourne, with
everyone on tenterhooks for the result of the RSPB Garden
Watch.

World leaders meet to discuss how to deal with the
crisis, but soon find themselves wandering off the subject.
'I spoke about the grave situation to the Chancellor of
Germany, and I said to him, oooh, my granddaughter's
married to a German, well half-German anyway, he works
in computers but they had to move to Canada which I

thought must be very cold . . .' To which the UN Secretary General interjects, 'Cold, yes . . .' The emergency summit is then suspended for an hour or so when a number of delegates suddenly have a little nap.

The M25 will look a little different with nothing but those electric shopping carts tootling along at five miles an hour. By now the greatest cause of greenhouse gases will be, well, greenhouses. Of course, pensioners of the future will be different to the old people of today. They'll have grown up with computers and the Internet, so they'll be able to shop online for example, even if the van driver gets a bit exasperated with having to deliver just one tin of rice pudding every single day. 'Young people today,' they'll say as he nods and looks at his watch, 'they've no idea what it was like for us using Windows 95. In my day you had to type in the windows prompt from the DOS operating system, and then it took a good twenty seconds to come up. None of your flashy Windows 2050 Edition flashing straight on to the screen in those days. Ooh and the problem we had dialling up the net, I don't suppose you remember that little noise it made, as it tried to connect. These super-fast computers are all very well, but those minutes when you were waiting for an attachment to download, well, it just gave you time to pause and reflect . . .'

The 1990s craze for tattoos will mean that every resident at the 2050 old people's home will have a faded blue splurge at the base of their spines.

'Oh my, is that a bruise?'

'No, dearie, it used to be a sort of Celtic symbol that peeked out above my Calvin Kleins.'

And there'll be an enormous demand for nostalgic ceramic dolls with safety pins through their noses and purple Mohican haircuts, wearing the punk outfits of yesteryear while every other advert in the colour supplements will be for a beautiful hand-painted plate to commemorate the fiftieth anniversary of Prodigy's 'Smack My Bitch Up'.

'Oooh, they don't write 'em like that any more,' they'll say on Radio 2's *Sounds Familiar*.

Our society is of course chronically underprepared to cope with having the majority of the population past retirement age. But there is something that we can do now. And that is warning our children that we are going to be an enormous burden to them. Start telling them now that we are going to expect them to pay our bills, ferry us around and on Sundays, when we've been awake an hour or so (say around half past six in the morning), we'll be ringing them up and saying, 'Can you come and mend the stairlift again?'

Medical advances, improvements in diet and healthier lifestyles have led to a significant improvement in life expectancy since the war. We regularly hear about huge reductions in the number of old people dying from heart disease or influenza. But this excellent news is often accompanied by a secret guilty thought: 'Right, so how exactly is everyone going to die then?' It's not something Jeremy Paxman can comfortably ask the Minister of

Health on *Newsnight*, even though half of his viewers are thinking it: 'Great, so deaths from smoking are down 50 per cent. But you don't want to cure everything though, do you? I'm mean, they've got to die sometime . . .' It's like when you hear about that marvellous old lady of eighty-eight taking up the violin; you guiltily think, 'Well, is it really worth it? I mean, frankly, by the time she's any good . . .'

Most people would agree that we don't actually want people living for too long, with the honourable exception of ourselves and everybody that we know. 'When I'm old I don't want to outstay my welcome,' we say, 'I'm just going to die, just like that, before I get all decrepit and ga ga.'

'Yeah, me too, maybe when I'm about, say, 103?'

Deport the English!

2 April 2004

In 1973 Britain joined the EEC and few who witnessed it will ever forget the uncontrollable wave of immigration that followed. Hordes of Dutch people pouring into the country and swamping our traditional British way of life, forcing us to wear clogs and eat waxy cheese. 'It was terrible,' said one scared pensioner. 'I mean you'd get one windmill go up in the street, and then another went up next door and before you knew it the whole neighbourhood stank of tulips and everyone was cycling everywhere, speaking impeccable English . . .'

'Oh yeah, and then the bloody Belgians moved in, with their fancy lager and yummy chocolates. And the Luxembourgers, remember them, with their bloody . . . um, well, I can't actually remember any distinctive national characteristics, but that's what we all hated about 'em.'

And now another wave of migrants are set to sweep into Britain from Eastern Europe as soon as they can get the Trabant started. The general presumption seems to be that this will have a negative impact on our economy and society, that they'll all sign on the dole and then blow the money on Beatles memorabilia and pickled root vegetables. It's certainly true that the Poles and Hungarians who are already working over here have no idea whatsoever about British culture. Yer typical bloody Polish handyman, for example, not only turns up when he says he will, but then works really hard and completely fails to attempt to rip you off or shout offensive remarks at passing women. I mean, it's just not acceptable, these are all precious British traditions that may disappear for ever if we're not careful. Once we start incorporating immigrant culture into our society our whole way of life is under threat. Imagine if everyone was as polite and attentive as a typical Indian waiter, for example? You wouldn't spend half an hour on the phone trying to get through to the right council department; instead they'd keep checking with you that everything was all right, offer you another lager, and when the council tax bill came, there'd be free mints with it.

We expect immigrants to learn to behave like British people, but only up to a point. For no English person would tolerate the amount of crap that Britain's immigrant population has to endure. Who stands there in his take-away shop taking endless abuse from drunken English youths after closing time? Is it the English kebab-shop owner who is insulted and intimidated? Is it the English mini-cab driver who has people being sick in the back of his car and then refusing to pay? (Mind you, they might not have been sick if that Turkish bloke hadn't sold them the dodgy kebab, but that's not the point.) Imagine if it was the other way round. Imagine the *Daily Mail* front page if every Friday night hundreds of Afro-Caribbean kids were spilling out of the pubs on to British high streets fighting and then staggering into the English Rose tea rooms saying, 'Oi whitey, turn off that bloody honky string quartet music, will you?'

It is true that Britain is a small crowded country but the answer to this is a simple one: the time has come to deport all the crap English people. This might sound a reactionary idea, but it's simply about allowing people to find their natural level. For example, this week Ann Winterton was readmitted to the Tories after her dismal, offensive joke about drowned Chinese cockle-pickers. But she is clearly not up to being an MP (her one spell on the front bench ended when she was sacked for another joke about 'Pakis') and there are a lot of hard-working highly intelligent Eastern Europeans who could do her job a lot better than her. Ann would be far more suited to being the local councillor for an impoverished suburb of Skopje. Robert Kilroy-Silk is another candidate for relocation to a more impoverished part of Europe. His hateful tirade against Arabs got him the sack from his job fronting his god-awful TV show, so now is the perfect time for him to start again hosting a local radio phone-in, say in rural Moldova where no-one is on the telephone.

Basically any Brit, from the racist football fan to right-wing columnist, who thinks they are really great and feels at liberty to snipe at racial minorities from their privileged position will have to move to a struggling country where nothing works and you have to toil long hours for low pay. And in their place let's give a really big friendly welcome to any new immigrants, who don't just bring new skills, hard work and enthusiasm – they bring humility, something which is in very short supply in this country when we discuss immigration and race. Except the French of course – they're bloody worse than we are.

Rushing roulette

9 April 2004

For the past few months a cross-party committee has been preparing a report on gambling. Reading their conclusions gives a window into the MPs' experiences during their intensive research. 'The committee recommends that the man who gives out the change in the amusement arcade should not use foul language just because Bernard banged the glass near that big pile of 2ps on the Copper Coin Cascade.' Or, 'The committee strongly recommend that someone should fix the little Grab-a-Gift crane because Sir John definitely had the watch with the £10 note wrapped around it and then the teeth just went all floppy and dropped it back amongst all the cuddly toys.'

Of course, when any group of middle-class people go out gambling together there is always a certain amount of macho posturing and pretending they understand it all.

'So why does it say "handicap" next to the horse's name here?'

'Er, well, they have to have a race for handicapped horses as well, you see, it's like the Special Olympics . . .'

'Right, I see, and what does "each way" mean?'

'Well, obviously they race down the course one way, and then, um, they turn around and race back again.'

And then all the MPs pretended to study the baffling columns of numbers and letters before placing a bet on the horse with the funniest name.

The report comes in advance of a Gambling Bill which is planned to update Britain's antiquated betting laws. Under rules laid down in the 1960s, anyone opening a new casino without Ronnie and Reggie's permission gets buried in the Hammersmith flyover. But now a new hardened operator is muscling into the gangster's traditional patch. Known as Tessa 'The Godmother' Jowell, she'll be making a few changes and seeing that 'Big Tony' gets his rake-off. All sorts of reforms are planned. For example, slot machines may be banned from fish and chip shops because the customer is already taking quite enough risks ordering that congealed red saveloy that's been kept warm for a week or so. Trades description legislation will apply to slot machine arcades in the high street, so instead of having names like 'Loads-a-Fun' these will have to be renamed 'Miserable Dive for No-Hope Losers'. And in future the DSS will pay child benefit direct to Ladbrokes so as to cut out the middle man. One of the hopes is that Las Vegas-type resorts will spring up in Britain's run-down seaside towns. The Americans might have Atlantic City, the French might go to Monte Carlo, but we'll have Blackpool, where you can bet on roulette, blackjack and whether that donkey will cope with the weight of the fat kid with the candy floss. These days you can bet on virtually anything: it's 2-1 that any single male you know will remember his nephew's birthday, evens that Tony Benn can talk about Iraq without mentioning the Crusades and 2/7 that any wine bar or restaurant will have Dido or Norah Jones playing in the background.

The current boom in gambling is due in part to the world-wide-web. Internet gambling sites are now programmed to make online betting just like going to the bookies; they even send round some sad-looking old blokes to hang around your front room smoking and dropping bits of paper on the floor. Most of the sites also boast 'Online Casinos', which are every bit as glamorous as the real thing. You say to your partner, 'Get dressed up, I'm taking you to the casino,' and then you both walk the ten feet over to the computer where you demonstrate just what a cool and cunning hustler you really are by typing in the same Internet password you use for everything else.

Some time ago the government recognized which way the wind was blowing, and did everything it could to encourage the online gambling companies to stay in this country, even abolishing the 10 per cent off-course duty. But liberalizing Britain's gambling laws even further does not come without risks of its own. 'Look how much we stand to win!' says Tony Blair, adding up the revenue from the new casinos and jobs in the leisure industry. But like any hardened gambler he's forgetting about how much it will cost him. Hundreds of thousands of people getting into debt, losing their homes, unable to support their families. More people turning to crime to pay for their habit. There are an estimated 300,000 so-called 'problem gamblers' in this country (which is twice as many as I bet my kids there would be). But it won't be the casinos paying for all the social costs of more addicts. Maybe the all-party committee should explain everything they have learnt to the Prime Minister and he might think twice about the morality of it all.

'So, guys, how do these big bookmakers maintain such enormous profit margins?'

'Well, it's simple really, PM: they take loads of money off millions of poor people, but keep them passive by occasionally giving small amounts back.'

'Hang on a minute,' says the Prime Minister. 'I thought that was what the Treasury did.'

If it wasn't for opening all those crisp packets I wouldn't get any exercise at all

15 April 2004

A well-established tenet of propaganda is that if you are going to tell a lie, tell a really big one: 'The Luftwaffe have destroyed all of London' or 'This watch is waterproof to a depth of 100m'. So it is with Walkers Crisps getting their brand associated with a new TV show aimed at tackling Britain's obesity crisis. If your product's biggest problem is that it's perceived as unhealthy then keep repeating the subconscious message that eating crisps is what healthy sporty people like to do. That's why Walkers sponsor Leicester City and Wolverhampton Wanderers. Because they want people to associate their brand with, er, desperate struggles to avoid relegation.

In the biggest row about inappropriate product

placement since the Home-Assembly Power Saw sponsored *Casualty*, Walkers Snack Foods has been criticized for getting involved in a new high-profile TV campaign to help Britons lose weight. Walkers are set to help fund the planned giveaway of around two million step-o-meters that measure how far people walk every day, which seems like a bit of a waste of money. Clearly it's five yards from the sofa to the fridge, and ten yards from the front door to the car. This forthcoming television campaign will be called 'Britain on the Move' and aims to tackle Britain's obesity crisis by getting everyone sitting around watching TV shows about healthier lifestyles. Walkers were presumably thought to be ideal because the central mission of this health initiative is to get everyone walking. 'Brilliant idea!' said the PR company. 'We want to make people walk, and these crisps are called Walkers! It's perfect!' Presumably they'd already been declined by 'Strollers biscuits' and 'Joggers, the deep fried chocolate donut people.' Of course, the great thing about walking as a form of exercise is that it keeps your hands free for stuffing Dorito Dippas in your gob.

This row follows persistent criticism of Britain's crisp producers that their crisps are poor value, that Wotsits are actually flavoured bits of polystyrene used for packing fragile parcels and that Monster Munch simply aren't scary enough. However, try reading the fat content for the average packet of Monster Munch and you'll realize they're actually terrifying. Britain eats more crisps than the rest of Europe put together and for some time now the government has been concerned about the way in which fried snack foods exacerbate this country's growing obesity problem. In the Department of Health recently, the politicians were presented with some typical packets of crisps and asked to read the alarming figures printed on the back.

'Hang on a minute, this can't be right,' said the Minister, 'in my day salt and vinegar always came in blue packets and cheese and onion was always green; this is the wrong way round.'

'Well maybe it's changed, Minister, but just look at the fat and salt values listed on the packet there.'

'But hang on, why have they changed the colours? Cheese and onion should be green, it just confuses everything.'

The MPs then opened a packet, allowing each other to sample the various flavours. 'Oi, don't take a whole handful!'

'Well, you don't have to hold the packet in the middle like that . . .'

In the end the government decided against banning junk food advertising aimed at children, perhaps because it was hard to imagine healthier foodstuffs stepping into the breach: 'The Premiership is sponsored by organic wholemeal pasta.' 'Welcome to the FA Cup Final, sponsored by lettuce.' But surely it won't be long until we have to watch our children at their school's sports day sponsored by the various junk food companies. Instead of throwing the discus, kids will have to lob a deep-fried pizza towards the lunch queue. In place of the shot put, kids will have to use all their strength to lift that enormous Easter Egg that they got from Aunty Vera, and then the race is on for who can eat theirs the quickest. A few years back Walkers was criticized for the way it encouraged school children to eat crisps by getting them to collect tokens which would be exchanged for books. It was a great deal; if every child in the school ate seven packets of crisps a day for two years, the school library got enough tokens for one new book explaining premature heart disease.

If ITV are sincere about wanting to improve the nation's health they should reject any involvement between Walkers Snack Foods and the Britain on the Move campaign. Britain's obesity crisis is a serious problem and should not be used as an opportunity for a bit of surreptitious advertising for unhealthy fatty foods. It's enough to make you switch channels. Except the remote control has slipped under the sofa cushions and I'm not getting up now.

Privacy campaigners should be named and shamed

22 April 2004

As part of the national curriculum, junior school children now learn how to produce their own class newspaper, the idea being to make it as much like the real thing as possible. It's been a bit distressing for one headteacher, having a press pack of ten-year-olds camped outside her bedroom window for a week following a wild claim from a child in Year 4. 'Mrs Johnson in Sleazy Love Tryst with Caretaker Colin!' screamed the front page, beside a photo of them chatting in the school hall, carefully doctored so that they appeared to be snogging during the nativity play. 'Inside: my booze hell by LSA Jenny' and 'Mr Harris who runs the football team in secret text affair with Miss Jones from Key Stage One'. The school were going to stop the photocopier, but when sales went up by

200,000 they realized they needed the extra school funds.

This week a poll apparently revealed that a large majority of the British population would be in favour of a law protecting celebrities from press intrusion. Eighty-five per cent of those polled said that they believe that David Beckham's affair should have been kept private, but they couldn't chat with the pollsters for long because they were just dashing into the newsagents to buy the *News of the World*.

'Have you seen the front page, "I'm Becks' Lover Number 2"?'

'All right, hurry up, I want to get back to watch *Rebecca Loos, My Story* on Sky One Mix.'

The idea of a privacy law is often mooted after a major celebrity exposé like this one. When the papers have run out of reasons to print pictures of Posh and Becks, there follows a serious commentary piece about press intrusion alongside a big picture of Posh and Becks helpfully reminding us of the sort of people who've suffered from over-the-top newspaper coverage recently. 'Should celebrities be protected from wild allegations like the ones we are now going to repeat once more, just in case you missed them?'

Media coverage of celebrities has been a problem ever since the *Anglo-Saxon Chronicle* ran that front page on King Alfred burning the cakes. 'It's Alfie the Grate – My Burnt Cake Misery by Wessex Housewife – More Engravings Inside'. It drove the king mad with frustration: 'They don't talk about me defeating the Danes at Edington, do they?

Or how I converted Guthrum to Christianity, or my translations of Boethius and Bede, no, no, it's always, "Ooh, here he comes, don't let him near the kitchen!"'

'Oh that's where I recognize you from!' said the newsagent. 'You're that bloke who burnt all those cakes.'

Respect for public figures got steadily worse down the centuries, until suddenly in the last decade or so it became inevitable that any major celebrity would be smeared by someone and at least one editor would be prepared to print it all. The most recent story had the bonus of containing the word 'text', which highly trained headline writers spotted bore a vague similarity to the word 'sex'. Although all credit to David Beckham for finding out how to do asterisks on his mobile phone. But of course these petty scandals are not real news stories, they have no bearing on the world at large. I mean who really wants to read details of Hugh Grant having sex with a prostitute when there is a fascinating article about US interest rates looking unlikely to change? What is so interesting about George Michael being caught in a public lavatory when you can read about the Belgian general election shifting the balance in the coalition at Brussels? No wonder the celebrities get fed up with it; apparently Michael Douglas and Catherine Zeta Jones are currently going to court over some unauthorized photographs taken by speed cameras on the M25.

Public figures have the right to a certain amount of privacy, but when celebrities work so hard to gain exposure and then talk about privacy from the media, what they really mean is they want control of how they are portrayed. Showbiz stars might call for a less intrusive media and tabloid readers might claim that they support this idea, but before we get a privacy law, what we need is a hypocrisy law. Perhaps a few celebrities could join the cause.

'But hang on, you only got famous by campaigning against a hypocrisy law and now you want one?'

'Oh yeah, but that was different . . .'

It might be argued that if part of your multimillion-pound brand is your wonderful family life, then don't have an affair. If you sell yourself as a wholesome children's TV presenter, then don't take cocaine. If you're going to be a Prime Minister talking about Back to Basics, don't have sex with Edwina Currie. In fact whatever the situation, just don't have sex with Edwina Currie.

Athens Olympics – nothing like the brochure

7 May 2004

The Greek Prime Minister shook his head in sorrow this week as he looked around the chaos of mangled steel and piles of rubble.

'So just how bad is this bomb damage?' he asked.

'No, no, Minister, the bombs went off miles away. This is just the Olympic village building site.'

It is sixteen hundred years since the Olympic Games ended in Ancient Greece, and it looks like it might be another sixteen hundred before the current Olympic site is ready. With just under a hundred days until the opening ceremony, the Greek government are putting a brave face on their state of readiness, admitting that the project may be a little behind, but that building work will definitely go up another gear as soon as the skip arrives.

'So, Minister, just how serious is this crisis?'

'We're not worried at all, now give us a hand mixing this cement, will you?'

Prime Minister Kostas Karamanlis has taken personal charge of the proceedings and yesterday was spotted looking a little lost wandering around the Athens B&Q trying to find the decking to go round the Olympic swimming pool.

Matters have not been helped by the presence of a Channel 4 TV crew filming *Olympic Village Makeover* with Kevin McLeod walking around saying, 'Week 27, and the project is months behind schedule and massively over budget . . .'

'Excuse me, mate, would you mind getting off my building site?'

'Yes, tensions are clearly rising as Kostas realizes he shouldn't have left all that cement out in the rain.'

'Right, that's it, someone arrest this bloke for plane spotting.'*

With the Games looking like they might have to take place in the middle of a chaotic building site a few adjustments are being planned for some of the events. The 400m hurdles will now involve jumping over piles of scaffolding poles and a generator. Competitors in the long jump will have to hurry before the sand is shovelled into a cement mixer. And most nervous of all are the

---

* Some British plane spotters had recently been detained by the Greek authorities for spying. The British public were shocked; 'Only three days at the airport? We were stuck at Luton for a week.'

competitors in the freestyle diving event, who've been told not to be distracted by little imperfections like the fact that the pool doesn't actually have any water in it.

Because there is no time to complete the roof on the massive new aquatic centre, they have rather brilliantly announced that the Olympic swimming pool is going to be open air. Next they'll announce that the living accommodation is going to be open air as well. 'It's nothing like the brochure', the athletes will all complain, pointing to the artist's impression and demanding to see their holiday rep. Now the swimming races are bound to be delayed; as soon as the starting pistol is fired all the athletes' mums will rush forward and start rubbing factor 30 sun cream all over them before they're allowed in the water. New events are also being added that don't require massive velodromes or expensive stadia and Britain is hoping for a gold medal in the 'scissors, paper, stone' event.

Although Greece was awarded the Games in 1997, construction work did not begin until 2000. The head of the organizing committee, Mr Gianna Angelopoulos-Daskalaki, remains confident that the site will be ready on time though part of the delay can be put down to the fact that every time anyone rang up they had to say 'Hello, can I speak to Gianna Angelopoulos-Daskalaki?' Of course there is some romance in the idea of taking the Games back to their original location; for example the marathon runners will be following the original route of Pheidippides after the Battle of Marathon, or 'the Battle of Snickers' as the Americans now insist on calling it. But a combination of corruption, legal quagmires, nepotism and strike action looks set to make this showpiece into a major humiliation, which leaves you wondering why any country would want the poisoned chalice of hosting the modern Olympic Games. And this week's bombs confirm the enormous security worries inherent in policing the event, especially when they've been told that the security fencing won't be delivered until the autumn.

Yet while the Greeks are being made into an international laughing stock, Britain is desperately bidding to be next in the queue.

'Please, let London host the 2012 Olympics, because English builders are famous for their reliability and reasonable budgets.'

'Definitely, and with Britain now so popular in the Arab world, a London Olympics would certainly never be a prime terrorist target!'

But a London Olympics might see a few records being broken. Nervous athletes would be told that they had to go and spend two weeks in the capital of America's closest ally and then they'd record their fastest-ever times – as they all ran off in the opposite direction.

Greece managed to complete its facilities at the last minute, and hosted a successful Olympics in which Great Britain did fantastically in all the sports that count: women's sailing (Yngling class), synchronized platform diving and K1 kayak slalom. Meanwhile London of course went on to surprise everyone by winning its Olympic bid – see page 277.

And now the weather – well, we're all going to die

14 May 2004

There was panic in Hollywood this week, when news came through that one or two meteorologists had criticized the scientific inaccuracies in Fox's new multi-million-pound blockbuster *The Day after Tomorrow*.

'You mean to say climate change wouldn't actually be as dramatic as we've made it in the film?' screamed the appalled Rupert Murdoch, horrified at the prospect of losing his reputation for integrity.

'It gets worse, sir. Professor Mike Hulme, director of climate change research at the University of East Anglia, has said that the film actually breaks the laws of physics.'

'Oh no, a man from the University of East Anglia has criticized it? Look, I think we're just going to take a chance and release the movie anyway.'

174

The Day after Tomorrow portrays a scenario in which New York is hit by a 100ft tidal wave, three vast hurricanes cover the northern hemisphere and even more implausibly a family have a caravan holiday in North Wales and it doesn't rain for the entire fortnight. Other scientists have praised the film for putting the issue of climate change back on the agenda, even if it is hard to imagine the British royal family actually freezing to death at Balmoral. Surely they'd just keep chucking back issues of the *Sporting Life* on the fire; there must be enough to get them through a short ice age. The film shows panicking Americans fleeing to Mexico while in Britain the calamitous climate news has people tutting and saying, 'I was hoping to pot those geraniums this weekend . . .'

'. . . Don't worry, we won't feel any effects of global warming just yet,' continues Michael Fish with the water lapping around his midriff as a couple of ducks swim past his weather map.

Back in the 1970s there was a rash of terrifying films such as *The Towering Inferno* and *Airport* which all ended in disaster when Charlton Heston survived. In some cinemas the film *Earthquake* was actually released in what was called 'Sensurround' in which your chair physically shook and looters nicked all your popcorn. Now Sensurround is back, and viewers of this new climate change disaster movie at the Streatham Odeon can really experience the freezing cold conditions portrayed on the screen. Witness complete electrical and computer meltdown as you attempt to collect your pre-ordered tickets. Feel the floods wash around your feet as a two-pint carton of Pepsi is knocked over by the teenagers sitting behind you. Are those giant hailstones falling all around your seat, or are those kids chucking toffee poppets down from the circle?

The difference about this new disaster movie is that it addresses a genuine and very real environmental danger. In the Maldives, for example, rising sea waters may well result in the entire country disappearing under the Indian Ocean at some point this century. It's funny how Cabinet discussions tend to always come back to the same thing.

'So what are we going to do about this strike at the tuna canning factory?'

'I think the best response to this dispute would be to move to Tibet.'

'All right, item seven on the agenda. Farm subsidies?'

'Again, I would say that all things considered, the way forward on this one is to move to Tibet.'

The earth's temperature is rapidly rising and the current American government, which Rupert Murdoch supports, is doing pretty well everything it can to make matters worse. Fox's latest blockbuster movie portrays the US government as complacent about global warming, which is about the only part of the film that is not exaggerated. It's lucky that drive-in movies went out of fashion in America, or George W. Bush would have gone to see the film and left his engine running the whole way through.

The Day after Tomorrow may have been criticized for distorting the facts to attract a wider audience. But the problem is that unless real events mirror the dramatic timescale of Hollywood movies, then no response is demanded of our politicians. Public opinion conditioned by thousands of years of the traditional three-act story shape wants its non-fiction stories to follow the same rules. So while the news agenda might be gripped by a terrorist atrocity or the soap opera of a footballer and his wife, interest cannot be sustained in a slow and un-theatrical narrative such as a major shifting in climate patterns. The weather used to come after the news. By the time it comes at the top of the news it will already be too late.

All over the world panic and disorder will prevail while the British will continue to greet each other with casual observations about the weather.

'It's turned out apocalyptic again, I see.'

'Yes, the radio said the whole of England will be under water tomorrow.'

'Still, mustn't grumble . . .'

Purple haze
20 May 2004

Isn't it always the way? You wait ages for one purple flour-filled condom and then three come along at once. Although objects get thrown from the public gallery every decade or so this is thought to be the first time that a Prime Minister has actually received a direct hit since Spencer Perceval was assassinated in the Commons in 1812. I bet the Whig MP who raffled those tickets was embarrassed.

By now most details of Wednesday's alarming attack are well known. Sometime before 11.45 the so-called 'purple haze bombers' passed through the House of Commons security, placing any large objects in the tray for the x-ray machine. The eagle-eyed police officers checked each item carefully: car keys . . . mobile phone . . . condoms stuffed with purple powder . . . Hang on a minute! Oh no, it's

OK, there's no nail clippers attached to those car keys. At 11.51 the attackers took their seats in the VIP section of the public gallery using tickets which they had won at a raffle. Other guests at the fundraiser such as Osama Bin Laden and a couple of men from Dundalk in sunglasses and black berets cursed their luck that they had the same number but on a different coloured ticket (though they did go home slightly mollified when they won the crystallized fruit and the bottle of British sherry). At 12.18 p.m. a protestor interrupted PMQs by shouting, 'I haven't seen my daughter in five years!' at which point Tory MPs with kids at boarding school mumbled, 'That recently?' Then the Prime Minister felt some sort of projectile strike him in the back. His first thought was that the obvious suspects could immediately be narrowed down to any one of around four hundred Labour MPs seated behind him.

The protestors were in luck; neither Tony Blair nor Gordon Brown were wearing their bright purple jackets on that particular day, so the powder was clearly visible. Gordon Brown did the nearest he does to panicking which involved slightly raising one eyebrow, while Tory MPs stampeded towards the exits in their rush to spread the anthrax virus all over London as quickly as possible.

Samples of the powder were immediately sent for analysis at the forensic labs and it was discovered that it was indeed dangerous. The flour was neither wholemeal nor organic; if you ate this stuff for forty years you could develop serious digestion problems.

Eventually PMQs were resumed but somehow none of Michael Howard's prepared one-liners seemed likely to catch the Prime Minister as unawares as a purple condom falling out of the sky. The correct procedure should have been for all MPs to remain in the chamber and remove all items of clothing. I'm not sure which is a more horrific thought: anthrax all over London or the vision of a naked Ann Widdecombe chatting to Nicholas Soames as he slipped out of his Y-fronts.

Though we have a right to be informed who carried out this stunt, it is important that the media do not give too much publicity to fathers 4 justice, or fathers-4-justice.org as they are known on the web. Too much free advertising in British newspapers might encourage similar pranks from Fathers 4 Justice, PO Box 7835, Sudbury, CO10 8YT, telephone 01787 281922.

The media responded to the incident with a suitable sense of proportion. 'Man who could have killed Blair,' said the *Mail*. 'They could all be dead,' screamed the *Sun*. 'Still no broadband for Hereford,' said the *Hereford Times*. Now there are fears that increased security will drive a further wedge between politicians and the public. No longer will bemused American tourists sit there watching an unknown MP talking out loud to an empty chamber. No more will the Prime Minister be able to shake the hands of ordinary members of the public who've just been hand-picked from Labour Party head office.

In fact the public gallery became irreversibly public in the late 1980s when TV cameras were finally allowed into the House and the British people now watch the Parliamentary Channel in their dozens. The real issue here is that our seat of government is managed by amateurs according to quaint and random archaic customs. When the men in wigs and gaiters expressed anger that the correct procedure was not followed on Wednesday, what they meant was that it's traditional that Honourable Members should not evacuate a lethally poisoned chamber without first doffing their top hat to Mr Speaker after hanging up their sword beside Black Rod's breeches and jigging around the woolsack. The Palace of Westminster needed a wake-up call and this was it. We should just be grateful that nothing really dangerous happened and no one got hurt. But only because several policemen managed to hold John Prescott back to prevent him from retaliating.

Losing face

28 May 2004

This week scientists in America sought permission to go ahead with the first-ever face transplant. It's an incredibly expensive procedure, but the good news is that afterwards no-one will recognize the patient who came in for the operation so he can walk straight past hospital reception without paying. The world's first face transplant will take a team of surgeons twenty-four hours to complete, lifting nose cartilage, lips and nerves and then reconnecting all the muscles and skin tissue to another human head. Then finally all the relations will be allowed to visit the recovery ward.

'Brian, you look fantastic!'

'I'm not Brian, I'm Kevin – Brian's in that bed over there.'

'No, I thought I was Sheila. Excuse me, I think there's been a bit of a mix-up.'

Until very recently this extraordinary concept was pure science fiction, and featured in the 1997 thriller *Face/Off*, starring Nicholas Cage and John Travolta, in which two of Hollywood's leading actors were suddenly faced with the challenge of playing each other.

'Why are both of you suddenly mumbling and performing so woodenly?' asked the director.

'Oh, I thought you wanted me to start acting like *him*.'

But now it won't be long before we will all be carrying face donor cards, although you wouldn't want to receive the face of just anyone.

'That's a very kind thought, Lady Thatcher. But you really don't need to carry a face donor card.'

'No, I think I should set an example. And whoever is lucky enough to get my face will be smiled on wherever she goes . . .'

The cards will probably say something like 'I would like someone to be screamed at after I have died' because there will of course be problems inherent in walking around with the face of someone who has passed away. The recipient might be sitting in a pub when suddenly a beautiful woman comes running over to him.

'David, at last I've found you. My first true love, I always dreamed that we would be reunited.'

'Ah, er, well actually there's something you ought to know.'

'Never mind that. Let's find a hotel room and make wild passionate love just like the old days.'

'Well, all right. But *after that* there really is something I have to tell you.'

There's going to be a few rules for people walking around with someone else's visage. The code of practice recommends for example that they do not burst into the funeral of the donor and shout 'Surprise!' And you would probably be best advised not to volunteer for identity parades, because it would not be the best time to discover that you had been given the boat race of some notorious gangster.

'No, you see this isn't actually my face, I just got it in an operation.'

'Sure you did, Fingers, mind your head on the cell door there . . .'

The pioneering work in this field has been done on behalf of people who have suffered facial disfigurement, but it won't be long before the process is hijacked by cosmetic surgeons for patients whose riches are matched only by their vanity. In private clinics in California, elderly rich women will be exasperating the staff in the face shops, saying, 'No, I don't like this one either, I don't know, it just isn't me . . .'

'No, well, that's because it isn't you, madam. It's a woman called Trisha.'

'Hmm . . . actually I quite like the one you're wearing, how much is that?'

Because you won't have to be dead to lose face; people

who fancy a change after a few years will be able to stick their passport photos up on eBay and see if anyone fancies a swap. *Forty-year-old face, one or two wrinkles. Will exchange for something a bit more intellectual-looking. No pierced noses.* And decades later if they want to see what they would have looked like if they'd stuck with the original, they can always meet up by logging on to Faces Reunited.

In fact all the ethical worries about this medical milestone are being exaggerated. Differing bone structure means that recipients will not look the same as their donor, and people who've had to endure disfigurements will be liberated from all the misery that blighted their lives before their faces were perceived as normal. And think about the other wonderful opportunities this presents. Imagine the moment when a patient regains consciousness, his bandages are removed and they hand him a mirror and ask him what he thinks of his brand-new face.

'Er, it's fine, except that I'm a leading figure in the British National Party, and you've made me black.'

'Yes, sir, but it's what's inside that really counts, isn't it? Now come on, up you get, you're addressing a rally this evening . . .'

Let them smoke fags

11 June 2004

Beneath the smiling exterior Tony Blair can be the most vicious of politicians. What sort of sadist calls the one member of his Cabinet who smokes sixty cigarettes a day and makes him Minister for Health?

'Of course, John, it will mean giving up the fags. I mean, we can't have a chain-smoking Health Secretary.'

'Er, no problem, Tony. Ha! Cigarettes, who needs 'em, eh?'

No decisions came from the Department of Health for weeks as John Reid just sat there, shaking slightly as he stared at the ripped up cigarettes in the wastepaper basket. Piles of chewed pencils surrounded him, his fingernails were long bitten away, gum wrappers piled up all around him; all he could think about was having a smoke.

'I know it's a fag, Minister, butt we really want to-bacco this scheme, so all we ash you is you put your ciggie-nature here.'

'Argh stop it!' he screamed. 'Stop going on about smoking all the time.'

'Who mentioned smoking? Though now we mention it, we do need a decision on banning smoking in public places.'

'Ah yes, smoky pubs and cafés . . . I think I have a responsibility to visit some immediately. To experience passive smoking at first hand just to see how bad this problem really is . . .'

John Reid has done a great deal for the National Health Service; in fact most of Labour's hospital building pro-gramme has been funded with the tax revenue from his smoking habit. But this week the now ex-smoker sparked a controversy. During a debate on banning smoking he suggested that cigarettes were one of the few pleasures left in life for people on sink estates, adding that smoking 'was an obsession of the learned middle classes'. The Tory health spokesman angrily lashed out at his opposite number calling his comments 'regrettable'. Boy, that must have hurt. Pro-smoking campaigners gave a hearty cheer, which then turned into a rather ugly hacking cough. News of the political row even reached George Bush, who asked Blair what all the fuss was about.

'Oh, people are upset because we slapped a big tax on fags.'

'Hmm, I might try that . . .' said the President, '. . . though they'd go mad in San Francisco.'

It is true that the campaign against smoking has always been led by the middle classes. When Native American chieftains passed around the pipe of peace, there'd always be one middle-class squaw smugly pointing to her lapel badge that said 'You smoke, I choke.' And when Sir Walter Raleigh first demonstrated tobacco to Queen Elizabeth, one courtier pointedly waved the smoke away and tutted, 'Excuse me, do you mind . . .' With this merciless technique the middle classes are now terrorizing smokers everywhere. Strong words like 'nuisance!' and 'honestly!' are muttered just within hearing distance. Annoyingly affected coughs can be heard immediately after anyone lights up. Perhaps the warnings on cigarette packets should reflect this. Instead of saying 'Smoking Kills' they should say 'Smoking may cause people nearby to sigh and noisily open a window.' Where the label currently screams 'Smoking causes heart diseases' they should say 'Smoking may cause the snooty lady sitting near you in the restaurant to frown and loudly ask to be moved to another table.' I say this as a confirmed non-smoker. I resent the damage that passive smoking does to my health when I go to the pub for six or seven pints, maybe a whisky or two and a few jumbo bags of crisps. But John Reid does have a point. It is easy to pontificate when your life is under control. It is easy to see the damage that people do to themselves and others when you are not totally demoralized and exhausted. 'I just don't see why I should have to breathe in all their smoke,' say the middle classes from their air-conditioned 4x4s pumping out carbon monoxide.

But the arguments here need to be examined on their own merits; we should never let a case be judged according to who it is that's making it (unless it's being advocated by Robert Kilroy-Silk; then we should definitely be prejudiced). Banning smoking in public places would not be without its problems. Does that include banning smoking in prisons? And if so who's going to tell Crusher McCoy in D-wing? But the bottom line is that passive smoking causes cancer. Smokers do not have the right to inflict that upon other people. The government should follow the example of the Irish and push through an outright ban in public places. They'd be saving thousands of lives; what more motivation can MPs possibly want? Okay and when they stagger home claiming they've been working late at the Commons, there won't be a stink of smoke betraying the fact that they've been in the pub all evening.

Bike weak

18 June 2004

Few people can have failed to notice that we are currently living through 'Bike Week'. This is a special seven days when white van drivers everywhere obscure their view with England flags so that they can cut up even more cyclists than usual. The dates were set ages ago. The cycling campaigners got their diaries out and said, 'Okay, how about 12–20 June for Bike Week?'

'Yup, nothing happening then; just England's first few games in Euro 2004, so if we want to gain maximum attention for our particular sport then that would definitely be the week to do it.'

The crowning PR coup came on Wednesday, when fifty MPs were persuaded to cycle around Westminster. It was the Parliamentary equivalent of the Tour de France; after twenty minutes all the perspiring MPs were huffing and puffing but had still not managed to clamber onto the saddle for the start. The Conservative MPs who took part didn't quite get the idea and drove round Parliament Square with their bikes in the boot of the Range Rover. At least this spared us the sight of Eric Pickles in a pair of lycra shorts, which would be enough to put anyone off cycling for life.

But Bike Week has been rather spoiled by the Department of Transport's admission that their ambitious plan to quadruple the number of cyclists in Britain has totally failed. In fact the number of people on bikes has actually fallen back since 2001. Apparently it's much quicker to drive to the gym to be first to the bike machines. (Or you might want to go on the rowing machine; in which case you'd have to put up with the people on bike machines pedalling next to you shouting instructions.)

Cycling in this country has suffered mixed fortunes ever since the invention of the Penny Farthing, or 'the farthing' as it was known when the inventor neglected to lock both wheels to the railings. Rising numbers of cars on our roads have made cyclists increasingly nervous. Cycling is of course by far the healthiest way to get about, and you can congratulate yourself on how much good all that exercise does your heart right up until the moment that you collide with a speeding juggernaut. It is also the quickest way round the inner cities, with no petrol or fares to pay, no parking space to find, the only minor expense being the cost of a new bike when you return to see a severed D-lock swinging from the rack where you left your lovely new Marin. If you share a home, nothing will endear you to your flatmates more than a bicycle in that narrow bit of corridor at the bottom of the stairs. 'How marvellous that my flatmate is doing so much for the environment,' they will think as they gash their shin on the steel pedals once again on the way in from a hard day at work.

Most cyclists will tell you that this country has an excellent network of super-fast cycle lanes, known to some people as 'pavements'. Cycle routes are clearly marked by signs that say 'No cycling'. Traffic signals now have their own special indicators for cyclists; a red traffic light means cyclists may whizz straight past the waiting cars causing pedestrians to leap back in terror and look confused that the little green man had said it was safe to cross.

But for all this it is still the best way to get about. Not only do you combine travel time with regular exercise, but the only pollution you produce is the rancid smell when you arrive at work with dripping armpits. You can get a decent bike for £200, which pays for itself in a few months with saved fares, and your mental health also improves as you develop a wonderful feeling of self-righteousness. 'Did I mention that I cycled into work today?' you beam. 'Yes,' groans the office, 'it took you twelve minutes, a new personal record.' Plus you get to engage in cheerful banter with so many lovely professional drivers. Oh how we laugh, the cabbies and I, when I point out that he turned left without looking or indicating and nearly knocked me flying!

I recently found myself angrily whacking the side of a taxi as he suddenly forced me off the road. Instead of apologizing, he leapt out and grabbed me by the scruff of the neck, but what he didn't know was that he was messing with a professional satirist! Instantly my trained writer's brain kicked in, rapidly searched for the devastating *mot juste* that would put him in his place. 'You know what you are?' I seethed. 'You're just . . . you're just a . . . a . . . NUISANCE!' I shouted. I bet he'll never mess with a cyclist again.

Overpaid, under-sexed and over here

25 June 2004

In British cities this week, pretty young girls from America have been going up to young men in the street and announcing that they want to talk to them about sex. 'Sorry, too busy,' they reply hurrying past, before suddenly halting and turning to exclaim, 'Sorry, what did you say just then?' The young Americans are over to promote the idea that young people should not have sexual relations before marriage, which is a complete inversion of the usual British tradition of abstaining from sex after marriage. These no-sex tourists are part of a movement called the Silver Ring Thing, so called because once you have taken the abstinence pledge you wear a special ring featuring a quote from the Bible so that all your mates know you are a virgin. Obviously British teenage boys are fighting to get hold of these things.

The campaign has received $700,000 from the Bush administration, which favours 'virginity training' in place of information about contraception. This represents a marked shift from the previous administration; for some reason Bill Clinton decided against a personal crusade to lecture on sexual abstinence. But now, overpaid, under-sexed and over here, the Silver Ring Thing are spreading their gospel in British cities. The UK has the second-highest teenage pregnancy rate in the Western world, so obviously we need a few lessons from the country that has the very highest. But, boy, are these Bible Belt Christians prepared to get right in there and brave the inner city ghettos to get their message across! The one 'London area' event for example takes place tonight at a church in Esher. This part of the Surrey commuter belt is famous for the sort of poverty and alienation where teenage pregnancies are endemic. Turnout might be a little disappointing, however; apparently all the local kids are still away at their single-sex boarding schools.

Over a million young Americans have already taken the Silver Ring pledge, including one young couple who were interviewed on *Newsnight* on Wednesday. 'Sure, we hug and cuddle but we both believe that's as far as it should go,' explained the girl as her boyfriend nodded uncertainly beside her, testosterone clearly pumping through his veins. 'We hear about other teenagers having sex all the time and we actually feel sorry for them, don't we?' she continued as her boyfriend started to turn a pale shade of green. 'That's why we pledged never ever to have sex out of wedlock and we don't mind if we wait another ten or twelve years.' At this point he started to convulse violently, retching and shaking as veins on his forehead looked close to exploding.

The Silver Ring Thing are not saying that young people shouldn't have fun with the opposite sex; indeed, they organize concerts and discos where teens can dance to such popular classics as 'Let's Spend the Night Apart' and 'Do You Remember the First Time (Nope)' and 'It's Raining Rain'. The crux of their message is that it is cool not to have sex, which has been going down a storm with a generation of Brits brought up wearing FCUK T-shirts and listening to songs like 'Hey Sex-bomb, I is Gonna Sex You Up with My Sex, Sex, Sex.'* In fact the message that it's worth waiting till you are a bit older to start having sex is actually one that many of us would agree with. The trouble is that these are the worst possible people to be associated with it. 'Wow, if a bunch of born-again Christians from Texas are telling me it's hip then that's good enough for me,' shout the youths of Britain's inner cities.

The depressing reality is that abstinence education actually increases teenage pregnancies. An American study showed that nine out of ten young people who took a sexual abstinence pledge went on to break it, and because they were so unprepared and guilty, they were far less

---

* Dana really changed after she left that convent.

likely to use contraception. (The moment after you first have sex can be an anti-climax, but you have to feel sorry for those kids who believe they're now doomed to rot in hell.) European countries such as Sweden and Holland that have the most accessible contraception and progressive sexual education programmes also have the lowest rates of teenage pregnancy. Of course, lower poverty rates may well be a more significant contributory factor, but the Republican religious right that spawned the Silver Ring Thing is no enemy of poverty. 'I know I pledged not to screw the American people,' weeps George W. Bush, 'but I couldn't help myself. All my friends were doing it, and I finally cracked.' Now, with George's backing, hundreds of British teenagers will be paying their ten quid for their silver ring. Still, they can always pawn it later to pay for nappies.

Defence lawyer for Saddam wanted (no win, no fee)

2 July 2004

In Iraq this week a young barrister who recently graduated from law school got a surprising phone call.

'Hi, we've got you your first case and it's a big one. Wait for this: you're getting the Saddam Hussein trial!'

'Wow, I can't believe it! Me, prosecuting Saddam! Oh I've got to ring my parents.'

'Erm, no, not actually prosecuting. You're defending him . . .'

'What! Defending the world's most infamous tyrant? But how can I do that?'

'Well, you know how it works: try and bring out his good points, his love of animals, his work for charity . . . I mean, we have to be seen to give him a fair trial.'

'Really?'

'Very much so. A fair trial, but one that finds him guilty.'

It's going to be a tough gig defending the most hated man in the world (except in Britain, where he came second to the referee who disallowed Sol Campbell's goal against Portugal). But all credit to the defence counsel for getting Saddam to smarten up a bit before he came to court. Frankly that big shaggy beard did nothing for him. One look at that matted grey fuzz and any jury was going to think, 'Well, I don't like the look of him.' And much better to trim it than shave it off completely, otherwise everyone might recognize him as that dictator bloke whose face is still on all their wrist watches. This was the first time the world's media had seen Saddam since he was caught in December and they shone a torch in his mouth announcing, 'Nope, the weapons of mass destruction aren't in here either.'

Things haven't been made any easier for the defence counsel by the fact the trial is taking place in a location so secret that no-one will actually tell them where the courtroom is. There will be video footage of the courtroom but the judge's face will be pixelated to protect his identity. This is the only trial where it is the judge who has his head under a blanket as he is bundled into the courtroom. Or perhaps this is just because he's so embarrassed to be involved with such a meticulously stage-managed piece of theatre. The West's biggest baddie could have been tried by a democratic Iraqi regime but that might have meant waiting until after the American elections. Iraq's new national security adviser, Mowaffaq al-Rubaie, insisted the process will not be a show trial, as he sold expensive ice creams and glossy programmes during the interval. In fact it is more than that, it is an international celebrity trial; as *Big Brother* ends, *Baghdad Brother* begins. A whole cast of ugly candidates will be paraded before us for the two-minute hate as Saddam stands trial with eleven of his former aides, or 'henchmen' as they are generally called in the interests of neutrality. These are some of the faces that became familiar after they were pictured in the US army's famous pack of cards: Abed Hamid Mahmoud, Ali Hassan al-Majid and, after a mix-up with some other playing cards, Pikachu from Poke'mon and Mr Bun the Baker. They are charged with countless human rights atrocities and the invasion of Kuwait but interestingly prosecutors have dropped the invasion of Iran from the charge sheet. Of course this is nothing to do with any embarrassment that this episode might have caused the United States. 'Ah yes,' Saddam might have recalled, 'I still have my good luck card from the White House. "Way to go, Saddam, whip those mad mullahs from Tehran. Weapons to follow. All the best, The President."'

They have also decided not to broadcast the audio of what Saddam is saying; instead a carefully phrased transcript will appear on the screen. Sentences such as 'Here are the details of the arms deals I did with the CIA' will be slightly tidied up and rephrased as 'I am guilty, that clever Mr Bush has stopped me and my buddy Osama from invading Utah.'

Of course, some sort of trial was required, if only to

provide closure and a modicum of justice for the thousands who suffered under Saddam's brutal dictatorship. But this sham isn't it. And as they rejoin the world community the Iraqis might just consider the bigger picture. This is election year in the United States and this public parading of Saddam Hussein is the best fillip the George Bush re-election campaign could hope for. So to test the idea of genuine independence, in early November the Iraqis should ring up Washington and say, 'We've finished the trial, George, and well, we decided to let him off.'

'You're not going to execute him?'

'Far from it. In fact we thought, all things considered, we thought we'd appoint Saddam Hussein as the new president of Iraq. He just seemed to have far more experience than all the other applicants. Sorry you went to all that trouble, George. And best of luck with your election on Tuesday . . .'

Microsoft Kevin

9 July 2004

When Microsoft turned up at the US Patent Office the other day, the man behind the desk did his best to understand what they were on about.

'We want to copyright the idea of using the human body as a conductor of data and energy.'

'Hang on, hang on, so it's something to do with computers, is it?'

'No, it's way beyond that. We're talking about integrating the human body into the network, so that software, information and programs can be transmitted through a person's skin.'

'Oh yeah, I get the picture. Sounds like the computer companies trying to take over the world again.'

The Microsoft delegation groaned at this tired old cliché

and then demonstrated their plans by connecting his index finger to a small palmtop. Then he said in a monotone voice, 'Patent is granted, whatever Microsoft wants is completely fine.'

Of course, the idea of the computer-enhanced human has already been widely explored in science fiction. In the 1970s we watched the US government splash out on the *Six Million Dollar Man*, though really they should have waited a bit because the prices always come down after a year or so. Then there was *Robocop*, the futuristic computerized police officer who was completely without emotion, spoke in simple sentences and was capable of extreme violence; so much like thousands of other policemen really. But now under US Patent 6,754, 472, 'Method and apparatus for transmitting power and data across the human body', Microsoft have exclusive rights to the ability of the human body to transmit digital information. Before now copying files from a colleague's computer involved all sorts of disks or cables, but soon you'll be able to access everything just by sticking your finger up their nose.

The way it works apparently is that our bodies are made up of millions of tiny vessels and tubes full of liquids all capable of transmitting messages at high speed. For example: your brain receives a message that you must tell your partner to ring Deirdre. So fast and efficient is the human information superhighway that only a week later you suddenly announce, 'Oh shit, I completely forgot – you were supposed to ring Deirdre . . .' Well, soon this network of nerves and capillaries (and on a busy day your long intestine), will replace the thicket of plastic cables that grow like weeds out of every port on your computer. No need for those giveaway white cables that tell muggers you got an iPod for Christmas; now the music will go directly into your body, up to your ears and straight down to your tapping feet as well. And still the person sitting next to you on the train will be able to hear the percussion. The technology also offers the possibility of monitoring health with a number of sensors fitted around the body. You'll know when you're unwell because all the fish on your screensaver will be floating on the top of the screen. (There'll be new medical problems such as 'slipped disk drive' and 'athlete's port'.) Apparently, palmtops, mobiles, MP3 players and the electronic tag you have to wear for nicking all those gadgets will all be replaced with a single keypad implanted in your forearm. And if there is too much information for the hard drive, then you can always delete useless stuff like the date of your wedding anniversary.

Trying to get the right hardware at PC World will never be the same again.

'Hello, I'm having problems with my laptop. It doesn't seem to be compatible with my spinal cord.'

'Let's have a look. Oh yeah, that sort of central nervous system has been discontinued I'm afraid. You want a USB hub.'

'Oh, right. And this "USB hub" will definitely do all the things that my spinal cord used to do, will it? Like carrying impulses from my brain, making my body function and all that?'

'Er probably. Any problems, just come back in.'

Call me an old paranoid conspiracy theorist, but I'm not sure I feel very comfortable with the idea of the world's most powerful company having access to my body's central nervous system. Once we are all physically connected up to the Microsoft network, their potential power will be limitless. Bill Gates will be able to control our minds; he might even be able to make us think that preppy jumpers and nerdy square glasses are really fashionable. But the reality is probably a lot more mundane. Incredibly advanced and complex technology will be used to listen to rehashed '70s singles and tell the office you're still stuck on the train. And then finally you'll get into work, and say, 'Morning everyone-one-one-one-one', before your head lands with a bang on the desk. And the rest of the office will groan, 'Oh no, it's Microsoft Kevin. He's crashed again.'

Going . . . going . . . gong!

16 July 2004

This week a group of MPs concluded their report into the British honours system. These meetings can be a bit dull at times so the Labour-dominated committee invited along one Tory MP who just happened to be a 'Sir', in order to create a bit of sport.

'Don't get us wrong, SIR Sydney, we're not saying that because you are a knight you must automatically be a toadying, sycophantic, goody-two shoes, busy-body, yes-man and total brown-noser; not at all, the thought never crossed our minds that you must have grovelled and sniffed, and bribed and crawled across the carpet while Maggie wiped her shoes on your golf club blazer . . .'

Their indignation was all the greater because their own efforts always seem to have gone unrecognized.

'I raised £23.17 in the Lurpak Fun-Run, but nobody's put any letters after my name . . .'

'Yes, well, I do lots to promote various charities. I mean, I try to use that free pen I got sent by the Woodland Trust . . .'

The Select Committee was reporting on the complex and arcane British honours system, and discovered that the meaning of dozens of different titles are rather lost in the mists of time. For example, the Order of St Michael originally gave the wearer exclusive rights to supply underwear to Marks and Spencer. A Commander of the Bath on the other hand is granted total jurisdiction over his bath, how full it is, how hot he has it; it's all completely up to him. These less well-known awards may be done away with completely. For the remaining honours, screening will be far more vigorous; you won't be able to become a Member of the British Empire unless you can produce two utility bills showing your current address. Another recommendation is that we do away with the imperialist overtones, so that the Order of the British Empire be renamed the Order of British Excellence; a plonky sounding compromise which was reached after five minutes flicking through the letter 'E' in the dictionary.

'Order of British Egg-nog? No, let's see. Echidna . . . no, Espresso machine . . . no, Epiglottis, no . . . Order of British Egomaniacs . . . Hmm, a bit too close to the truth . . .'

'Look, why don't we just go the whole hog? MBE stands for "Met Blair's Expenses", OBE stands for "Obviously

Brown-nosed Everyone" and CBE stands for "Cynically Bankrolled Election".

There is criticism that the awards haven't always gone to the people who might deserve them most. For example, why hasn't the Queen ever got an OBE? She does loads of work for charities, she's always going round the country supporting British good causes, but every year the chairman of the honours committee sits down with her and goes through all the nominations and every year she does her best to hide her disappointment.

'Um, not many elderly ladies this year, I notice,' she hints, 'you know, who might have done a lot of work for the country at large . . .'

'Ah yes, I get your drift, Ma'am – another gong for Esther Rantzen perhaps?'

'No, no, no, I mean, you know; what about a certain old queen?'

And so every year Lord St John of Fawsley gets yet a few more letters after his name.

The real problem with the existing set-up is that you have to be a certain type of establishment person to really value a little silver medal on a ribbon. It seems unfair that that is the only gift that the nation can bestow. Instead the Queen should offer a choice, so that when the civil servant is kneeling before her, she should say, 'Now which would you prefer, an OBE or an iPod?'

'An iPod?'

'Yes, it's the new system. Instead of a medal we can offer something your wife said you really wanted. Or you could have one of those mobile phones that take photos, a mountain bike or a bread maker: I've got a lovely Panasonic bread maker with an automatic nut and raisin dispenser if you'd prefer that?'

Of course, it is nice to be able to commend people when they have achieved something of note. But as well as acting as a carrot, the honours system should also contain an element of stick, so that people get to have special letters after their name if they have done something particularly rubbish. So the England captain would become David Beckham KMP (Keeps Missing Penalties), the exiled former council leader would be known as Dame Shirley Porter GCBKM (Got Caught But Kept Money) and Chris Woodhead would go to the palace to be conferred with a much-deserved TBE (Talks Bollocks about Education).

This week's report was more damning of the honours system than many expected, and by calling for a complete overhaul and the abolition of most honorary titles the MPs have left Tony Blair with a tricky problem.

'You don't have time to do this, PM, but if you ignore their radical suggestions, the MPs may well criticize you in public.'

'I know what I'll do,' says the PM without hesitation, 'I'll just give them all knighthoods. That'll shut them up for a bit.'

Help, we're all going to die!

30 July 2004

In the next few weeks a leaflet on surviving a terrorist attack will be dropping through the letter box of every home in the country, quickly followed by another seven leaflets offering two pizzas for the price of one. Then in millions of homes across the country this vital document will be placed next to the phone for a few days, then tucked on the kitchen shelf with that letter from school and finally put away in the drawer with the balloon pump and those old batteries that haven't been thrown out because you're not sure if they're dead or not.

The leaflet explains what precautions you can take to increase your chances of surviving a major terrorist attack. 'Move to the Hebrides' was crossed out of the first draft. But it does recommend that you have a torch handy, some tinned food and enough bottled water to last you the weeks you may have to spend hiding in the cellar. You might also consider packing *A Suitable Boy* by Vikram Seth because you're not going to finish it in any other circumstances.

Under the section entitled 'The bleedin' obvious' it tells you to pack matches with your candles and a tin opener with your tinned food. It also advises you to keep a list of useful phone numbers handy though it's thought the Samaritans will be turning on the answerphone. A battery-operated radio is also recommended in order that you can keep up to date with the crisis, although different radio stations will convey the news in different ways. On Radio 4, a Home Office spokesman telling listeners that the whole of London is on fire will never get to the end of his sentence because John Humphrys will keep interrupting him. Capital Gold will bring you those classic nuclear scares of the 1970s and '80s, while Radio One will announce 'Celeb gossip update; and Ant and Dec were just some of the stars who had to take cover when the whole of London was destroyed by terrorist attacks (sudden sound effect of electronic raspberry), massive bombs went off all over the capital (Crowd goes "Boo!") and germ warfare has been unleashed on the capital (comedy sound effect of lots of people sneezing).'

When deciding whether or not to go ahead with a national campaign such as this the government have to find the balance between ensuring that people are prepared and informed and the risk of creating panic in the general population. Some critics fear this leaflet entitled 'Help! Help! We're all going to die!' may not have got the balance exactly right. The bit about trying to get near a radiator if a building has collapsed on top of you does not leave you smugly thinking, 'Well, I'm going to be all right because I've taken the trouble to check where all the radiators are . . .' And I don't want to be alarmist or anything, but what if al-Qaida break into the warehouse where all the leaflets are stored and contaminate all of them with ricin before they're individually delivered to every home in the country?

Given that people will generally do the opposite of what any government tells them, perhaps the leaflet's advice should be to panic; to tell Dolores in data processing that you love her and then loot Dixons. But the general thrust of the pamphlet is if there does happen to be a major terrorist attack, old chap, just stay in your house and watch television. 'That's money well spent,' they're saying at the Home Office, 'millions of pounds to tell people to sit in their houses watching television.' They've been very gratified to see the large numbers of families across the country already practising this on a regular basis. Dummy runs are an important part of being prepared, and last year the government itself conducted an exercise to practise exactly what they would do if a hostile dictatorship possessed weapons of mass destruction. For the purposes of this rehearsal, the country in question was Iraq and the practice bombing, invasion and occupation were conducted exactly as if there had been a genuine threat. Unfortunately, soon after this exercise, the threat of a terrorist attack in Britain actually seemed to increase rather than diminish.

Before the leaflets are finally delivered to every home in the land, a few adjustments have been made to the copy being pushed through the letter box of 10 Downing Street. After the bit about what you can do to reduce the chance of being a victim of a terrorist attack, it says, 'Don't bomb Arab civilians on the basis of invented evidence. Don't ally yourself with a US government with a disastrous Middle East policy and make sure you've got lots of bottled water under the stairs.' 'Oh well,' says the householder brightly, 'one out of three's not bad.'

Mark Thatcher: I blame the parents

27 August 2004

Who among us can honestly say that our children have never done anything a little bit naughty in the past? Sneaking a chocolate from the second layer in the box when no-one was looking; going into next door's garden to get their ball back without asking; funding military coups in Third World countries with an eye to making an illegal fortune. No child is perfect and they grow out of these things, he's only fifty-one, for goodness' sake.

The news that Sir Mark Thatcher had been arrested for alleged involvement in a botched coup attempt seemed to chime with the other headline of the week that boys are finally catching up with the girls. Unless of course Carol Thatcher suddenly gets caught flogging AK47s to Colombian terrorists in order to secure lucrative cocaine smuggling contracts; nothing would surprise me any more.

News first leaked out six months ago of an attempted coup in Equatorial Guinea. Early details were sketchy though first reports suggested that it was possibly in Africa or maybe in South America – oh, hang on, that's Ecuador and Guyana, isn't it? Anyway no-one in the news room had ever been there on holiday and since no Americans were involved the story was quickly forgotten. But recently it emerged that the ex-Etonian organizer of the coup was an old friend of Mark Thatcher (they were joint winners of Upper Class Twit of the Year 1982) and from his cell in a high-security African prison he wrote a letter demanding that the son of the former PM help get him out. That'll teach Mark to put his details on Friends Reunited. Sir Mark was arrested on Wednesday morning in his pyjamas at his home outside Cape Town, and if found guilty of involvement in the conspiracy could face a lengthy gaol sentence. Lefties in the 1980s sought inspiration from prisoners in South Africa, so look out for Tories at next month's party conference sporting T-shirts saying 'Free Sir Mark Thatcher!' Incidentally a large payment to the leader of the coup was also made by someone with the name J. Archer, while it's been reported that Lady Thatcher is 'extremely distressed' at the news of the affair. It just gets better and better!

However, this African adventure does leave the rest of us wondering if we lead rather mundane lives. None of my old school friends has ever asked me to lend a helicopter to assist his ex-SAS mercenaries stage a Third World coup with a view to making millions out of oil reserves. I was invited to a bring and buy sale to raise funds for the new rubber matting under the school swings but somehow it didn't have quite the same dangerous glamour.

Sir Mark (who owes his knighthood to his mother's inspired idea of bringing back hereditary honours just before she herself retired) has never been very far from controversy. Despite the thousands spent on his education at Harrow School he only managed three 'O' levels and then failed his accountancy finals three times. Apparently examiners were not impressed with the way he answered every hypothetical funding problem with the answer 'Just get Mummy to have a word with them'. Yet he has since accumulated a fortune of around £60 million with no-one being very sure where any of it comes from. Perhaps he just cuts a lot of money-off coupons out of *Take-A-Break* magazine. Heaven forbid that he might have ever used his family connections to secure any dodgy business deals! The allegation that he was in Oman in 1981 to act as an intermediary for a £300 million deal secured by his mother is completely without foundation. No, he just happened to be in the Middle East because he took another wrong turning in the Sahara desert. Neither is there any truth in the allegations that he made £12 million in commission on the al-Yamamah arms deal with Saudi Arabia signed by his mother, no, he was on a CND demo at the time. Of course, by the time Mrs T was thrown out of office, America also had a leader with a stupid son who seemed to make a curiously large amount of money out of some rather shady deals, so I suppose we should just be grateful that Thatcher Jnr hasn't followed his mother into 10 Downing Street.

In fact, episodes like this remind us of the type of morality that prevailed during the greedy Thatcher years. Thank heavens things have moved on. Can you imagine our current Prime Minister being associated with the sort of people who'd embark on some ill-thought-out military adventure because they hoped to install a regime that would allow them to get their hands on the country's oil reserves – it's completely unthinkable.

Computer carbon-dating

3 September 2004

Apparently there are certain tell-tale signs you should look out for if you suspect your husband of getting back in touch with his first-ever girlfriend: increased time spent on the Internet, furtive texting on his mobile phone and having a huge love-bite on his neck and 'Gary 4 Shazza 4 Ever' scratched into his forearm with a fountain pen. This week the divorce rate reached its highest level in seven years and part of the blame was laid at the door of Internet sites such as Friends Reunited. It's been one of the unforeseen by-products of the Internet revolution that people can easily contact old flames instead of using computers for their intended purpose, which is stealing music and downloading hardcore pornography. The problem is getting so bad that in a few years' time they're launching a new site called Divorcées Reunited, where all the people who left their partners for their childhood sweethearts can find out what their ex-spouse has been up to since the big split.

You can occasionally spot these former puppy-lovers desperately trying to re-create those magical moments they shared together as teenagers: completely unsuited middle-aged couples hanging around in bus-shelters in dead-end provincial towns mumbling, 'So only another three years till we can get into the pub. Shall we go and get some more chips or have another fag?' At last a chance to revive all those hot topics that your husband doesn't want to talk about any more: 'Who's more gorgeous, Donny Osmond or David Cassidy?' 'How can you stop your flares getting caught in your bike chain?' And then just when you've lost your wife and home because you got back with the girl you imagined you loved when you were fourteen she goes and chucks you for Degsy 'cos he's got a better moped.

Of course, it's always interesting to see where your friends ended up – I was a bit lonely at school so I had to look my old mates up on Imaginary Friends Reunited. One of them's doing quite well actually, in fact he married my imaginary sister and they're living in Droitwitch. The problem comes when you think you can recapture that naïve happiness of youth; those innocent days when you promised to love each other for ever, or at least until the following Tuesday. But of course that first kiss in the multi-storey car park was thrilling precisely because it was all so new – no amount of mid-life crisis will ever bring back his unique scent of Hai Karate aftershave mingled with Player's No. 6. You know his life is now just as mundane as yours; that's why he too is spending hours on the Internet every night.

And don't be flattered if your old girlfriend happened to get back in touch – it's not surprising after she read all the incredible things you've achieved in the last couple of decades. Okay so you may have exaggerated your potted biography a little here and there: 'recently made investments with aim to securing multi-million-pound profit yield' means 'just bought another lottery ticket', and 'currently dividing my time between London and Wiltshire' means 'took the kids to Center Parcs this summer'. Of course, one of the great things about Friends Reunited is that you don't have to limit yourself to just making things up about yourself. If it still rankles with you that that bloody Piers Johnson got better 'O' level results than you, then just pay your fiver and you can post an entry in his name; making up an entirely new life story in which everything went horribly wrong for the smug bastard: 'jailed for fraud, drunk driving and exposing myself in public, now bankrupt, bitter and fat and realize that my life started to go wrong when I grassed on that bloke in 5G who let off the fire alarm.' On such a huge site it is quite hard to monitor exactly what gets put up there; for example, the last time I looked some wag had posted an entry for Osama Bin Laden. Actually it was quite surprising to read what he's been up to, he was always such a quiet type at school.

But you can't blame the website for the weaknesses it exposes in marriages. It is a wonderful thing that email and the Internet make it physically easier for people to contact one another from around the world, even if it turned out that I wasn't really the millionth visitor to that website and hadn't won a holiday in Florida. But contacting old flames is playing with fire. Just look at the example of the anonymous caller who rang that radio phone-in the other night: 'So I looked her up on the Internet and said my god Camilla married that Parker Bowles bloke! Oh well I'll just send her an email anyway – no harm will ever come of it . . .'

Another one bites the dust

10 September 2004

On Wednesday, NASA scientists watched in shock as their Genesis solar project ended in disaster. 'I can't believe it,' they all said. 'A space mission that went wrong? This is completely unprecedented. I mean, the last time a major space project ended in embarrassing failure was way, way back in January when our Mars rover broke down, and then before that the Beagle 2 project lost contact with their probe, oh and then there was last year's Columbia disaster, oh and the Hubble telescope fiasco, but apart from that our record is very impressive. From now on NASA are going to launch their rockets on 4 July, just so that everyone thinks they're meant to explode.

We had been promised a dramatic re-entry for the Genesis capsule, which was set to return its precious payload of atomic solar particles after a three-year mission. Stunt pilots hired from Hollywood for the occasion were on stand-by waiting to hook up with the capsule as it entered the earth's atmosphere, but they failed to connect because they couldn't see out of their Jedi helmets.

'Sorry, can we go for another take on that one?'

'Er – no, actually.'

After the parachutes failed to open the capsule crashed to earth and the scientists found their precious parcel smashed open and the contents strewn* all over the ground. It couldn't have been worse if they had paid the extra for Royal Mail Registered Post. The whole point of this trip was to bring back pure uncontaminated atoms from the sun. Now they're going to have to gather up everything they find on that patch of ground in Utah and painstakingly analyse all of it. 'It's amazing, solar explosions seem to be emitting old burger cartons, cigarette butts and Wal-Mart shopping bags.'

The team did their best to remain positive. 'There are a lot of things that had to happen in series and we got just about all of them done and we just did not get the last two or three done,' said Genesis project manager Don Sweetnam. Oh well, that's all right then. Maybe I'm being a little picky, but if I was plummeting to the ground at two hundred miles an hour, and one of those last details included the failure of my parachute to open, I'd struggle

---

* Why is there no present tense for the word 'strewn'? You don't get postmen saying, 'I think I'm going to strow these elastic bands all over the pavement.'

to be upbeat about all the other things that had gone so well.

How do they get the insurance for all these missions? Perhaps they just have to hope they get a particularly dim telesales rep when they ring the insurance company.

'So are there any additional drivers you would like listed on the policy?'

'Well, there are no actual "drivers" as such, it's a remote-control space-explorer capsule costing two hundred and fifty million dollars.'

'Right, no additional drivers . . . and will you be using it for business or leisure?'

'Well, mainly for catching atoms ejected in solar explosions.'

'I'll click "leisure", and can I have the postcode where the vehicle will be kept, please?'

'Well, for the next two years it will be in orbit at temperatures of thousands of degrees, trying to dodge solar explosions, meteorites and collisions with the planet Mercury.'

'That's all right, sir, as long as it's not going to be parked in Hackney or Liverpool.'

The so-called Genesis project received its massive funding before they realized that it had nothing to do with taking Phil Collins into deep space. In fact the naming of the craft is not without an irony of its own, since the purpose of this trip was to inform us about the origin of our solar system. Yet the President who is paying for it all has passed an education bill allowing creationism to creep back into American schools. Why does he need to spend millions on the Genesis space probe, to find out what he says Americans can read in the Book of Genesis? Could it be that he's only claiming to take the Bible at face value in order to secure votes in America's Bible Belt? Or maybe they just told him that with all that fire coming off the sun there must be some oil in there somewhere?

With the tide of Christian fundamentalism that is increasingly directing scientific funding in America, soon NASA won't be able to send out any more probes unless they are looking for a big bloke with a white beard sitting on a cloud surrounded by angels. But though their latest mission has ended in disaster, maybe this week NASA just settled the science versus religion debate once and for all. A huge lump of metal comes flying out of the sky at two hundred miles an hour, crash-lands in the United States, but it completely misses President George W. Bush. Clearly there is no god; what more proof does anyone need?

Sell us your votes!

17 September 2004

Researchers in Maryland, USA, recently completed a worldwide poll to see how citizens of countries beyond America would vote in the forthcoming presidential election. They rang millions of random numbers all across the globe, with one particular call certainly taking Osama Bin Laden by surprise.

'Hello, we are phoning from the United States to see if you are a supporter of George W. Bush.'

'Um . . . no, not really . . .'

'Do you think he has done enough to catch Osama Bin Laden?'

'Yes, plenty, there's nothing else he should do.'

'OK, could we just take your name please?'

'It's Mr Bin—, I mean, Robinson, Monty Robinson, from Reykjavik, oh yes, I love fish.'

As it turned out, Osama suddenly began to worry that Kerry might be lying about his war record and so ended up plumping for Dubya.

But just about everyone else seems to be hoping for a Democrat victory. In Norway, the margin was 74 per cent for Kerry and only 7 per cent for Bush, with the President getting the same level of support in Spain and only 5 per cent in France. Bush isn't worried about these figures. Even if he gets this share of the vote at home, he'll still somehow manage to fiddle it so he wins. It is hardly surprising that John Kerry has inspired so many people around the world, because his outstanding attributes are plain to see. Firstly who can have failed to notice that wonderful 'not-George-Bush' quality about him? Plus there is that certain 'un-Dubya-ness' that he seems to possess, not to mention what the French call the *'il n'est pas George Bush'* aspect of his personality. Many of us have been moved to tears by his speeches. 'Is that the best the Democrats can do?' we wept. And there is the fact that he served in Vietnam, where he was seriously injured by enemy fire, leaving army surgeons with no choice but to amputate his charisma.

But the tragedy is that while millions of us in Europe and beyond desperately care about who becomes the next president, none of us has any influence over the outcome. The time has come for European liberals to get together and do something about this. One possibility might be to make some commercials of our own to put out on American TV. Obviously we couldn't let on that we were a bunch of lefty foreigners – we'd have to give our organization an authentic-sounding alias – something neutral like the 'American Creationist Freedom Rifle Patriots for Truth'. But imagine the impact of some grainy footage of a young Dubya, with a gravelly voiceover whispering, 'Everyone knows that George Bush did not fight for his country during the Vietnam War. This is because he was actually fighting for the Vietcong; leading the infamous "Gay Jihad Atheists Squad" who captured American soldiers and forced them to become vegetarians and play soccer.' Never mind that every time we express outrage that George Bush wriggled out of going to Vietnam, we privately think, 'Excellent move, George, that's exactly what I would have done'; by the time the facts were checked the damage would be done and Bush would be twenty points behind in the polls.

The only trouble with this idea is that the various European directors would never be able to agree on a style for the commercial. The French would want to film it as an allegorical three-hour internal monologue from a chain-smoking poet who was battling with writer's block. The British would have Hugh Grant as a lovestruck ex-Beatle who gets mistaken for John Kerry by Emma Thompson. In the end the whole project would be handed over to the experimental Prague Cartoon Workshop who had just won lots of awards for their unusual animation style when in fact they're just not very good at drawing.

If the advert idea is a non-starter, there is a more direct

way that non-American liberals can get involved in the US election. Why don't we just offer to buy the votes of all those US citizens who aren't really that bothered? A majority of Americans probably won't even take part in the most important election in the world, and I'm sure they'd appreciate twenty or thirty dollars that lots of us would willingly pay to cast their votes for them. So I call on all apolitical skint Americans to get themselves a postal vote and auction it on eBay. What could be more in the spirit of American capitalist democracy than dis-enfranchising yourself for cash? The laws of the free market would settle the price of a ballot paper; votes from swing states would go for that much more of course, although personally I'm hoping for a vote in Texas, because it will be so humiliating when Bush even loses his home state. Sadly in my first attempt to bid for a vote I lost the auction to someone calling themselves GBW@whitehouse.us.

Still, the winner was kind enough to send me an email. It said, 'Nice try, limey, but we've got a lot more money than you and you're not the first person to have this idea. P.S. How do you think I got in last time?'

The Prince of Whiteness

24 September 2004

You can always tell when Tory leaders are in trouble – they resort to playing the race card. But I hadn't realized that Michael Howard was in quite that much trouble. On Wednesday night's evening news the Prince of Darkness appeared in a carefully stage-managed walk towards the TV cameras to talk about immigration. On either side of him were respectable looking black people chuckling along with him to send out the message 'Of course our leader isn't a racialist, look, here he is with some coloured chappies!' No wonder they were laughing; Michael had just asked them if they were Tory MPs. This embarrassing gap in the Conservative benches made setting up this photo opportunity a nightmare. At the planning meeting,

Oliver Letwin and Theresa May helpfully offered to black up and hum songs from *Motown's Greatest Hits*.

'No, that won't work, Theresa, the press might notice that you don't have a natural sense of rhythm.'

'I could be eating rice and peas,' suggested Oliver, 'and talk about how good I am at sport.' In the end they found some black Conservatives that they'd managed to keep as party members by desperately preventing them from ever meeting the rest of the grassroots Tory membership (who probably would have screamed and called security).

The Conservative Party have come a long way since the days of Enoch Powell. It has to be much more subtle these days: they have learned to start by saying, 'I'm not a racist but . . .'

'Yeah that's great, Michael. But can we try it again, this time without the pointy white hood and the burning cross in the background?'

But the core message is still the same: 'If you don't like all these immigrants, we're the party for you.' At a time when the number of asylum seekers entering Britain is at its lowest point since 1997, the Tory leader chose to go on the offensive about immigration; 'offensive' being the operative word. He advocated a quota system to set a limit on the number of immigrants and asylum seekers entering the country, which would certainly make for some tense scenes at Harare airport.

'Hello, I'm from British Airways, I'm afraid this flight to London is over-booked, would you be willing to be put on tomorrow's flight instead?'

'No, you see if I don't get on this plane right now, I'll just miss the cut-off point for Britain's asylum quota, and be sent back to Zimbabwe and certain execution.'

'Right, not even if we offer you a glass of bucks fizz and some complimentary travel vouchers . . . ?'

Maybe the RNLI could have a quota for the number of sinking trawlers they rescue? Our hospitals are under a lot of pressure; how about a limit on the number of emergency resuscitations? 'I'm sorry we can't send out the ambulance, we reached our annual quota of lives saved back in August.'

The curious thing about this week's pitch for the anti-immigration vote is that even from the basest Machiavellian point of view it was not even good politics. In a week when the focus was on the Liberal Democrats (the greatest threat to Tory marginals), Howard chose to lurch to the right; trying to shore up the votes that he is losing to UKIP and the BNP. If you are going to sell your soul, you should at least try and get a decent price for it. When Howard first took over the ailing Tory party, some of us feared that the Conservatives might finally have a competent leader to lift their pitiful poll ratings. Of course, we should have trusted the verdict of those who knew him best. Tory MPs gave their judgement in 1997, the last time Michael Howard actually had to fight a leadership election. I suppose coming fifth isn't so bad, even if there were only five candidates. But his own party decided he was less appealing than John Redwood, less charismatic than Peter Lilley, less of a fresh face than Kenneth Clarke and less likely to win an election than William Hague. So in 2003 he was the only candidate – and this time they thought they'd better not risk a vote in case he still didn't win it.

But this week marked a new low-point in Michael Howard's fading political career; he demonstrated that his integrity is even lower than his charm rating. The presenters of *Blue Peter* can feel that much more secure that he won't be getting their job. More significantly he showed he just doesn't have the skill or judgement required for the one he has at the moment. What greater case could there be for welcoming more foreigners to our shores? We desperately need immigrants so that challenging jobs like Leader of the Opposition can be done properly.

2004: A Space Holiday

1 October 2004

This week Sir Richard Branson announced his plans to fly the first commercial passengers into space. For around a hundred grand, members of the public will be able to fly sixty miles above the Earth and enjoy the view. 'We will be giving people something they will remember for the rest of their lives,' he promised, which if recent space adventures are anything to go by, may not be that long. Who can blame people for being so concerned about the risks involved? You might pay all that money and end up sitting next to Sir Richard Branson.

At £640 pounds a minute, this trip looks set to be the most expensive journey in the history of travel, and they'll probably still charge you extra for the headphones. And with only four minutes to look down at Planet Earth there's going to be a hell of an argument over which of the kids gets the window seat.

'It's not fair – all I can see is the wing.'

'Never mind, dear – why don't you colour in the Disney pictures in your fun pack?'

Passengers will be required to undertake three days of astronaut training before coming on board, after which they will be expected to demonstrate a thorough knowledge of space travel. 'No, James Earl Jones only did the voice for Darth Vader; the man in the suit was Dave Prowse.' In fact the first space plane will rather un-originally be called the VSS *Enterprise* – as Virgin seek to mix contemporary air travel with the iconic myths of *Star Trek*. The search is now on for a gay Vulcan to be an air steward. Whether British Airways hire Klingons to try and poach Virgin's customers remains to be seen.

Take-off will be from a special airfield in the Mojave desert of California, because all the slots at Stansted had already been nabbed by Ryanair. Passengers will be securely strapped in while the craft accelerates to 2,000 miles an hour in twenty-five seconds. Rather worryingly there is no toilet on board, presumably because with that sort of take-off the passengers will have wet themselves already. But once the seatbelt signs are switched off, passengers will literally float around the plane, peeking out of one of the portholes or trying to catch the last little cheese triangle that floated off their plate as they left the Earth's atmosphere.

Then there are four short minutes spent listening to

everyone saying, 'Hmm, you know, when you see the whole Earth like that, it makes you realize how insignificant we all really are', while the bloke next to you just missed it all because he was still trying to get his plastic knife and fork out of the cellophane wrapper. As tourist attractions go, three days' wait for 240 seconds of excitement puts it roughly on a par with the Dragon Falls at Chessington World of Adventure. After that it's the long flight back home nervously listening out for any announcements. 'This is your captain speaking. Space traffic control say there may be a slight delay in re-entering the Earth's atmosphere, a little bit of bad weather up ahead so we may have to divert to the Moon unfortunately – anyway just sit back, pop on the headphones and watch the in-flight movie channel. *Apollo 13* is just starting.' That is of course if the whole thing isn't an elaborate con and customers are secretly seated aboard a sophisticated flight simulator. (Suspicions that the incredible view of the stars is actually stock video footage will not be helped by the little sign in the corner that says 'London Planetarium – Exit via Gift Shop'.)

This is only the first step towards a projected space tourism industry that it is predicted will see orbiting hotels being built within our lifetime. Why anyone would want to go on holiday to outer space remains a mystery; if you want to pay a fortune to stay in the middle of a lifeless vacuum, there's a hotel in Worthing I could recommend. But basically, if your stag weekend is still just a booze cruise to Prague, you'll be a laughing stock.

A hundred thousand pounds is probably not a particularly astronomical price for the multimillionaires who are already queuing up for an 'out of this world' experience. But of course the real cost will not be paid by the super-rich thrill-seekers. Increasing air travel is a major cause of greenhouse gases and the advent of space tourism will take pollution up to a whole new level. So that's why they need a fully functional space hotel up there. Where else to sit back and watch the Earth die from all the pollution caused by unnecessary air travel and commercial space rockets? Our best chance of saving Planet Earth will be that Richard Branson's latest pet project will come up against some insurmountable obstacles between now and take-off. Let's just hope all the passengers get Virgin trains to the airport. That should delay things another year or two.

Hungrey and homless

8 October 2004

Newspaper headlines are generally designed to terrify the public while the journalists who concoct them remain totally indifferent. But a story this week had completely the opposite effect; ordinary readers shrugged and turned the page while reporters everywhere spluttered on their pints, skipped breakfast and dashed straight into work. 'The outsourcing of journalism,' declared yesterday's *Guardian* as the news agency Reuters began shifting its financial coverage to Bangalore. 'This is an outrage!' said *Telegraph* leader-writers who'd just finished an editorial about how British workers must accept pay cuts to compete with call centres in India. 'These Asians,' ranted the *Daily Star* hacks, 'they stay over there and take our jobs!'

Reuters financial journalists had been writing for some

time about how cost-efficient it might be for corporations to take advantage of India's highly educated workforce. Well at least now they know that their bosses bother to read their stuff. 'Breaking news will continue to be reported from the world's financial centres,' wrote the media company's press secretary, struggling with the two removal men who were carrying out his desk. 'Journalists miles away from the actual stories?' exclaimed one outraged cub reporter. 'How will they check for mistakes?' At which point the entire news room looked at him with one eyebrow raised and he was quietly shown the door.

Without anyone realizing, this has been happening in local newspapers for some time. Trainee journalists in India get to their computers at 8 a.m. and by lunchtime have produced all the news stories that you read in your local freesheet. The template is pretty straightforward; the software simply prompts the operator to make a series of simple choices to create a typical local news report: 'Pensioner Mugged for Only 10p/50p/£1.20 (please delete accordingly).' 'A cowardly attack on a local pensioner was carried out [in broad daylight/in the park/in this court report I just read] earlier this week. The attacker was wearing [a bomber jacket and jeans/a hooded top and trainers] and fled the scene with only . . . p (insert pitiful amount here). Police said this was a particularly despicable/ shocking/vague story and are warning pensioners to take extra care/stay inside/not to read their local newspaper and live in permanent terror.' To balance up this routinely depressing item the would-be journalists are then presented with a range of heart-warming reports such as 'Hospice Hero Cycling to Scotland!' and 'Brownies Cake Sale Takes the Biscuit!' to put above 'notice of planning application for new conservatory'. Then they just press 'send' on their computer and the next day four copies of the local advertiser are pushed through your letterbox to make sure you have something to line the hamster cage with.

But now the software has been refined so that Indian computer operators can write the stories for British national newspapers as well. Of course, the range of subject matter differs according to which newspaper the journalist is writing for. Click on the *Daily Mail* icon and you get the headline 'Asylum Seekers Threat to House Prices' and the piece pretty well writes itself from there, although the software will not allow you to delete the words 'mother of two', 'fear' and 'Islamic extremists'. Click on the *Sun* and you get 'It's Christine Agui-Leera!' and you just have to write the caption for a photo of an attractive young singer with a low-cut dress and faulty bra. Soon central London will be full of unemployed British journalists – Fleet Street's finest former wordsmiths holding up cardboard signs saying 'Hungrey and Homless – Plese Halp'. And the placards of the Murdoch journalists will include a plug for whatever's on Sky One that night.

But this is pay-back time for centuries of colonization. Britain occupied India, imposed the English language and left the country significantly poorer so that two hundred years later it is still much cheaper to get Indians to compile our crosswords and review the new Dido album. Of course, some former colonies are in a better position than others.

'Right,' says the finance minister of Surinam, 'we're going to set up an on-line news agency.'

'But we were colonized by Holland. I'm afraid there's not much call for Dutch financial journalism.'

'Not even in the Netherlands?'

'Nope, they speak even better English than the Americans.'

Unless of course this is all an elaborate plan to halt immigration. The presumption was always that Third World workers desperately hoped to come and work in the paradise that was Europe or America. Give them a few months of learning about the sort of newspapers we read and they'll all be saying, 'Er, actually I think I'll stay right here, thank you very much.'

NB Although this comment column will continue to be credited to John O'Farrell it has now been outsourced to topical comedy writers in southern India. No discernible change in standard is anticipated.

Some like it not

15 October 2004

It's always a shock when you actually meet 'one of them'. One of those strange misfits who unlike everyone else in modern society is not completely obsessed with sex. They ask you back for coffee but when you get into the flat they offer you filter or decaff. So you wink and say, 'So what about these "etchings" you were going to show me? Eh? Eh?' and they slip out and return five minutes later with their portfolio. It's disgusting, it really is, and far more widespread than you'd imagine. You know those little cards in the newsagent's windows? They're not advertising what you think at all! No, you ring the number that promises 'French lessons' and they explain yes, they can do GCSE and 'A' level French or just beginners' conversation. You go round to the dingy flat that promised 'Large

Chest For Sale' and they show you a big piece of furniture.

The shocking truth is that asexuality is on the rise. This week's *New Scientist* reports that growing numbers of people are coming out of the closet and proudly declaring that they are simply not that bothered about sex. Even the *Sun* gave the story a few column inches, adding, 'And here's a photo of a naked lady that asexuals would have no interest in whatsoever.' Forums such as the Asexual Visibility and Education Network (AVEN) are urging their members to be more vocal as asexual chat-rooms spring up on the Internet (although dirty old men can get special software to block these sites out). In a society that is so completely dominated by sexual imagery and suggestion, most of us would find this idea completely repellent. I mean, what they don't do in the privacy of their own homes is their own business, but why do they have to flaunt it so?

Some of these more obscure websites are pretty graphic. Ladies with their eyes blacked out, pictured sitting in comfy chairs wearing cardigans. Pixelated video clips of middle-aged gentlemen sipping a cup of tea. And the personal accounts that people post up there . . . 'One thing led to another and well, we ended up doing a jigsaw puzzle together. It was amazing, she was obviously really experienced – "I like to separate all the edges," she moaned. "And then do all the clouds . . ."'

Advertisers are working hard to appeal to this newly identified target group. They're going to show Häagen-Dazs ice cream being eaten from a bowl after dinner.

Cadbury's Flake will no longer be pronounced 'phall-ake'. And at this year's motor show, the new Ferrari will be put on display with Ann Widdecombe draped across the bonnet.

It is important here to distinguish between asexuality and celibacy. People who feel sexual urges but decline to act on them are 'celibate', people who feel little inclination to have sex are referred to as 'asexual', and people who used to have a lot of sex but have now ceased are called 'married'. The AVEN website explains it in terms of a stereo. 'Everyone has a volume knob and a tuning knob . . . there are some who have their volume knob turned right down.' Unfortunately most men would find it hard to follow this mature treatise on sexuality, because they would still be giggling at the word 'knob'.

Of course, there are other creatures in the animal kingdom that manage to get by without sexual reproduction. Amoeba teenagers listen in horror as their parents describe how they never had sex.

'And then Mummy's cell divided in two and I was nowhere near.'

'Urgh, that's sick, I don't even want to think about it.'

'And Granny and Granddad, they never had sex either.'

'Urgh, no, stop it, they must have done . . .'

Of course, if asexuality is an inherited trait, then as a gene you would think its future must be pretty bleak. But as a cultural counterweight to Western society's snowballing obsession with sex, then the advent of assertive asexuality is more than welcome. Say it loud, you're 'A' and you're proud! Because our media is at the point of sexual overkill, every advert, T-shirt, TV chat show and tabloid story seems to be loaded with sexual innuendo. It might be quite refreshing to get some spam email offering us knitting patterns and a recipe for biscuits. But everything these days seems to be preoccupied with sex, I mean, even ornithologists concerned about global warming can't type 'hot chicks in action' into a search engine without one or two of the sites turning out to be sexual. Thank goodness there's still a few of us who manage to resist every chance for a bit of smutty innuendo, we have better things to do with our column inches. Oh damn, I did that one already.

Grand Prix (pronounced as it's spelt)
22 October 2004

One of the important things about living in a democracy is remembering that just because you couldn't care less about something, it doesn't mean it isn't very important to other people. However, when it comes to motor racing, I'm afraid the rest of us are struggling a bit.

'Do you realize what's about to happen?' the enthusiasts have implored all week. 'No F1 race at Silverstone next year! No British Grand Prix! Is that the sort of country you want to live in?'

'Um . . . well, you know, we'll just have to do our best to cope.'

British motor sport is in crisis. Talks broke down this week between the British Racing Drivers Club (who own Silverstone) and Formula One's commercial supremo

Bernie Ecclestone. Neither side was able to find answers to some very difficult questions, such as 'Why do the cars just go round and round like that with nothing ever changing?', 'Why does the winner have to waste all that champagne at the end?' and 'Does Murray Walker really sound like that or am I just thinking of Rory Bremner's impression?'

Of course, Formula One is not always boring, but generally you have to wait ages for a crash. These days you can get dreadful pile-ups far more regularly on *When the World's Weirdest Police Chases Go Bad!* over on Sky Car Crash +1. Unless this dispute is settled soon Silverstone's place on the Grand Prix calendar may be lost and we will never know who would have come second to Michael Schumacher. The famous venue isn't just a racetrack, it's also used as a driving school, although they generally try and get the nervous learners off the course before any of the races.

'There's someone very keen to overtake me,' says Mrs Johnson doing 20 mph in the Nissan Micra with a roaring high-powered Ferrari almost touching her L-plates.

'Good, you're using your rearview mirror, that's good . . .'

'He's swerving around right behind me, trying to squeeze past.'

'OK, Mrs Johnson, let's have another go at the emergency stop.'

They could still use the circuit for other sorts of motor racing of course, mums in 4x4s dashing to get the last parking place outside the nursery school maybe, or a race in which minicab drivers have to go once round the track and still manage to get lost on the way there.

There is also talk of holding a Grand Prix through the streets of London, which would certainly liven things up a bit. First the cars attempt to pull away while squeegee merchants are still cleaning their windscreens. Then they accelerate into the long straight that is Park Lane, before suddenly hitting the brakes at the same time as they all spot the first speed camera. Michael Schumacher nearly crashes into Jacques Villeneuve, because he's fiddling with his mobile phone to try and pay the congestion charge and finally down the Mall the cars hit 120 mph, but now everyone has to stop because a four-year-old has pressed the button on the pelican crossing even though his mum isn't crossing the road. Meanwhile the British driver is stuck in the pits because he pulled over to get his tyres changed and the guys from Kwik-Fit say, 'Naah, we don't keep those in stock, you'll have to go over to our Croydon branch.'

Logistical problems surrounding this event means that such speeds will not be witnessed on British roads for many years unless Princess Anne starts driving again. Ecclestone has got himself into such a powerful position within the sport that he can basically demand any price he likes or leave Silverstone out of next year's F1 calendar. His grip over the sport is such that even Scalextric sets now come with a tiny little plastic figure of a grey-haired man with glasses with a glamorous young wife towering over him. Once a secondhand car dealer, Ecclestone is now a billionaire in control of one of the world's most glamorous sports, touring the world's hotspots surrounded by fast cars, champagne and beautiful women. Yeah, but is he happy?

The F1 supremo claims that Silverstone's facilities do not come up to scratch compared to brand-new government-funded circuits in places such as China and Malaysia; the subtext being that the government should cough up the millions he is demanding. This is the BRDC's solution as well. 'Look, I'm afraid Bernie Ecclestone is being rather greedy, so could the government fund that, please?' It's a really tough one. The government has a set amount of money to put into sport. Would these millions be better spent on developing grass roots facilities across a range of games and activities, or should they just hand a huge cheque over to Bernie Ecclestone? Hmmm, it's one of those really agonizing dilemmas that make you glad that someone else has to take those impossible decisions. One way or another Ecclestone will emerge from this even richer than he was before. And that's what's so boring about F1 racing. The same bloke always wins.

A short history of humans

29 October 2004

It is the most exciting anthropological discovery for a century. Until just twelve thousand years ago, there was a species of little people walking around who would have only come up to our waist. Finally they were wiped out, possibly following encounters with the much larger *Homo sapiens*, who it's feared may have patronized them to death. Things got off to a bad start after that first meeting and never really improved.

'Halt! I am the chief of this island. What is your business here?'

'Hello, little fellah, is your mummy or daddy around?'

'I don't have a mummy or daddy, I'm thirty-seven years old.'

'Of course you are dear, now run and play while we do a bit of hunting.'

Indeed it's thought that the slightly flatter skull of *Homo floresiensis* may be a result of being patted on the head so often.

The tiny human remains were unearthed alongside charred bones, basic little tools and two-inch lifts that they slotted into their shoes. The creature was immediately nicknamed 'the hobbit', which was a little optimistic. There will never be as much interest in a major rewriting of evolutionary history as there is in a mythical dwarf endlessly over-interpreted by teenage boys and 1970s heavy metal stars. The discoveries were made in the remote Indonesian island of Flores, where this sub-species of humans probably evolved. When a population is cut off from the mainland, there is an evolutionary tendency for them to shrink in size; witness all the little old ladies on the Isle of Wight. At the press conference where the tiny skull was put on show, the scientists excitedly described life on an island where hominids the size of two-year-olds hunted pygmy elephants, giant lizards and rats 'the size of golden retrievers'. At which point the journalists at the press conference went, 'Yeah, right, and I hear they've taken the word "gullible" out of the dictionary.' But yesterday an artist's impression of this naked man was reproduced in newspapers across the world, except in some of primmer states of the American Bible Belt where they put him in swimming trunks. He is posing with a giant rat that he's just killed, and looks pretty pleased with himself, tragically unaware that lots of other much bigger people are about to arrive and start laughing at him.

One of the fascinating things about this discovery is that stories of a race of tiny people living in the forests still survive in local folklore. It may well be that this oral history is based on truth and that the race were still around at the time that the first white men arrived, when the islanders probably committed suicide rather than face the indignity of Australian dwarf-throwing contests. It also raises the possibility that some of our own popular myths might be based on fact. Perhaps there really were seven dwarves who lived in a remote cottage deep in the woods? Travellers to a site north of Paris have actually reported seeing some of these figures, posing with children and waving at the camera. Maybe the myth of leprechauns is based on other tiny people who lived on the fringes of Western Europe making little ceramic figures of each other to flog to Americans arriving at Shannon Airport? Perhaps there really was a David 'Diddy' Hamilton who presented *Top of the Pops*?

Twelve thousand years ago is incredibly recent in terms of the development of mankind. In other parts of the world our ancestors were already learning to become farmers by planting grain, domesticating animals and filling out complicated subsidy forms. Other contemporary humans were attempting rudimentary pottery, organizing plate-painting sessions for children's birthday parties. Meanwhile these three-feet-high hominids were probably more attracted to occupations usually associated with short men: aerobics teachers, driving instructors . . . that sort of thing. We know from evidence found in the Liang

Bua caves of Indonesia that Flores man was able to start a fire and cook meat, which puts him ahead of most modern males struggling with the new barbecue. But it has been a long-held belief that we *Homo sapiens* owe our intelligence to the size of our brains. That is why we are much smarter than a gorilla, for example (though you might not want to say so to his face). But with a brain only the size of a grapefruit, *Homo floresiensis* were able to make tools, hunt and probably employ some sort of language. So it isn't just the size of the brain, it's what you do with it that counts. Men have been saying that about other parts of their body for centuries. But now it's official; having a tiny brain doesn't necessarily make you some sort of chimp. Somebody should tell the President.

'President Bush' and other oxymorons

5 November 2004

It was a very tense night. All over America millions of viewers stayed up late waiting to find out the result of that referendum on a regional assembly for the north-east of England. In bars in the Mid-West, tattooed truckers and Vietnam vets anxiously bit their lips as CNN reported that exit polls from Chester-le-Street made the referendum too close to call.

'Jeez, if the Welsh and Scotch can have assemblies, why not the Geordies?'

'Because it's an unnecessary tier of bureaucracy, you schmuck. Bishop Auckland and Hartlepool already have local councils . . .'

And again these bitter divisions spilled over into physical violence.

Taking this much interest was the least the Americans could do after the rest of the world had sat up all night waiting to see who would win the US Presidency. And what a thrilling night's television it was! The BBC wheeled out heavyweight American commentators, like the former assistant speechwriter to Gary Hart's friend, telling us it was too early to say one way or the other.

'When might we get to the situation when people are no longer saying, "It's too early to say"?'

'It's too early to say.'

Then we'd cut back to Peter Snow pointlessly jumping around a giant map of the United States, dodging animated graphics of Ohio that kept popping up and nearly knocking him over. There was not much more information over on CNN or Sky News (although by accidentally landing on the WWF wrestling channel you could at least get a reminder of what a more dignified contest looked like). Early signs were encouraging.

'No incumbent president has ever won in the same year that the Minnesota Bluebirds have come third in the ice hockey play-offs.'

'Yes, and just as in 1960 the Democrats have a candidate with the initials JFK who is a senator from Massachusetts and a Navy war veteran.'

Yup, and then Kerry went and got murdered by a nut-case from Texas. Like Charlie Brown kicking the football, yet again we had allowed ourselves to believe the exit polls (so called because putting your faith in them makes you want to join Exit). To make it even more annoying, people who hadn't really been following it would glance at the telly and say, 'Wow – that looks promising!' seeing the great wash of red across middle America. 'No,' we groaned, 'the red states are Republican ones. The Democrat states are those tiny blue ones up in the north-east.'

Finally, when it became clear that there are lies, damned lies and exit polls, we went to bed in disgust, having left a message at work to say we wouldn't be in today because we were emigrating to the planet Jupiter. Damn, they went and made the bastard legitimate! Up until Tuesday 'President Bush' was an oxymoron. Now he's thrown off that tag. Or at least shortened it a bit.

Meanwhile John Kerry will have to find something else to do with his leadership skills. Apparently there's a vacancy coming up at the PLO he might consider. But there are shreds of hope to be taken from all of this. This was not the electoral catastrophe for the Democrats that some commentators are making out. An unimpressive Democratic candidate polled more votes than any Republican had ever received before Tuesday, a million more than Reagan got in his landslide of '84, more votes than Nixon got in '72 when he won 49 states out of 50; in fact, John Kerry got the second-highest number of votes for any presidential candidate ever. The only negative (admittedly quite a big one) is that the new record was set by his rival on Tuesday. In one sense Global Village Idiot does now represent all of the American people; one half of his smile is smug and happy, the left-hand side of his mouth is turned down in a bitter sneer. But there's not much evidence to suggest that America will have more to smile about in four years' time.

Because on the Wednesday morning, the Republicans stumbled back into the White House with a terrible hangover, looking at their wrecked offices the night after the party. 'Oh no, we completely trashed the place! We thought the other lot were going to have to clear up this mess. We're billions in debt, industry's destroyed and the rest of the world hates us; how the hell did we get landed with sorting out all this?' Dubya was quick to clarify things. 'We're gonna reunificate the country; continuizing our economical strategums and re-envigorizing the Middle-Eastern Peace Processor.' Still, it could be worse; he could have a dreadful brother ready to replace him in 2008. Yes, Tuesday's result was a disaster but hey, it's not the end of the world. Oh, apparently that's pencilled in for early next year.

Never say Di

12 November 2004

Occasionally in courtrooms around the world, judges and juries are exposed to some pretty horrific images: violent scenes from security cameras, graphic descriptions of cruelty and neglect or horrific photographs of murder victims. But in a courtroom in Los Angeles last week, even hardened police officers visibly winced as Exhibit A was put on display. It was the porcelain Princess Diana tea set, featuring the exclusive English Rose motif and gold-effect embellish. Worse was to come, as the cover was whisked off Exhibit B: a ten-inch Queen of Hearts collectable china doll, in the dress that Lady Di wore on her wedding day, perfectly capturing her unmistakable blue eyes and bright red lips, individually hand-painted at some sweatshop in Costa Rica. Some in the courtroom were forced to avert their eyes, others wanted to be sick, as each one of these stomach-churning over-priced pieces of tat were passed around the courtroom. No-one had seen anything as ghastly since finding themselves unable to look away from QVC the shopping channel.

Perhaps it was to avoid months of this trauma that the case was settled out of court this week. The Princess Diana fund had looked set to lose millions after an ill-advised attempt to block one of America's biggest memorabilia companies, Franklin Mint, from marketing souvenirs in the late princess's image. To help get some of that money back Camilla kindly offered to allow her own image to be put on souvenir plates, but the charity said, 'No, I think we're all right, thanks.' Meanwhile Mohammed Al Fayed claimed the whole court case was a result of a conspiracy between M15, the Duke of Edinburgh and Mossad.

But somewhere in the middle of this suing and counter-suing, it appears that the real victims have been forgotten, the tragic cases who the charity was originally set up to help. Take a typical sufferer like Mrs X from Didsbury. Once Mrs X was a normal well-adjusted middle-aged woman, but following a car accident (which happened hundreds of miles away in Paris) there seemed to be a rapid deterioration in her sense of good taste. She rushed to London, stopping at a garage to buy some wilting carnations to bung on the pile outside Kensington Palace. But this only fed a tragic addiction that saw her spending her last few quid on an entire Queen of Hearts dinner set, a Princess of Wales Jewelled Tribute ring and a realistic

Diana Enchantment Doll which said, 'You could say it was a crowded marriage' when you pulled a little string in her back.

The really frightening thing about all this fantastically kitsch Diana memorabilia is that there really are thousands of people out there who are buying it *unironically*. You'd think it was just gay couples giving each other the stuff for a laugh but there really are people who want to spend their Sunday lunches dolloping mashed swede on to the face of a dim sloane who died in a car crash. Images of royal celebrities have always been in high demand. After the death of Anne Boleyn every Tudor corner cabinet gave pride of place to a hand-painted little ceramic doll with no head. But the death of Diana raised this macabre fascination to a new level as all sorts of inappropriate merchandise flooded the market. Frankly I thought that special edition 'Di and Dodi vs the Paparazzi' Scalextric was in poor taste.

But it turns out that no-one actually owns the image of Diana, Princess of Wales, Queen of Hearts, who I think lived her life a little bit like a candle in the wind. This particular legal battle had raged back and forth since 1998. And now all those members of the public who gave their savings to the Princess Diana Fund will be delighted to learn that their charitable donations have been passed on to those who need it most, namely American lawyers.

'Remember, for every copy sold of Elton John's rehashed tribute song, £1 goes directly to millionaire ambulance chasers who gave completely the wrong advice about copyright law. And just look what else we've been able to do with your cash. Fifty pounds allowed us to buy a two-minute phone call with a Californian barrister. A hundred pounds paid for another silk tie for the law firm's accountant. A thousand pounds helped that Harvard law graduate pay off the loan on his second sports car. But please keep your donations coming in because now it's time to get on with what this charity does best.' Yup, the Diana fund is now suing the original lawyers who urged the charity to sue the Franklin Mint. Ah, it's what she would have wanted. At least when Diana walked into a minefield somebody had had the sense to check it first.

The prince and the P45

19 November 2004

Below is an exchange of letters and memos between Prince Charles and a private secretary which have come into the Guardian's possession after they were flogged to us by a dodgy-looking bloke in the pub claiming to be the former Keeper of the Royal Trouser Press . . .

Your Highness,

The royal household is getting a lot of bad publicity following an employment tribunal brought by a former servant of yours. It is my judgement that we are faced with three choices: refute all charges, come to a quick settlement or set Princess Anne's dogs on her. In the meantime this might be a good time to promote one or two of your highness's lowlier staff to get a bit of positive coverage. I was thinking in particular of that assistant ghillie at Highgrove whose job it is to lie across the puddle outside the back door. He's been in that position for five years now, and has put in an early application for promotion, i.e. he wants to know if he might lie face up for a couple of hours a day when you're up in London?

Dear Servant-chappie whose name escapes me,
What is wrong with these people? Where do they get these ridiculous delusions of grandeur from? One gives them a privileged position and still they want more, I mean, one cannot possibly consider having a junior ghillie lying face up when one is wiping one's feet on him! Why do people think they are capable of tasks beyond their natural abilities? I blame all this modern child-centred learning; education shouldn't be based around children, for god's sake, any idiot knows it should be centred around badgers and other nocturnal mammals. And another thing: why have car keys got bigger? I mean, it's really annoying having a great big key in your pocket, oh, and why do we have to wait so long for the next page on Ceefax, I mean can't people read any more? I think I might make a keynote speech on this.

Dear Prince,
Thank you for these very interesting thoughts; might I humbly suggest that it may be prudent to keep these views private just for the time being? Apparently there was a drunk bloke on a radio phone-in last night pretending to

be you, complaining about 'uppity servants', 'bloody modern architecture', 'Internet designer babies' and how impossible it is to re-fold Ordnance Survey maps.

Dear Thingy,

Er, no that was me actually. I would have phoned up before except I couldn't work out the fancy cordless phone, I mean what was wrong with the old Bakelite with a dial and a curly wire you could twiddle with when you were flirting with Camilla? I blame social workers, MMR jabs and modern agriculture; do you know in school these days they don't even teach kids to plough with oxen; and another thing, there are too many different remote controls for everything these days, you can never find the right one.

Your Royal Highness,

Yes, very interesting thoughts. It is important, however, that we are not perceived to be totally out of touch and obsessively formal as I think you yourself mentioned to your Rouge-Croix Falconer at Arms. One radical suggestion, for example, is that since I am in the room with you right now, we might communicate by 'talking' rather than this rather formal exchange of letters written with quill on parchment.

Dear Footrest,

What is wrong with you! Far better to write everything down, that way there is less chance of embarrassing comments finding their way into the newspapers. When you've worked as hard as I have to get the job I do today you will understand these things. It seems as if even you are getting ideas above your station. Next you'll be wanting a chair. I blame political correctness, the BBC and intrusive medicine. From now on, no promotion happens to anyone in the Royal Household, unless it is based on merit, intellect, and um, merit. Understand?

Dear Charlie-Boy with the big ears,
I have enacted your wishes to the letter and as such, I'm afraid your application to be promoted to the position of 'King' has been rejected. You simply do not have the intelligence, qualifications or temperament to be elevated to the post of a modern head of state. Frankly I don't know where you got such arrogant delusions from – I blame a private education system that filled your head with more crap than you put on your organic allotment. So forget about advancing beyond your current so-called job, we'll get someone with a bit more brains, one of the Millibands maybe, and you can pursue an occupation more suited to your particular communication skills. The black cab's being delivered at the weekend.

Finally, after five years, a column about cricket . . .

26 November 2004

Nobody in the cricketing establishment ever imagined that things could possibly reach this stage, but recent events have shocked the world of sport. England have finally got a decent cricket team. Angry protests have been made by British comedy writers, furious at this flagrant breach of years of satirical tradition; shell-shocked sketch writers have called on the government to invest far less at grass roots and build luxury flats on school playing fields in the hope that we might see a return to the golden age when England were all out for five against Tellytubbyland. (Atherton 0, bowled Dipsy, caught La La.)

However, any competence that the English cricketing establishment may have discovered on the field of play has been more than made up for by a staggering incompetence behind the scenes. A couple of years ago when they were pawing over their dusty old atlas that still had the British Empire coloured in pink, they agreed that the perfect place for a nice trouble-free winter tour would be Southern Rhodesia, or whatever it's called these days.

'Are you sure? Why does it have to be Zimbabwe?'

'Well, all the hotels in Iraq were fully booked.'

After two years of planning England were due to play the first game of their tour in Harare today. But then the tour was off. And then it was back on again. Then it was about to be called off but was confirmed as definitely on. Finally they changed their minds for the hundredth time and there was light applause from the pavilion. The BBC's Jonathan Agnew said that Zimbabwe 'kept moving the goalposts', which makes me worry that he knows even less about cricket than I do. Events hung in the balance as the players themselves made their own feelings plain.

'We the England team have decided that there are basic ethical principles at stake here. As such we will not be going into the war-torn hell-hole that is Zimbabwe, but will make a moral stand by seeing out the next week of the winter tour here in this five-star hotel in sun-kissed South Africa.'

'Two more pina coladas?'

'Over here, please.'

'Great news – Zimbabwe have relented; we might be able to go!'

'Oh no, but I've got my trunks on now. And the cocktail waitress agreed to rub sun cream on my back . . .'

267

It was right that the players were prepared to make a stand because this time the Zimbabwean government had really gone too far. The cricket correspondents were not being given their press accreditation. 'Okay, tyranny, torture and oppression we can live with, but denying those chaps from the *Telegraph* and the *Times* their press accreditation – now that's off the scale!' The team were supported in their wish to call off the tour by such moral lodestars as Mike Gatting: 'There has to be a very serious dilemma about representing your country on the cricket field in a land where people are suffering so much at the hands of their government,' said the captain who led the rebel tour to apartheid South Africa. Calls for the games to be cancelled were even made by John Major, to which the press said, 'Hmmm, the name definitely rings a bell; did he use to bowl for Glamorgan?'

The Zimbabwe cricket authorities insist that this tour is in no way a political stunt, though they have demanded one or two changes. Opening for Zimbabwe will be their new star batsman, President Robert Mugabe. England bowlers have been asked to bowl underarm and not to use such a hard ball. If he hits it into next door's garden, he can keep on getting hundreds and hundreds of runs even if the other team are angrily shouting, 'Lost ball!'

The fact that a cricket team actually got Mugabe to back down on something, succeeding where economic boycotts and UN resolutions have previously failed, has proved just what a potent political force sport really is. 'We must keep sport and politics apart,' said a

Zimbabwean minister, whose despotic president also happens to be the patron of the Zimbabwe Cricket Union. Sport is political because everything is political (with the possible exception of a couple of back-bench Liberal MPs). But while the cricketers in Harare will be wearing pads and helmets, the protestors outside the ground will have no such protection. If the players are to be forced to take part, they should use the occasion to make the most pointed passive protest possible – standing back and letting themselves be bowled out for a duck; deliberately knocking down their wickets with their own bats; standing completely still while easy catches bounce right next to them. It would send a heartening message around the world about what England still symbolizes. 'I see the English cricket team are back to their usual form then.'

New Home Office catch-all form: everyone gets caught

3 December 2004

Following Home Office reforms and the resignation of David Blunkett,* the following form HO/7b(1) will be used for all applications for Identity Cards, British Citizenship and Fast Track Visa Applications.

Please read this form carefully. Please complete all sections in black ink, putting the postcode in the wrong place before crossing it out and putting it in the box marked 'Postcode'. Please enter your name, address and any other personal details that may be of interest to the tabloids when this form is leaked to the *Daily Mail*. Please enter your gender, date of birth, and the value of your luxury

---

* David Blunkett was soon brought back into the Cabinet so that he could go back to what he did best: resigning from the Cabinet.

house. Please attach a passport-sized photograph, unless you are female and attractive in which case a large colour one of you arm-in-arm with a major public figure would be preferred. Do not forget to tick the appropriate box to indicate your marital status: (a) single, (b) married, (c) divorced but having a brief fling with a married woman which will all go horribly wrong when we split up. Do not forget to include details of children. These will be reproduced inaccurately on the front page thereby causing maximum personal distress to all concerned.

Please note that applicants for British Identity Cards are strongly advised not to have an identity. Demonstrating interesting character traits, wit, personality or any hint of individuality (Boris Johnson, David Blunkett etc.) will count against you. Indeed, having no identity will become compulsory in 2008. As well as ID cards there are also plans for the introduction of 'id cards', which will list your subconscious evolutionary desires as defined by Freud, i.e. 'everyone needs to have it off from time to time' and 'ex-lovers can become incredibly bitter'. You do not need to include details of previous employment – how well you have done your job or otherwise is of no interest to anyone. Applicants with a visual impairment may require assistance filling out this form, and should also expect people to think, 'Why should a blind bloke have a girlfriend who's quite pretty? That's not fair on the rest of us.' It is advisable to get Visa applications thoroughly checked before submission by a magistrate, councillor, GP but definitely not the Home Secretary, I mean honestly, what are they expected to know about it?

If you are formally applying for a visa to live and work legally in the United Kingdom, then frankly you will be in the minority. By being kosher and above board you might find yourself priced out of a job. Please note that British employers generally prefer their foreign workers to be here illegally so that they can sack them at a moment's notice having paid them paltry wages to dig potatoes, do the laundry in the top hotels or indeed look after their kids while they go off to edit national newspapers.

Having completed the above section, naturalized Britons may be invited to take part in a British citizenship ceremony which has been introduced following successful pilot schemes in various parts of the United Kingdom and Marbella. Applicants are asked to make the following oath: 'I promise to uphold modern British values of liberty, justice and the belief that a person is innocent until proven guilty by a newspaper headline. I pledge to believe the worst in every MP, local councillor and MEP and I promise to only use the word "politician" as a term of abuse. I pledge to always believe a conspiracy theory when the duller explanation of a simple cock-up is far more likely. I will of course do something for charity (buy a scratchcard) and may vote if it's made really easy for me and I think there's a chance I might gain personally from the outcome. I think "civic duty" is the car tax I have to pay on my Honda.'

The ceremony will include the national anthem and other appropriate national songs in other parts of the UK such as Scotland or Wales. In Somerset, you may opt to sing along to something by the Wurzels. You will also be expected to swear loyalty to her Majesty the Queen, unless you are Greek or German, in which case that's already a given.

Congratulations, you have completed the form and if successful will have the right of abode in the UK and dependencies (a small corner of Southern Iraq). If you wish to contribute further to British public life, by entering politics for example and spending years helping ordinary constituents and trying to make the world a better place when you could have earned far more money working shorter hours in the private sector, if you would like to expose your private life to endless scrutiny only to have your career ended after one minor slip, then you are advised to complete form HO/3(b): Application to be Sectioned under the Mental Health Act. And if after that you are still determined to find a way to serve your community without being hounded and vilified then please fill out form HO/8(a): Application to Emigrate to Mainland Europe or Scandinavia. We regret that these guidance notes have not been available in Braille.

Witness for the persecution

9 December 2004

On Wednesday senior judges heard an appeal that Gloucestershire police behaved illegally when they stopped three coachloads of protestors travelling to a US military base to protest against the Iraq war. Below are the witness statements of those involved in the original incident.

Statement of PC Hooper: In July of last year my colleagues and I were carrying out our normal duties on the M4 motorway (deliberately making people go extra slow past the smelly sewage works at Slough West), when we noticed a coach driver behaving suspiciously; i.e. he was not doing 90 mph while texting on his mobile phone. There were banners in the windows saying 'No blood for oil', 'US of Oil' and another asking 'How do you spell

WAR? O.I.L.' which I have checked and is incorrect in all three letters. The spelling of the Prime Minister's name also had a very basic error. I became concerned that I would not be doing my duty as a police officer if I did not pull over this vehicle and point out that these spelling mistakes constituted an offence under the new anti-terrorism laws so I ordered the coach driver to leave the motorway.

Statement of anti-war protestor known as 'Spider': So where did the Old Bill take us, right? To a motorway service station, where they sell OIL, like did you know that for every litre of Esso sold George Bush gets five dollars direct into his campaign fund so Tony B-liar has instructed his police to force everyone to go to motorway service stations and spend money there and they don't even have veggie samosas in the Harry Ramsden's, which is part of global-ization, but anyway I got searched right, cos they'd found a smoke bomb but like what about the bombs they drop on Iraq which they're only doing because of the oil.

PC Hooper: I then received intelligence which led me to believe that if these protestors proceeded to RAF Fairford scenes of violence would ensue. This was based on excited comments from a number of my officers who were saying, 'Please, sir, let them start protesting so we can kick the shit out of this twat Spider.' I strongly refute allegations that we were heavy-handed with the protestors, illegally detaining them without charge, constantly filming them and

275

deliberately saying 'luv' in a patronizing manner to the spokeslady just because she was one of them 'strong women' types with a big jumper and no make-up.

Spider: So the police right even searched inside the coach engine, but what did they see? Yeah OIL, exactly; so that proves what they were really interested in because it was Britain and America who sold Iraq all their weapons of mass destruction except they don't have any because Bin Laden was actually in the pay of George Bush who's actually an old family friend who helped the CIA organize 9/11 so Bush would get re-elected and that's why the fourth plane didn't hit the White House and that's true because I read it on the internet on www.its-actually-all-about-oil.

PC Hooper: When they had been held on the coach for two hours I tried to interview them, but became doubtful about the details given; e.g. name? 'Oh god I need a wee.' Address? 'Oh god, I really, really need a wee, I'm going to wet my pants if you don't let me off the coach to have a wee.' No postcode was given. I was also suspicious about the way the lady in question was squatting at the back of the coach with a water bottle, but at least she subsequently offered us a sip of some 'organic kumquat juice', which I have to say was far too salty for my liking. In the circumstances I decided that my best course of action would be to force the protestors to return to London. I have a duty to uphold the democratic rule of law and

I was anxious for the safety of the weaker members of our society, i.e. the United States Air Force, who could potentially have been the target of some hurtful name-calling. The protestors became very angry that they were not going to be allowed to be angry where they'd planned to be angry and called my actions 'totally undemocratic' which is actually an offence under the new Incitement to Hatred Law for which I now request that they be detained indefinitely and bound over not to say the word 'oil'.

Based on this evidence the appeal judges decided that the police were right to prevent the demonstration ever happening. The protestors have said they will take their case to the European Court of Human Rights at Strasbourg. Police will be waiting for them on the M2 to Dover.

The Good Brit Guide

17 December 2004

'Excuse me, have you got any of those handy new government booklets explaining British history, custom and character?'

'You wot, mate? Oh them, nah they were supposed to be delivered Thursday, but they never turned up.'

'Thanks, that's all I needed to know.'

It's a tough job for anyone, cramming everything that defines this country into one small publication. How do you possibly explain *How Clean is Your House*? How do you prevent them from finding out about Swindon? Do you talk about the wars that Britain has fought against its neighbours or do you emphasize the culture, and tradition of tolerance of others? I suppose whichever most annoys the French.

The history of Britain is a rich and fascinating narrative except for that bit in the sixth form where they make you study the Whig Oligarchy. But history is just old spin; there is no single incident in our island story on which everyone can agree, with the exception of 'Yeah, that was pretty funny when Kilroy-Silk was covered in pig slurry.' Any official government history is going to depend on whichever party is in power. The Tory version of the olden days would have been all Nelson, Kipling and Maggie scoring a hat trick in the 1966 World Cup final. If the booklet had been written by well-meaning lefties it would be full of things like 'Describe how you think the chimney sweeps would have felt.' Even the Liberal Democrats have their own emphasis: 'In 1485 Henry Tudor defeated Richard III but amazingly still didn't introduce pro-portional representation.' But now we have a New Labour government guide to British history and customs. 'Guy Fawkes broke the terms of his anti-social behaviour order and managed to plant the gunpowder because necessary anti-terrorism legislation had been opposed by the Hampstead chattering classes.' 'Shakespeare's plays played to packed houses at the Globe Theatre, and he managed perfectly well without an Arts Council subsidy and didn't attack the government just because he never got offered a knighthood.'

Asylum seekers skimming through this potted history of Great Britain may be angered about what has been left out. 'Why no mention of John of Gaunt? What about the Battle of Malplaquet? And who is this Princess Diana you mention?' There are of course certain quintessential British icons that still resonate around the globe: Shakespeare, Churchill, Mr Bean. So most people come to Britain with a certain amount of advance knowledge, which is more than you can say for every nation. If you were asked about the Central African Republic, for example, you could probably have a stab at its approximate location and its system of government, but after that you'd be struggling. But nothing can be presumed, so this Good Brit Guide has had to start with the basics: 'Britain is a country off the north-western corner of Europe. It has a unique culture comprising Indian restaurants, mock-Irish pubs and American television. It is a constitutional monarchy, which means that the Queen is head of state, though of course genuine power was handed over long ago to the likes of Paul Dacre and Rupert Murdoch. We used to have a band called the Beatles. We won the war. We invented football. Er, what else? Did we mention the Beatles? Well, anyway, you only have to look at the postcards on the London newsstands to see the symbols that define Great Britain. Big Ben, Princess Diana, and for some reason a solitary bosom with a funny face painted on it.'

The idea of an official guide to the UK for uninitiated newcomers is a perfectly laudable one. The trouble is that the wrong version has been published and distributed. You know how these things happen, you dash out a joke version, you're off work for a day, and suddenly the cod guide to Britain that was being emailed round the office is now being religiously followed by every nervous foreigner desperate to make the right impression. 'Free accommodation is widely available from any of the landladies whose cards may be found in telephone boxes. Pints of beer in pubs do not belong to anyone in particular and are placed on the tables for you to help yourself. There is an amusing pub game where people try and pretend that you are stealing their drink, and it would be rude if you did not join in the fun by shouting, "Oi, gaylord, in the pub car park, now!" After this you may encounter a traditional British policeman. Remember that he expects courtesy, so you should address him by his formal rank which is "Oink! Oink!" If you didn't get a bed for the night earlier, you'll be sure to have one now.'

Fortunately this mistake has been discovered and the proper booklets are now available. But imagine if no-one had noticed; we might have had asylum seekers being verbally abused, discriminated against or unjustly imprisoned. We might have had drunken brawling and ugly arrests in our market towns after closing time. Thank goodness the real Britain's nothing like that. It can't be or I'm sure the booklet would have mentioned it.

Tony's round robin

24 December 2004

Every year the British PM sends a Christmas card to all the other prime ministers and presidents around the world. This year for the first time Tony Blair included an American-style round robin to tell everyone what Britain had been up to during the previous twelve months.

Well, it's been another wonderful year for us here in the Great British family. 'Reach for the skies,' I said to our football team as they set off for Euro 2004, and when it came to the penalty shoot-out that's exactly what David Beckham did. (Perhaps not the best moment to text him, Rebecca!) Meanwhile in Athens, Team GB did us all proud at the Olympics. A quick look at the medal table will confirm that Britain was right up there with Cuba and South

Korea, and it was quite obvious that not a single British athlete had taken any performance-enhancing drugs. Britain can also claim credit for some of the fastest running times ever recorded after some delegates spotted Sebastian Coe coming over to lobby them about London's bid for 2012.

The British royal family have been great ambassadors once again. Our heir to the throne raised some interesting points about people foolishly imagining they can just become head of state, which made us think maybe we should jump straight to William after all! Sadly we did lose our eldest royal, Princess Alice, who died aged 102. News of her death was greeted with a minute's silence (no, not as we tried to remember which one she was) and the family asked to have a quiet funeral so they could mourn in private and so that Prince Harry didn't punch any more photographers.

On the domestic front there was an awkward moment in the House of Commons when a Fathers 4 Justice campaigner caused an embarrassing scene. I had to say 'Shut up, David, you're supposed to be Home Secretary!' On another occasion I did get covered in purple flour (thanks to Bill and Hilary for the great suit-cleaning tips) but I think we were all relieved that we hadn't finally located those weapons of mass destruction! There was another huge demo by the Countryside Alliance, though I think the numbers marching may be exaggerated. My deputy pointed out that the police were probably making the mistake of counting the farmer's wife and his sister as two separate people! Meanwhile we have continued to make Britain a safer place, with immediate on-the-spot fines and anti-social behaviour orders for people who walk away from photocopiers leaving jammed paper in the feeder tray.

On a personal note, I announced that I would step down as Prime Minister at the end of the next parliament and I was touched by the distraught look on Gordon's face when I told him this. I also said that the moment I became an electoral liability for the Labour Party I would leave, at which point the whole Cabinet leapt up and held the door open for me, which just goes to show what a wonderful sense of humour we still have in this country!

The British army have been very busy as always, but times change and we are having to do away with some regiments (no, not by sending them to Fallujah, thank you, Jacques). Last year I said that there would be peace in Iraq in twelve months' time, and nothing has made me change my position that there will be peace in Iraq in twelve months' time. I was very gratified when President Bush told me that using British troops to replace Americans in the most dangerous zones this autumn was crucial to a victory he'd been planning all year. Indeed Dubya himself said that whenever he felt he might have been licked, he knew Tony Blair was right behind him. Like everyone else I watched the presidential election and after his success I called the President to congratulate him, told him I looked forward to our two nations continuing to work together and cementing our unique special relationship. Then the message tape ran out. On a final note, I'd just like to add how saddened we were by the death of the former President Ronald Reagan back in June. People used to joke that he was the most bigoted right-wing simpleton who would ever occupy the White House. Well, they don't say that any more.

Happy Christmas everyone – and a peaceful 2005. No, er, a prosperous 2005. No, er, look I'll get back to you . . .

Freedom of Information Bill

7 January 2005

This week the thirty-year rule was abolished. Actually it was abolished thirty years ago but they didn't tell us until now. Since 1 January we have been able to request all sorts of interesting information about the workings of government that was hitherto kept completely secret. For example, '30 November 2000: The Cabinet agree to pass the Freedom of Information Act. 1 December 2000: Cabinet order 350 paper shredders and the keys to Parliamentary archives. 2 December 2000: Cabinet spend three hours trying to sellotape together Magna Carta after erroneously feeding it through machine.'

As far as the government is concerned the Freedom of Information Act is a pain in the neck. With the worry that their every word will be made available for immediate public consumption, Cabinet meetings will now consist of various ministers waiting their turn to say things like 'By the way, I'm sorry I was late this morning, I was doing a sponsored fun-run for disabled children from my constituency. After all, children are our future and my only ambition in politics is to bring a little happiness into the lives of those less fortunate than myself.' There will still be just as many conversations to be had that MPs would rather keep to themselves, but now these will have to be conducted in hushed tones in places where no-one would ever consider looking for them, like in the chamber of the House of Commons.

The new act is also a splendid way to wind up a politician who might have annoyed you. Even a completely innocent minister might start to feel distinctly edgy when they learn someone keeps submitting written requests for the addresses of all motels he has visited after 11 p.m., plus details of his overseas bank accounts and a list of mobile phone calls made in the area around Soho.

So now the government is planning the second stage of the Freedom of Information Act, to extend it to the rest of British society. Ministers have realized that as soon as the rest of us start having to be as honest and open as we expect them to be, we'll soon be clamouring for the Act's immediate abolition. For example, as from next year married couples will be forced to disclose all information that is formally requested by their spouse.

'You were up late last night surfing the Internet, darling.'

'Yeah, just keeping in touch with the rest of the world, you know.'

'Yes, well, under the new Freedom of Information legislation, I'd like to see a full list of all websites visited please. Plus photo print-outs of any jpg that you enlarged.'

Children too will be able to demand honest answers to difficult questions: 'Why did Father Christmas give all my friends at nursery Playstation Grand Auto Drive-By Shooting 7 when I only got a soft toy and a sponsored donkey?' Elderly parents will also demand information that was formerly restricted: 'Yes, I know it seems odd that Keith has to work on Christmas Day. That's because he's really visiting his secret love-child from an affair he had with his life coach; we just hadn't been planning to tell you how everything got totally screwed up.'

Idle curiosity can be satisfied by demanding the truth from total strangers. 'Why do you have a stupid pointy beard?', 'Doesn't your midriff get cold sticking out like that?' or 'I like your convertible sports car. Do you in fact have a very small penis or is that just one of those myths?' The same strict regulations will be applied to businesses. It will now be the right of any television viewer to ring up the advertising agency responsible for the Cadbury's Happiness commercials and ask, 'Exactly which drugs were you on when you came up with this campaign then? I mean, did you genuinely believe that showing us an unconvincing talking puma strumming a guitar would make us want to buy your chocolate?' Sir Alex Ferguson will be forced to say, 'Obviously I knew it was a goal, but my players are under strict instructions to cheat.' If you are phoned up at home only to hear a recorded advertisement, you will now have the right to obtain the home number of the company's chief executive so you can ring him up in the middle of the night informing him that he's been selected for an exclusive opportunity to purchase the unopenable walnuts that have been on your sideboard since Christmas.

Within twelve months the whole nation will be clamouring for a Restriction of Information Bill. Newspaper editors sick of having their expenses published alongside details of how many glasses of wine they had before driving home will be demanding more privacy for politicians and celebrities. The National Archives will take all those dusty old papers down to the recycling centre as we revert to our historical culture of secrecy and obfuscation. And overseas observers will ask, 'Whatever happened to that Freedom of Information Bill you passed?'

'I'm afraid we're not at liberty to talk about that.'

Hitler Youth

14 January 2005

Yesterday's press review at Buckingham Palace was an awkward affair.

'I understand we made the front page of the *Sun* today?' said the Queen excitedly. 'Was it my tour round the new stable block at Sandringham?'

'Er, no, I don't think they covered that at all, Your Majesty.'

'Oh dear. Well then, it must have been Anne's attendance at the industry initiative luncheon.'

'Er, no, that didn't seem to catch their imagination either, Ma'am. For some reason they decided there might be more interest in this big photo of Prince Harry dressed as a Nazi.'

The Duke of Edinburgh was incandescent. 'A Nazi

armband! Do you know what Nazi means, young man? National Socialism! I will not have the British royal family being associated with these soppy left-wing views.'

'And it's bound to upset the Germans,' said the Queen.

'Let's keep your relations out of this, dear.'

The Duchess of Kent was just as upset. 'That was my dad's armband. Don't borrow it again without asking!'

As soon as the photo was published, the media's contrived outrage machine went into overdrive. Rabbis were phoned up and expected to have a view on whether the Nazis were goodies or baddies. War veterans were asked if having British royals sporting swastikas was an appropriate way to remember the British war dead. Journalists quoted those MPs who are always available for a comment: 'I'm sorry I am not in at the moment. However, I am shocked or disgusted because whatever it is, it's disgraceful and he or she should immediately resign or apologize or remove the said painting from the Tate.' Of course, the swastika has always been a symbol guaranteed to provoke instant outrage. It was the same when Adolf Hitler was photographed wearing a Nazi costume at Nuremberg. 'I'm sorry, I just didn't think,' grovelled the Führer, 'it was supposed to be a joke, I didn't mean to offend anyone.'

To help us put Harry's costume in context the *Sun* helpfully published a short history of the Second World War explaining that it ended in 1945 and that the Nazis lost. Blithely giving away the ending like this has completely spoiled those *World at War* reruns on the UK Nazi Channel. You'd think they could have put something like

'If you don't want to know the result look away now.' The paper also published a request for further information or more photos. 'Were you at the party? Ring us on this number. Forget the cost – we'll call back.' As if members of the British upper classes were thinking, 'I was going to stab my old friend Prince Harry in the back, but blimey, 10p to ring the *Sun*'s news desk – it's not really worth it!'

In fact he only wore the armband to distract attention from the fact he was holding a cigarette, so in one sense it worked perfectly. But officials at Clarence House agreed it was a poor choice of costume. 'I mean, the theme of the fancy dress party was "natives and colonials", and he went as a Nazi – it doesn't even work.' More relieved than ever that they managed to dissuade Harry from wearing his comedy Hitler moustache to the Cenotaph on Remembrance Day, his advisers are now engaged in a frantic damage limitation exercise.

Prince Harry has been told to do something to show himself in a more positive light.

'I could wear my Ku Klux Klan hood for Martin Luther King's birthday?' suggested the Prince helpfully.

'Hmmm, no, I don't think that quite does it, sir . . .'

'I know, how about a walkabout along Belfast's Shankill Road in IRA black beret and sunglasses? They'd love that,' offered the third in line to the throne.

What's almost as distressing is that taxpayers' money was spent sending this boy to Eton and this is the best they could do. Surely some sort of refund must be in order? Did Clarence House check the league tables for percentage of pupils gaining grades A–C in racial purity? So that's why his art teacher at Eton said she helped him with his 'A' level coursework; she had to paint over that great big portrait of Ribbentrop. Despite endless scandals and embarrassing gaffes these privately educated right-wing wasters are still the only people that the royals mix with; it's no wonder that our royal family have absolutely no idea about what is normal or appropriate behaviour. The fancy dress party in question was hosted by one of the pro-hunting upper-class twits who invaded last year's Labour Party Conference. The fact that one of the guests sold this picture to the tabloids tells us as much about their morality as Harry's costume. Last time he got into trouble for punching the photographer. This time you can't help feeling he was a bit slow off the mark.

Haven't you got second homes to go to?

21 January 2005

In the richer parts of our cities you often see mud-splattered Range Rovers or Volvos with stickers in the back window saying *Support Your Countryside Now*. Well, spending more than two days a week there might be a start. For the children of the rich it is not enough to have one doll's house, they have to have a second doll's house out in the sticks and every Friday evening the dolls pack up all their stuff and join the traffic queues heading out of town. The number of people with second homes has shot up as the gap between rich and poor has widened. Very few of London's homeless have a little cardbox box in Gloucestershire where they go at weekends.

The boom in second homes has turned some of Britain's prettier villages into ghost towns. Village schools, post offices, doctors' surgeries, these are just some of the buildings that are being closed though fortunately they can be converted into charming little bolt-holes. One angry villager organized a mass meeting about this problem but it was a Wednesday so everyone else was in Kensington. As local people are priced out of the housing market, jobs and essential services disappear. Few young people tell their careers adviser their ideal vocation would be popping into the Johnsons' cottage every Friday lunchtime to turn on the central heating.

But in Yorkshire they are finally fighting back. Soon cottages in the National Park will only be available to outsiders if they are deemed to be key workers essential to the traditional way of life in the Yorkshire Dales, i.e. vets, people making amusing films about vets and people putting up signs saying 'Welcome to Herriot Country'. Unfortunately, since estate agents could never qualify as key workers in any area, there'll be no-one to sell these people any houses any more. But from now on, if you want a second home in Yorkshire you will have to choose from some of the rougher estates in Rotherham and Doncaster. Ensuring that the remaining rural homes only go to local people will require an elaborate series of tests. For example, to qualify as a genuine Yorkshireman you have to be absolutely furious with the Labour Party. Not for stealth taxes or the war in Iraq but because back in the '80s they adopted a red rose as their symbol rather than the white rose of Yorkshire. Points are also scored for complaining about London beer or sending back an espresso coffee saying, 'Two bluddy quid? The cup's half empty!' Finally the interviewer will casually say what a good idea it was to divide Yorkshire up into metropolitan areas with names like Humberside and Cleveland and give a few bits to Lancashire. At this point the successful applicant should be convulsing violently and foaming at the mouth.

In other parts of the country many of our ancient parishes are already over-run with part-time visitors, which makes normal village life impossible. In Sussex, for example, locals at the Gatwick village feel completely swamped.

'Ooh-arr, there's a stranger in the Gatwick village!'

'Ee, and there's another one coming out of Sock Shop and look, two more heading for the sushi bar . . . They're bloody everywhere . . .'

A few years back in North Wales, this problem was tackled by burning down all the cottages owned by English weekenders. Fewer second homes were bought in that area, with the result that local families were finally able to afford to put a down-payment on their very own smouldering pile of cinders and ash.

Of course, you don't have to go to all the trouble and expense of buying a place in the country to enjoy the lifestyle of Britain's wealthier middle classes. When Friday evening comes around why not load up the car with chunky jumpers, groceries and wellington boots, then drive all the way round the M25, before heading straight home again and having a lovely relaxing weekend in the place where you live? Of course, by Sunday lunchtime you're already starting to sigh at the prospect of doing that four-hour drive all over again, but at least you've had a couple of nights in your own bed and you've finally met the people who live next door. Plus it's saved you all that effort of demonstratively closing the gate behind you or slowing down far too much for horses. Or why not decide to spend your money by just visiting different parts of the country? Rural communities would not be undermined and by continuing to go away every weekend you'd also be safe-guarding some of the traditional occupations of our inner cities – like burglary.

His-Tory paper

28 January 2005

Yesterday the Conservatives announced that they would make the teaching of history compulsory up to the age of sixteen. Below is an exclusive preview of the proposed Tory history exam paper.

History (British Empire and 1966 World Cup Final) Compulsory GCSE. Please write on only one side of the paper as this uses up more trees. Name (please put all your surnames; those at private school may use a separate piece of paper if necessary). On completing the exam you will be notified by post of your failure because frankly far too many children are doing well in their exams and what's the point in spending all that money if our kids don't come out top?

Part One

Q1. Who beat the French loads of times? (a) We did. (b) We really whopped them big-time. (c) Agincourt, Blenheim, Waterloo, Eurovision song contest 1976 – they never stood a chance! (You may tick more than one box – it's called multiple freedom of choice.)

Q2. Who beat the Germans in two world wars and one world cup? (a) That would be us plucky Brits again. (b) All on our own it was, with perhaps a little help from our good friends the Americans, but that's all, the Russian commies didn't do anything to help, especially that linesman at Wembley. (c) Winston Churchill was a Conservative, you know. And 'Nazi' is short for National Socialist.

Q3. The abolition of the slave trade was: (a) 'political correctness gone mad.' (b) The only way to set quotas for immigrants coming into the Empire. (c) Forced through Parliament by the Islington liberal elite who had no understanding of rural life in the colonies.

Q4. The olden days were much better because: (a) We began the industrial revolution without woolly environmentalists moaning about pollution and pandas and stuff. (b) There weren't all these petty bureaucratic regulations preventing young people from seeking employment in the chimney-sweeping industry. (c) We used to win elections.

Part Two. Now look at the map of the British Empire. Doesn't it make you feel good? See how big Canada looks? Okay, move on. Write an essay on one of the following questions (those at state schools just paint some yoghurt pots). Remember to use up all your allocated time before you realize there is another whole section overleaf.

1. Imagine the everyday problems confronting an ordinary family from the olden days. For example, father is sacked by the factory boss for going on strike. Mother takes the sick children to the hospital but is turned away. The family are evicted as they cannot pay the rent increases. (Marks will be deducted for confusing this period with 1980s Britain.)

2. Why was the Hundred Years War 116 years long? What does this say about the liberal teaching methods used for maths at the time? Describe how Conservative education reforms had improved numeracy by the time of the excellently titled 'Seven Years War'.

3. Write a profile of any one of Britain's greatest modern leaders. You may praise any politician you wish, irrespective of when she was Prime Minister.

4. Write an essay explaining how Anne Boleyn should have made more effort to make the marriage work.

5. Describe the influx of Normans from France in 1066 with particular reference to what it tells us about security at the Sangatte detention centre.

Part Three. You should now be one hour into your exam. It is likely that government education policy has changed during the past sixty minutes and another directive/press release has been dashed off saying that something else is compulsory. Please check with your invigilator; it may be necessary for you to complete the rest of the paper while jogging on the spot because we've just realized we had to cut PE to make room for history.

1. Explain how you have benefited from the compulsory teaching of history if it was a subject you would have chosen to drop. Is history more important than science, computer skills or learning a foreign language? Also, describe how a distorted, jingoistic view of history has held Britain back in Europe and has provided bogus moral authority to racists, football hooligans and the creators of *'Allo 'Allo*.

2. Write an essay analysing the behaviour of British opposition parties who know they are heading for defeat. Why do you think they make headline-grabbing policy announcements that are not thought through? Why do they imagine the electorate will not perceive that they are clearly unready for government? Do you think Michael Howard knows anything about ordinary schools having sent his own kids to Eton (who did such a fine job teaching history to Prince Harry)? Was it good judgement to launch a campaign celebrating British imperial conquests on Holocaust Day? And whose bloody idea was the slogan 'The Conservatives: We *are* history'?

You CAN kill a burglar

4 February 2005

There was no doubting the big story for middle England this week. 'You CAN kill a burglar!' screamed the front page of the *Mail*. 'You CAN kill a burglar!' echoed the front page of the *Express*. The identical headlines were in fact nicked from the London *Evening Standard* the night before, whose editor went straight round with his shotgun to test out the new guidelines.

These tabloids will soon be launching a range of competitions for their readers: 'Top a Robber and Win a Luxury Cruise!' 'Romford heads Dead Burglars League Table – House Prices Soar!' And look out for some unfunny cartoons of an English country home with stag's antlers above the fireplace, beside the stuffed head of a villain with a stripy jersey and a mask. Perhaps these guidelines are a trade-off with the pro-hunting lobby. They're not allowed to kill foxes any more, but if they leave the house unlocked at night, they can now sit on their stairs waiting to shoot anyone who climbs through the window. The Duke of Edinburgh was said to be delighted. The next time a protestor in a baggy Batman costume climbs up on to the balcony, Philip will be straight out there with his twelve-bore.

The Home Office leaflet was supposed to reassure the public that the forces of law and order are still on the side of the victims. The whipped-up fear of crime has not gone unnoticed at 10 Downing Street. Indeed, Tony Blair has been becoming increasingly paranoid about a man climbing over from next door to try and steal his job. Police said they couldn't help him, they were too busy looking for whoever it was who stole all the Tories' lines on law and order.

Even though the recent crime figures showed domestic burglary continuing to fall, crime, or rather the fear of it, continues to preoccupy a large swathe of the population. So this is just the first in a series of new guidelines to come from the Crown Prosecution Service; proportionate responses are also being recommended for other types of crime. You can't physically attack a litterbug for example – for that offence they suggest that you tut quietly and glare at them a little bit. If you are on the fast lane of the motorway and another driver overtakes you on the inside, you are urged to go dangerously close to the car in front to stop them cutting in. But you will be allowed to slap young boys sticking chewing gum in the coin slots of parking meters and if someone calls at your door collecting for a bogus charity the police say you may either (a) pull their hair or (b) give them a Chinese burn. But it should be stressed that physical attacks are permitted only for serious crimes like fraud, robbery and eating apples while driving.* And if you attack someone who turns out not to be a burglar, he may then seek official retribution, which would permit him to formally give you a dead leg and a poke in the eye.

For the CPS and the Association of Chief Police Officers to be telling people that 'A rugby tackle or a single blow would probably be reasonable' is very bad advice. What the leaflet should be saying in large letters is 'At all costs avoid getting into a fight with a burglar, it's really not worth it. You could never set that video anyway, he'll suffer enough when he tries to work out the 28-day timer.' Contrary to the impression that may have been given in old British films, if you break a vase over a burglar's head he doesn't roll his eyes and then swoon. He gets very cross and tries to hit you back and there is an outside chance you could end up being stabbed or, worse, receiving counselling from a police officer.

So in the event of a burglary I am a firm believer in the proportionate use of cowardice. Climb up into the loft and pull up the ladder. If your partner was too slow to join

* There was outrage this week that a motorist was prosecuted for eating an apple while at the wheel. Drivers heard about this story on their car radios and immediately rang each other to warn about this crackdown.

you, that's too bad, tell them they'll have to find their own hiding space. Trembling in terror should then be followed by acute embarrassment when you realize the gang of burly intruders was in fact a solitary fifteen-year-old. But the loss of property is preferable to risking serious injury every time. So what if he got your laptop? Yes it's a pain, but it was insured. Okay, it's got your files on it, but they were backed up. And all right, so he'll be able to see just how much money you lost on the Internet Casino when you were supposed to be working. 'Actually, come back here, you bastard, I'm going to kill you!'

Ils pensent que c'est tout fini

18 February 2005

This week another football landmark was reached when a Premiership team fielded an entire squad of foreign players. 'What is Arsène Wenger doing?' said the pundits. 'I mean okay, so Arsenal are 4–1 up, but they completely lack the home-grown talent of their opponents . . . oh hang on, now they're 5–1 up.' In fact it should have been six but we're stuck with these useless English referees. 'Where, oh where are the top British players?' asked a fan at half-time, sensing that he vaguely recognized the bloke serving him a reheated hotdog.

This milestone match came as UEFA were trying to establish quotas for domestic players, to compel European clubs to field a certain number of footballers from their own country. 'Oh great,' said the chairman of Monaco. 'So do I play Princess Stephanie up front or at right back?' And as for Vatican City's famous goalkeeper, well frankly, the physio is worried.* Most European associations are in favour of the idea of domestic quotas, realizing that it will help develop a stronger national squad and ensure match experience for their best players, but this week it emerged that FA Chairman Geoff Thompson was a lone dissenting voice at UEFA's meeting. A cynic might say that he was simply safeguarding the Premiership's position as the richest league in the world, but that would imply that English football is getting too commercial and I don't think anybody is suggesting that we might be approaching that point just yet.

There was a time when our national team was simply the cream of the best players in our top division but today if England played in the English Premiership they would struggle to finish in the top six (or avoid relegation if Graham Taylor was manager). We may yet see the captain of England lifting a cup above his head, it's just that we may need to prepare ourselves for it being the LDV Vans Trophy. There is no doubt that there's a crisis in English football – it isn't English any more. For younger British players coming up through the ranks this means less chance of getting into the first team and less likelihood of them fulfilling their potential as players so that they may never enjoy the happy and fulfilled lives of former football greats such as George Best and Gazza. For the clubs

* For much of the winter Pope John Paul II had seemed close to going to heaven. (The afterlife, not the gay disco.)

the influx of international talent has presented an enormous language problem and now the top players have to be tutored in the correct obscenities to scream at the referee. But outside football's elite there is a very real concern that unless action is taken the England team may cease to win international tournaments with the regularity that we've enjoyed over the past thirty-five years.

This issue is a strange twist in the traditional Marxist battle between capital and labour, for in this instance the worker becomes the commodity. Marx himself foresaw this syndrome: 'In bourgeois society capital is independent and has individuality, while the living person is dependent and has no individuality, unless that individual creates such wealth as to become the living capital – ' adding 'but what was Sven doing playing Andy Johnson on the wing, he's a striker, for God's sake . . .' Politically speaking the intellectual left should be in favour of the free movement of labour while safeguarding the employment rights of lower-paid workers in the same industry, all the time bearing in mind the over-riding philosophical consideration that it would be really brilliant if we could thrash Germany 5–0 in the World Cup final with a stunning hat trick from Wayne Rooney.

If English football is going to have to sacrifice foreign players perhaps a trade-off could be made in which we selflessly give up some of the English catering outlets around the ground. 'You can't have Louis Saha, but you can have a French patisserie in place of the pie van.' 'You can't have Jose Reyes but his brother is welcome to open a Spanish tapas bar next to the burger stand.'

Or perhaps the way to make it harder to bring foreign players into the Premiership would be to put Michael Howard in charge of the FA. Football stars wanting to come here from overseas would be detained for months in offshore prison ships, forced to undergo humiliating tests for HIV before being compelled to learn by rote the various triumphs of the British Empire.

'So, Thierry, hero of the French team. Who did Nelson beat then?'

'Er, Nelson? Did he maybe play for Preston North End?'

'He beat the French at the Battle of Trafalgar 1805, Garlic-breath, so that Britain wasn't invaded by thousands of Frenchmen and dominated ever-after by Gallic culture. Now send in Pires, Cygan and Viera, would you?'

Royal wedding: who's bringing the karaoke machine?

24 February 2005

There are times when the British establishment suddenly discover they have finally pushed the people too far and an angry backlash erupts onto the streets of England. So it was this week with the royal family's careless disregard for the Marriage Act of 1836. As buildings burned and angry mobs hurled missiles at a line of police officers, the government found themselves totally unprepared for the depth of feeling on this issue. 'The heir to the throne is constitutionally barred from a civil marriage service,' screamed the youths of Brixton over the noise of sirens and alarms. 'Yes, it's not enough to have the marriage formally blessed by the Archbishop of Canterbury – the subsequent 1949 statute is very clear on this,' shouted a masked anarchist as officers in riot gear found themselves forced back by sheer weight of numbers.

Finally the police had no choice but to unleash the ultimate deterrent. Crouched behind a burning van, an officer shouted through his megaphone, 'Disperse now! Or we will send in constitutional expert Lord St John of Fawsley!'

'He's bluffing!' said one of the rioters. 'They wouldn't dare.'

Suddenly an armoured police vehicle reversed at speed towards the mob, the back doors flew open and out stepped a dandy-looking grey-haired gent talking about his good friends Charles and Camilla . . .

'Arggh!' screamed the retreating crowd, blinded by his pink tie and blue striped shirt, but still he continued. 'There is of course a royal precedent for the monarch not attending an heir's wedding; if you go back to when the Duchess of Rutland was engaged to the Prince Consort . . .' he droned as Jennie Bond did her best to nod and look interested. Five minutes later the streets were completely clear and the big clear-up had begun.

It's not been the easiest of months for Prince Charles. First he announced that he and Camilla are finally going to do the honourable thing and get married at Windsor Castle. Then they discovered that this would mean having to let Barry and Shaz who work at the Drive-Thru McDonald's get married in the Queen's bedroom while she was trying to have a lie-in, so now the heir to the throne is getting hitched at the local registry office and then it's all over to the Market Tavern in Slough for the vol-au-vents and brown ale. This prompted the Queen to let slip that she isn't coming to the wedding after all as she had discovered she is busy that day watching Channel 4 racing.

'But, mother, you have to come – we agreed the date; Camilla might think you are freezing her out.'

'Camilla who? Never heard of her,' pouted Her Majesty.*

'Oh don't be like that. Just because you caught her trying on your crown. I mean, she wasn't to know it was yours . . .'

Like any mum the Queen finds it hard to deal with her little boy loving anyone else, even if he is fifty-six and it's high time he settled down.

'What happened to that other girl you were seeing?'

'We split up and then she died in a car crash, remember?'

'Well sometimes you have to work at these things . . . Anyway, I bought the bride this little jar of something by way of a present.'

'Sudan 1 Food Dye? Hmm, that rings a bell . . .'

Finally it turns out that the whole wedding is illegal anyway and that Thames Valley Police will wrestle Prince Charles to the floor the moment he tries on his morning suit at Moss Bros. But apart from all that, the wedding preparations couldn't be in better shape. Look out for

---

* The Queen did finally acknowledge the existence of her new daughter-in-law. She put a sticker in the back of her Range Rover that said, 'Warning! I slow down for Camilla.'

headlines revealing that the invitation to be best man has been accidentally sent to Andrew Parker Bowles and that Charles has booked the Paris Ritz for their honeymoon.

There have been question marks about the competence of Charles's advisers before this series of fiascos. Only last year there was that embarrassing evening when they'd been given the job of organizing a piss-up in a brewery, and they turned up at the wrong brewery, without a bottle opener, having only invited devout Muslims. The Lord Chancellor did his best to patch up the embarrassment by concocting a ruling that this union was legal 'because of, um . . . human rights, er yeah, that'll do . . .' Given their recent record, you would have thought the Human Rights Act might have been invoked to keep people out of the royal family. But what could have been a positive bit of PR for the royals has turned into a series of public humiliations. The newspapers of Middle England have been completely consumed with this soap opera, with each twist and turn filling the front pages and editorials on how the crisis might affect house prices. Thank goodness nothing important slipped through this week, like the introduction of detention without trial* or most of the country might have missed it. I never quite understood the role that the royal family played in the British government until this week, but gradually it is becoming clearer.

'Thanks for all your efforts, Charles, much appreciated.'

---

* Of course, no-one was suggesting a return to the days when the monarch could lock people up without charge. Now it would be down to the Home Secretary.

'You're welcome, Prime Minister. Oh and here's your invitation to the wedding.'

'Um, hang on a minute, that wasn't part of the deal . . .'

Identity theft: which one of you rings the insurance company?

3 March 2005

There was a big scandal at the Serious Fraud Office recently. It turned out they weren't the Serious Fraud Office at all, but a bunch of impostors. Identity fraud has been in the news this week with the publication of a *Which?* report claiming one in four people have been directly affected, while the rest of us just feel vaguely uneasy when we look at our bank statements and think, 'I don't remember going to a curry house after closing time that Friday night.'

There are many ingenious ways that criminals employ to get us to try and part with our money. (How was I to know that I hadn't really been specially selected for a free sample of Viagra?) But there is something particularly creepy about discovering there is a criminal out there

315

using your name and address in all sorts of dubious transactions. There might be a Blockbuster video card in your name that has you down as renting *Porky's Revenge*. Your Amazon account might show you ordering books by Edwina Currie. Your name might appear on a petition with which you don't particularly agree. Oh, no, that really was you; you were just too embarrassed to say no.

Simply by going through your rubbish, a criminal can get details of your bank account and bills and can see that you obviously have far too much money judging from all those organic yoghurt cartons. Just by sifting through your paper recycling, criminals can reconstruct your entire personality – 'She's addicted to *Puzzler* magazine, she reads the *Daily Mail*, she sends off for loads of Royal Doulton catalogues . . .' And then they think, 'Eurggh, I don't want an identity like that, thank you.' Obviously fraudsters are going to want to impersonate some people more than others. Rosemary West is probably pretty safe for the moment. I'm taking what steps I can against identity fraud by wearing particularly unfashionable and ill-fitting clothes, that should put a few of them off.

The Home Office are alerting people to this problem by running a TV advert featuring Alistair McGowan telling us how easily he could impersonate one of us. And it's true, he really does do a fantastic Mrs Johnson from Number 3, Station Road; it's much better than Rory Bremner's. Apparently these problems will all be solved with the introduction of identity cards, until the following week when the criminals start forging identity cards. But till then we have to take extra care to shred our bank statements, mobile phone bills and just trust the hamster not to piece his bedding back together.

It was back in the Second World War that encryption and technology began to really present a challenge to decoders. The Nazis believed their famous Enigma code to be impenetrable.

'I've had a brilliant idea for the four-digit code number we could use,' declared Adolf Hitler. 'How about my year of birth!' There was an uneasy silence among the assembled senior Nazis.

'Er, mein Führer – you don't think that might be a bit, er, obvious?'

'Nein, nonsense. And for the totally secret password . . . my mother's maiden name!'

Sadly it took the boffins at Bletchley Park three years before they tried these two options and the code was finally broken.

Today we are advised to have a variety of passwords and codes. This seems like the perfect solution until the waiter presents the little machine for you to enter your pin number just as you're finishing the second bottle of wine. 'Er, 1066 – no, that's my burglar alarm . . .' you slur loudly. 'Er, daughter's birth date? No that's my cashcard number. Try 1234,' you continue until the machine starts bleeping and flashing and the police van is pulling up outside.

Meanwhile today's impersonators are getting increasingly sophisticated, often operating for years undetected. Some years ago a young barrister submitted an application to get himself a Labour Party card. Using the name A. L. Blair he successfully gained access to one of Britain's main political parties, without anyone checking whether he really was committed to civil liberties or a major redistribution of wealth. Like many identity fraudsters he used more than one identity – sometimes he posed as a tough law and order man, on another day he might claim to be a friend of this or that celebrity. But over a period of years, millions of pounds that was supposed to go straight to the poorest in society was funnelled into private companies posing as deliverers of health-care or education. Using contacts in the United States, he diverted vast amounts of money into the Persian Gulf, funding activities that were later declared illegal. Apparently he's sending out a lot of unsolicited mail at the moment. Damn, that was the letter that persuaded me to send off another donation this morning . . . For one group of people have suffered from this type of theft more than any others: the socialists who have remained as Labour Party members – their identity got stolen years ago.

Red Nose/Rose Day (or 'O'Farrell realizes the election is approaching')

11 March 2005

Today is Red Nose Day in Great Britain. All over the country people will be dressing up and having fun while raising money for charity. Cardinals leading prayers for the health of the Pope will be wearing nothing but spotty boxer shorts. Policemen calling round to inform relatives that a loved one has been killed in a car crash will be wearing funny red plastic noses. And Sir Jimmy Savile will be sitting naked in a bath of jelly, making various farmyard noises and pulling funny faces, although this is nothing to do with Comic Relief, that's what he does every day.

There are of course those who prefer to remain aloof from the entire circus, who adopt a cynical air of politically superior contempt for the compulsory fun and zany vulgarity of it all. Janet Street Porter went on the record yesterday to proclaim that she hated Red Nose Day. 'The enthusiastic participants in Comic Relief are performers and singers with brands to maintain and . . . profiles to keep polished,' said the star of *I'm a Celebrity, Get Me Out of Here*.

'I couldn't agree more,' says eleven-year-old Kigeri from Rwanda. 'When I was a baby my parents were murdered in the massacre and then Comic Relief paid for my orphanage and my school. But frankly to see all those stars raising their profiles sickens me; I'd much rather go without the food and foster parenting scheme than have to listen to Dawn from *Monarch of the Glen* singing Abba hits out of tune again.'

What about the profits of the banks, goes the argument, what about the multinationals? 'Dawn, Lenny and their mates . . . should focus their attention on the fat cats in business who give so little,' says Spart-Porter. Yeah, right, that would get the viewers tuning in: 'In place of *The Vicar of Dibley* this evening, BBC1 presents Dawn French holding on the phone while she attempts to get through to the chairman of HSBC.' The real reason that many of the opponents of Comic Relief strike up this sneery posture is because they are worried that aligning themselves with this jolly shared national experience might make them look uncool. But if they think that dressing up and shaking a bucket is a little demeaning, they should try begging for food on the streets of Nairobi. It's rubbish, you get hardly anything, even with a red nose on.

Fortunately hostility to Comic Relief remains the

minority position. But virtually no goodwill is extended to another bunch of comedians who have done more for Third World Aid than Comic Relief could ever do. Since coming to power the Labour Party has almost doubled overseas aid, has written off 100 per cent of the debt for forty-one countries and led the campaign against poverty in Africa. And of course along the way they have also given us plenty of laughs as well. Who can forget the hilarious 'Prescott punches a voter sketch', or Tony's sweaty-shirt routine or Gordon's endogenous growth tongue-twister? Who would have missed Ron Davies declaring, 'I'm the only gay in the village!' Ordinary Labour MPs have consistently been prepared to make fools of themselves as they recited ludicrous lines they obviously never wrote themselves, but they knew it was worth it in the long run because people far worse off than themselves would benefit enormously. And just as with Comic Relief, it's not only in Africa that poverty has been alleviated; there are millions of people here in this country who are much better off because a few do-gooders put on a red rosette in the hope they could make a difference. Last year alone, the government's overseas aid budget was greater than all the money ever spent by Comic Relief over the past two decades. And by way of a bonus we never even had to watch John Prescott singing 'My Way' on *Celebrity Fame Academy*.

'Yeah, but I'm fed up with them now, it was all right when it started, but it's beyond a joke now,' say all the people who are willing to risk another government after

5 May. Well, that's your right, but like the people who sneer at Comic Relief, you're lucky you can afford to. It'll make no difference to you when Michael Howard slashes overseas aid, or cuts the minimum wage in the UK, and you can comfort yourself that at least you weren't tainted by associating yourself with that uncool bunch wearing red roses. Then when Michael Howard is waving on the steps of Downing Street you can tell the people who desperately needed this government to continue, 'But I thought everyone else was going to vote Labour, and I could keep my pride and abstain.' Only eight weeks to go, Friday, 6 May, Red Face Day.

England's national day, begorrah

18 March 2005

There are a lot of people waking up with hangovers this morning. From Cumbria to Cornwall, plastic shamrocks adorned the pub windows, the Guinness flowed to the sound of the *Riverdance* soundtrack as the English showed they really know how to celebrate a national festival. Okay it wasn't actually England's national day but at least when the Brits spilled out of the Irish theme pubs they went on to enjoy a traditional English kebab or chicken tikka massala.

Ireland just happens to have been in fashion for the past decade or so. Who knows, in a few years' time the trend might be for all things Siberian, and we'll be celebrating Russia's national day walking around in furry hats trying to launder money from illegally acquired oilfields. But yesterday's contrived parties demonstrate that England still does not have a proper national day of its own. We have the occasional royal wedding of course and next month gives us the chance to celebrate in the same manner as the royal family by staying home and reading *Sporting Life*. But there is no bank holiday in the calendar in which the whole country comes together and says, 'You know, when I think about St George and the fact that he was Turkish and was supposed to have killed a dragon, which is clearly nonsense, it gives me a really strong sense of who I am and what we stand for.'

It seems bizarre that the patron saint of the English is someone who's famous for killing an animal. If St George had done the deed in this country, he'd have faced angry demonstrators demanding the setting up of a dragon sanctuary. The government would have been forced into banning the hunting of dragons with saints, while the Countryside Alliance claimed that the reptile actually enjoyed the sport. England should have a patron saint who excelled in something we can identify with. St Cuthbert, for example, the patron saint of queuing. Or St Botolph, who Christian legend has it defied Roman planning regs and built a conservatory.

Another reason that we lack a meaningful national day is because we have never had a proper revolution. It looked possible for a moment when the BBC axed *One Man and His Dog*, but the English have never suddenly overthrown all the landowners and chopped their heads off. We were far more vicious than that, we made them open their gardens to the public and provide llama rides for the kiddies. Nor have we had to depose foreign rulers; the nearest the English have come to rebelling against an oppressive power was Hugh Grant being slightly rude to the American President in *Love Actually*.

So the search continues for an autumn bank holiday in which we can celebrate something that's important to us. The Tories have suggested 21 October become 'Trafalgar Day', which is as about as appealing as spending Halloween with Michael Howard. November the 11th is a possibility, but thinking about the millions who died in the trenches is not always the best way to kick off a party. 'Hmmm, there must be something in November to celebrate . . .' ponders the committee sitting around in Westminster, 'a day when people could let off fireworks and light great big bonfires, if only there was something already in place . . .'

This year is the four hundredth anniversary of the Gunpowder Plot. The official inquiry into the Gunpowder Plot is expected to report any day soon. Some say that this inquiry has been an expensive waste of time and money but at least we might find out why the conspiracy to blow up Parliament on 5 November really failed. Apparently Guido repeatedly tried to light the blue touch paper but it kept fizzling out, while his anxious wife called out, 'It says on the box that you're not supposed to go back to them – come and have some mulled wine and a baked potato.'

Guy Fawkes was of course the original terrorist. The fear of further outrages allowed the government of the day to curtail civil liberties and bring in all sorts of draconian measures, a response that obviously is hard for us to imagine today. As a Catholic plot, it was eagerly seized upon by the Protestant establishment as a perfect propaganda opportunity. 'The discovery of this fiendish plot of dire combustion shall be celebrated evermore,' wrote James I, 'by teenagers chucking bangers at the swans in the park, and the letting off of airbombs outside the old people's home at two in the morning.' And so four hundred years later from the beginning of October to the middle of November we celebrate the fact that an explosion didn't happen by letting off 2,000 decibel explosions in the shopping precinct after closing time and seeing how many fireworks it takes to set a telephone box alight.

But our national day is staring us in the face, we already celebrate it. The Americans let off fireworks on 4 July, the French let off fireworks on 14 July, while every autumn the English stand around in damp back gardens wondering why it is not possible to invent a Catherine wheel that actually goes round. Of course the events themselves vary from one area to the next. In Eastbourne, the public don't gather for the fireworks, they just watch the public display through their net curtains and then tut at the noise. In one particularly Old Labour council there were gasps of astonishment at the suggestion that maybe a woman could light the fireworks this year. Surely that's taking feminism too far. But the day that Parliament was saved should be celebrated as a national holiday – 5 November could become a party for democracy, the day we celebrate the Mother of Parliaments. Admittedly Westminster wasn't exactly a model of democracy at the time, though Jacobean Conservatives promised they'd have lots of black and women MPs in the near future. And we'd have to bury all that anti-Catholic stuff and ignore the fact that Guy Fawkes was probably fitted up by the West Midlands police force. But the fact that the Palace of Westminster survives is something to be celebrated and 5 November is the perfect fixture in our national consciousness for the mooted Autumn bank holiday. What's more English than standing out in the drizzle and watching expensive fireworks fizzle out? We could even have a slogan like 'the British Parliament – it's a real Mother!' Of course, Downing Street might need a bit more persuading but there's one argument that might just clinch it: 'We have to celebrate the Gunpowder Plot, Prime Minister – it was the last time the government found any weapons of mass destruction . . .'

Because this decision to honour our historic debating chamber couldn't be left to Parliament to decide, it would be imposed by the Prime Minister and the House of Commons would just have to go along with it. But it would be a holiday on which the people celebrated their chosen system of government and remembered where the power lies in this ancient democracy. 'Okay,' says the Prime Minister coming off the phone from Washington, 'July the 4th it is then.'

Speak of the devil

25 March 2005

Following a review of computer security at Conservative Party headquarters, the following document by the Leader of the Opposition was emailed to all the other political parties this week. Here we are able to reproduce the main points from all the keynote speeches to be given by Michael Howard between now and polling day.

Our slogan for this election is 'Are You Thinking What We're Thinking?' Common sense, fair play, respect for traditional values. Short sentences. Some without verbs. Or subject. Individual. Words. Saying. Nothing. I think the time has come to say, 'Enough is enough.' To stand up for the silent majority. An end to soundbite cynicism. Did you get that? It's got a ring, hasn't it – 'soundbite cynicism'?

This Labour government have accused me of desperation and bigotry. Of inspiring hatred against alienated minorities. No, I'm not talking about the Conservative Party. They somehow claim that my attacks upon travellers are just the thin end of the wedge and next I'll be desperately targeting other types of mobile home owners. Well, I'm sorry if it's not politically correct, Mr Blair, but it's time someone spoke out against some of these other groups of so-called travellers. We all know who we mean. Married couples in their fifties who take it upon themselves to go on caravanning holidays. 'Scum of the Earth' the *Sun* called them and here we have clear photographic evidence of one of these bogus 'sunshine seekers' attaching the tow-bar of the Alpine Sprite on to the back of his Vauxhall Astra. Using the Human Rights Act and the A303 Ilchester by-pass these so called 'middle-aged travellers' clog up the dual carriageway with their beige caravanettes and then turn up in Devon expecting to be put up in some sort of holiday camp. They claim they want to be part of mainstream British society and yet they insist on wearing these strange clothes: sandals with socks, crimplene fawn trousers and zip-up cagoules with a perspex map holder swinging around their neck. I spoke to one distraught local resident who told me how these outsiders had swamped the village and bought every last barbeque briquette at the Esso Mini-mart. But apparently we are not allowed to criticize travellers or anyone vaguely different or foreign. They say I'm constantly scrambling around for yet another group of overseas visitors to attack. Well, there is nothing desperate about repeating that a Conservative government will introduce strict quotas for so-called French exchange students. Under Labour, these Gallic teenagers have been arriving on our doorstep in ever-growing hordes, blocking the aisles in the Virgin Megastore and looking unimpressed in Madame Tussaud's. They come here on the understanding that they will learn English. But all they do is mumble an embarrassed 'no zank you' whenever you offer them microwaved pizza parcels or mini-chicken kievs and then spend the next hour on the phone weeping to their parents. Well, enough is enough. It's not racist to say we don't like the French because they are a bit smelly. It's just common sense.

No doubt Labour will accuse us of scaremongering about Europe. Of coming up with yet another Aunt Sally, or 'Tante Sylvie', as we are now compelled to call them. Many people are not aware that if Labour get back in they will allow the European Union to force us to adopt standardized European hand-signals. When you ask for the bill in a restaurant, you will no longer be allowed to mime scribbling on a piece of paper. It's true. You will have to pat your head and rub your hand in a circle on your tummy. Many people, especially pensioners, will find this very difficult. Sticking two fingers up at fellow motorists will also be replaced with a standardized European gesture of flicking your thumb from the end of your nose. Well, we in the Conservative Party give these barmy ideas the traditional English thumbs down, not the shadow-puppet mime of the little rabbit that we would be forced to adopt by Labour's friends in Brussels. But most of all I repeat our core message that this country should never have allowed in so many so-called asylum seekers. They came over here claiming they were escaping persecution and were welcomed to the shores of this tolerant and liberal country. Are you thinking what we're thinking? Yes, then they changed their surname to 'Howard' and then produced boys who grew up to be poisonous and opportunistic leaders of the Conservative Party – hang on, who the bloody hell's been tampering with my speech?

Michael Howard's unique anecdotal after-dinner witticisms will be available for your corporate events after 6 May. He will be available as an after-dinner speaker, a novelty Halloween party guest and for Channel 5 celebrity nostalgia shows. Please note that Michael will not be available after sunrise.

Pay a visit to the soul gym

1 April 2005

I became a blood donor recently. It was really very easy, there are just a few everyday questions that they ask you before you do the quote from the Tony Hancock sketch and roll up your sleeve. The trouble is that the precise nature of the questions makes it very hard to be sure you're giving an accurate answer.

'Have you accepted money for sex during the past five years?'

'Hmmm . . . five years? Let me think . . . No, I think it's just over five years actually . . .'

'Have you accepted drugs as payment for sex during the past five years?'

'Oooh, let me see, now when was the last time I did that exactly?'

'During the past five years, have you had anal sex with an intravenous drug user in any of these African countries?'

'Oh for God's sake, I don't know, you can't expect me to recall every subtle nuance of every single dinner party and book launch.'

The best time to give blood is the summer so that you can wear short-sleeved shirts that prompt people to ask why you have a plaster on your arm. Whether the blood is used to save a life is not actually the point; this wonderful outpost of the welfare state is actually there to provide a service for the donors. It's there to make people feel good about themselves for the rest of the week. Even if no-one notices that you are walking around with the inside of your elbow pointedly facing outwards, you still feel a munificent glow of moral superiority that goes some way towards cancelling out that Nestlé Easter egg and the way you cut up that Variety Club minibus at the traffic lights.

But giving blood is just one of a thousand ways in which you can selfishly make yourself feel better. Even more valuable than blood is time. All over the country people are needed to give up a few hours a month, help-ing out charities, becoming school governors or running voluntary organizations. 2005 is the official Year of the Volunteer and there is a Home Office website you can look at to see all the things you could do if you weren't so busy mindlessly surfing the internet. You can visit old people who live alone and have no relatives or friends, and then try and steer the conversation around to who they are going to leave all their money to. You could spend an hour or two helping in the Oxfam shop and be first to lay your hands on the latest batch of raffia-work table mats. You could mentor a young person who's been in trouble with the police, and drop hints about wanting one of those new 3-G mobile phones. But whatever you do you will find yourself in a win–win situation, because not only do other people benefit, but you gain an enormous amount too. How could you possibly feel worse after helping a former convict adjust to life outside prison? Well, you could be given Jonathan Aitken I suppose, but it's a long shot. But imagine the sense of fulfilment and well-being, meeting and talking to a former burglar about ideas for another job, passing him a cup of tea as you notice him clocking all the silver in your corner cabinet and writing down the make of your DVD player – hang on, this example is going nowhere, I'll start again.

The point is that as we head into an election campaign, we're going to be demanding more than ever that politicians do something for this group or that, but it's not just down to the government to make society better, it's down to us. And do not think that doing good work for others is the preserve of the left. Norman Lamont searched hard and low for a really good cause and settled on organizing a campaign for General Pinochet. Mary Archer worked tirelessly for the poor and oppressed Lloyd's names whose investments went down instead of up and were not offered millions in compensation. Let these good Samaritans be your inspiration. People take up jogging to get fit, and join book clubs to improve their minds, but how many of us ever visit the soul gym? How many of us stand in front of the bathroom mirror and sigh, and say, 'Oh dear, look how lazy and selfish I have got over the past few years, it's time I did something about it.' So make yourself feel better – volunteer to do something for someone else. Right, there, I've said it, I've done my bit. Now I can just send off a fiver to that Greenpeace campaign to adopt a whale* and then spend the rest of the year watching telly.

---

* The Adopt a Whale campaign ran into a few problems when social services kept coming round to see if people's homes were suitable. 'Our department can't help noticing that your home does not have any oceans.' 'No, it would be a big change for the whale, we're not denying that.'

A severe case of the blues

8 April 2005

It's been a tough week for Chelsea manager José Mourinho. His pay has been increased to £5.2 million and he doesn't have to go to matches any more. That's the sort of job I was looking for when I left university. They just never seemed to come up when you flicked through 'Creative and Media' in Monday's *Guardian*.

His punishment from UEFA meant that at Wednesday's Champions League game he was not allowed on the touchline, to talk to the players in the dressing room or converse with Chelsea staff in any way. He did think about secretly communicating a substitution but by the time he had texted Yves Makaba-Makalamby the game was over.

Banning football managers from the dugout seems like a perverse sort of punishment. None of the players understand those hand-signals anyway. Rolling your hands over one another; what is that supposed to mean? 'Gather up some wool while you're in defence' maybe? Moving the palms of your hands away from each other and then back together again? 'Pretend to be a seal?' Most managers scream and shout their instructions from the side while not a word of it can be heard above the din of the crowd. American footballers actually have little speakers in their helmets and individual instructions are communicated to them by radio. 'Um, throw the ball a long way!', 'Er, run and jump on one of the other players – sorry, I don't really understand this game at all.' And then of course the interference from another signal cuts in and the quarterback drives a taxi round to 87 Clarence Avenue to take them to the station.

The Chelsea boss was forced to watch his club's biggest game in years on the telly, which made for a very tense evening in the Mourinho household.

'I'm sorry,' said his wife, 'but I'm watching *Grand Designs Revisited* – you said you'd be out this evening.'

'But it's the quarter-final of the Champions League.'

'Well, you can record it.'

'No, not since we got cable; you can't watch one channel and tape another any more.'

As well as the two-game ban, Mourinho will now have to find a £9,000 fine out of his £5 million salary. That'll make him think twice. His massive hike in wages is actually a direct result of his spat with UEFA. Having behaved badly, Mourinho indicated that he was dissatisfied with the support he'd had from his directors so they immediately put his pay up four million a year. It was going to be three million but they forgot the biscuits with the coffee and he frowned for a split-second. Some have suggested that this salary might be slightly too high for the bloke who just picks the team. I have myself managed a football team so I know the pressure that Mourinho has to endure. Gudjohnsen's mum angrily demanding why he isn't on the starting line-up. Makelele bursting into tears because the ball was kicked at him too hard. Three of the players forgetting their boots and having to play in their school shoes; it's a very tough job. But you have to wonder if Chelsea's billions haven't completely distorted the English game. In the old days our football stars played for the love of the sport, got crippled by one crunching tackle and lived out their lives in abject poverty with arthritis and a drink problem. Marvellous. But today the ludicrous wealth of the Premiership's runaway leaders looks set to remove any element of competition. Next season they're ending any pretence and arranging the league table according to share value like the FTSE index. If Delia Smith can write another hit cookery book Norwich will be straight back into the top flight. But Abramovich can buy all the best players and hire the best manager and even afford spare printer cartridges for the office. You'd think with all that money that he could afford a razor, wouldn't you? And having bought the best team and coach, would it not be possible to purchase a better class of supporter, delightful though it was to be gobbed on by those Chelsea fans in the tier above us last time I sat in the away seats. We've been used to the top clubs being wealthy, but Chelsea's chairman is simply too rich. As it turned out, Chelsea thrashed Bayern Munich and played even better with Mourinho absent than they did when he was there. José's agent was straight on the phone. Either my client gets another ten million or he turns up to training on Monday . . .

~~Chelsea's wealth means they can brush aside any other club and it's clear that Liverpool will stand no chance against them over two legs.~~ But it's still eleven men against eleven, and I'm going to stick my neck out and predict that Liverpool will beat Chelsea in the Champions League semi-final and will go on to win the final in a penalty shoot-out having been three-nil down.

Time for a Muslim pope

15 April 2005

Things are not going well in the election for a new pope. 'I don't see the point in voting – it won't make no difference,' shrugged one gum-chewing cardinal in the Vatican yesterday. 'I mean, they all say that they're gonna bring man closer to God and all that, but nothing changes whoever gets in.' To counter this growing apathy among the senior bishops, new ways of voting are being piloted. A postal scheme was abandoned when over 1,000 ballot papers were received all proposing the same pontiff: an English councillor from the West Midlands. Papal candidates dressed in identical red robes have insisted that they are not all the same, while fears grow that indifference might encourage support for extremists who oppose equality for women, birth control and stem cell research – oh no, hang on, that's all of them.

But with faith under fire across the world and an increase in fundamentalism in various religions, the question that surely has to be asked is, 'Has the time come for a Muslim pope?' By electing a senior Islamic cleric the cardinals could avoid exacerbating the split in the divided Catholic church, while simultaneously holding out an olive branch to another great world religion. 'Ayatollah John Paul III' would then be in a position to bring East and West closer together, to end religious mistrust and oversee the introduction of halal Eucharist wafers. But frankly it looks like a long shot. After a considerable amount of research I have discovered that all popes have to be Catholic. Not even the Reverend Ian Paisley would be allowed were he to put himself forward.

Campaigning in a papal election is by its very nature low key. They can't pull off the same populist tricks as normal candidates; for example, for one of them to show off his new baby this week would be a definite minus, no question about it. They also have to appear neither to expect nor to seek the job. One archbishop lost support after he was caught ringing Vatican Autos to get a quote for installing a CD player in the Pope-mobile. The election process itself is steeped in tradition and ritual, so not much chance of introducing all-women shortlists. The cardinals are locked away in the Vatican, from where they do not emerge for many days until they've either selected a new pontiff or have been voted out of *Celebrity Conclave* by a TV phone poll after the video diaries. No, hang on,

I'm getting mixed up. They're not allowed TV, radios and newspapers; they're not even permitted to use mobiles to ring the bookies to put a bet on who'll be the new pope. They each receive a ballot paper which bears the Latin phrase *'Eligio in summum pontificem,'* which they then turn over in the hope that the answer is printed on the back. Having made their choice, they carry their vote to the altar and place the paper into a sacred chalice covered with a silver plate (except for cardinals from certain regions who are also electing their local councillors on the same day). Outside the Sistine Chapel, worshippers awaiting a decision look to the chimney for any sign of progress. Black smoke signals failure to reach a decision, white smoke conveys that a decision has been reached, and no smoke indicates that the Vatican converted to gas fires years ago and no one thought to mention it.

Electing God's representative on Earth is of course a huge responsibility. Choosing the wrong man could prove a major setback in the eternal war between good and evil. But beyond these traditional two camps a third way is emerging. For some time now, the bookies' favourite to win this election has been advocating putting aside all that negative old dogma of 'Get thee behind me Satan' and instead has called for a heaven/hell partnership which will benefit both sectors. 'Some people on our side have been too ready to demonize Beelzebub,' he says, criticizing former supporters for only ever seeing the bad side of eternal damnation. 'I think we should put aside these petty tribal loyalties about whether this person has horns or a halo, cloven hooves or a harp, and try to work together.' Of course, many cardinals are uncomfortable about this, but frankly the alternatives in this election look far worse. Perhaps that's why they are affecting indifference, because they'd rather leave the decision to someone else. But it's an age-old dilemma. Do you support someone who may be tainted and increasingly less popular or do you risk allowing the devil himself to rule? Surely that's an even easier question than 'Is the next Pope a Catholic?' You vote for the least worst of two options and hope that other bloke takes over in a couple of years' time.

Internet voter survey

22 April 2005

Late at night behind closed doors men across the country are secretly logging on to certain Internet sites and furtively entering a few details. They click their way through their private predilections and feel a shiver of guilty anticipation as they wait to see what will pop up on the screen. *Based on your answers you are a Liberal Democrat.*

Suddenly the door opens and a shocked wife is standing there in her dressing gown.

'What's that you have accessed? "You are a Liberal Democrat" – urgh, that is disgusting! How could you sink so low?'

'Darling, it just popped up on the screen! Honestly, all I did was tick the box saying I was in favour of higher taxes and banning smoking in public . . .'

'What if people find out you have these secret Liberal fetishes? Can the computer people trace your identity?'

'I'm not a Liberal, honestly, I'm Labour. Although if we had a local income tax . . .'

'God you've got it bad, haven't you? You can sleep in the spare room tonight.'

One of the unforeseen crazes in this general election has been the popularity of voter questionnaire websites. One of the most popular is HowShouldYouVote.com; then there are HowShouldIVote.com and Should-I-Bother-to-Vote.com but not many people have got to the end of that one. There is also one for teenagers: Which party would you support if under-18s were given the vote? (a) Dunno. (b) What election? (c) Beyoncé.

Because we so enjoy answering questions about ourselves, hundreds of thousands of voters have done one of these electoral tests and been quite surprised by the results.

'Oh dear, it says here that according to my answers I should be voting for the UK Independence Party or the BNP!'

'So what's the problem?'

'Well, I'm supposed to be the leader of the Conservative Party.' (This embarrassing Internet result comes on top of the Tories' other recent technical problems when the white hoods were all the wrong size, and the burning cross kept going out.) On the website The Public Whip I dutifully entered my postcode and as an experiment entered 'don't know' for every single issue. The website told me (and I'm not joking), 'You should vote Conservative in Vauxhall.' I actually found this vaguely reassuring. So that's who all those Tory voters are: the people who haven't got a clue about anything. On the site WhoShouldYouVoteFor.com, every single combination of policies seems to produce a vote for Charles Kennedy. I clicked on the dot for annexing the Sudetenland, declaring an Anschluss with Austria and invading Poland: 'Based on your responses you should vote Liberal Democrat in this election.' These sites are of course incredibly simplistic; your views on foxhunting are judged to be of equal value to your views on, say, the economy, education and the health service, which they are not; I feel far more strongly about abolishing those crappy little UHT milk capsules and that doesn't even feature. And not a single question asking if I was in favour of a weather report on *Newsnight*.* They also ignore local factors and the tribal nature of our political affiliations. I'm Labour, that's just part of who I am. Cut me and I bleed red. Oh, hang on, that's everyone, isn't it?

The worldwide web is a wonderful thing. But the Internet also has its hazards. For example, it's ages since I emailed my credit card details to claim that surprise win in the Nigerian lottery and they still haven't got back to me. And look at Robert Kilroy-Silk, a warning to us all of the dangers of buying sun-ray lamps on eBay. Clicking on

---

* There had been some minor controversy about having the weather on BBC2's flagship news show. Jeremy Paxman asked the weatherman whether it was going to rain this weekend, and then interrupted him seventeen times demanding a direct answer.

buttons in response to twenty questions cannot even begin to penetrate the complexity of the issues in front of us. Inside the brain of every thoughtful voter are hundreds of competing concerns and counter-arguments: 'I was against the war in Iraq but I'm in favour of Labour big increases in overseas aid.' 'I might be in favour of the Liberal's higher rate of tax, but I'd rather have Gordon Brown running the economy than – er, actually who would it be under them?' 'I'm concerned about some of Labour's negative campaigning but on the other hand I don't want to risk getting that racist vampire as Prime Minister.' And finally on 5 May it suddenly ceases to be complex and becomes incredibly straightforward as your mental cursor hovers over one simple last question. 'Who do you want to run the country for the next four or five years: Tony Blair and Gordon Brown or Michael Howard and Oliver Letwin?' Why would anyone need a computer to help them with that one? Remember, under Maggie Thatcher we never even had the internet. Do we really want to go back to those days?*

---

* Reading this back I am a little embarrassed at how clearly terrified I was that the country was about to elect Michael Howard as Prime Minister. It felt like we were that close to having a right-wing government bringing in private companies to run health and education while allying themselves with US Republicans and curtailing historic civil liberties. So thank God that never happened.

The view from overseas

29 April 2005

With only a few days to go, the British general election has caught the imagination of the entire world. Printed below are a selection of newspaper extracts that give the international view on the campaign.

Baghdad Times: Britain's fragile democracy hung in the balance this week as millions looked unlikely to go to the polls next Thursday. Unlike here in Iraq, where voters only had to defy death threats and dodge car bombs in order to vote, British electors are being kept away from polling stations by insurmountable obstacles such as 'not much caring for any of them' and 'wondering if it's a bit of a foregone conclusion' and the fact that *Footballers' Wives* is on Thursday evenings. Meanwhile, Saddam

Hussein said from his cell, 'What happened in Iraq is not a big issue for me. I want the British voters to focus on health, education and the economy. Will you let me out now? I want to go and canvass for George Galloway.'

Zimbabwe Daily News: President Mugabe has condemned the disgraceful state of British democracy as thousands of postal votes have been discovered to be from legitimate voters intending to vote by post. Asked to explain the huge increase in postal applications, a local council spokesman said, 'Well, with increasing apathy we were asked to promote the option of postal voting as a way of increasing turnout.' 'Oh,' said Mugabe. 'That does explain it, I suppose.'

Sydney Courier: Ozzy politicians have united in outright bloody condemnation at the vulgar and unseemly tone of the Pommy election campaign. 'Those bastards wanna learn some bloody respect,' said John Howard, 'especially that Lynton Crosby. Honestly, where do they get these scumbags from?' added Prime Minister Howard. On hearing the words 'Prime Minister Howard', a number of British holiday makers burst into tears and asked if they could apply for indefinite asylum.

Washington Post: There was no doubt about the big contest on everyone's mind this week. It was all to play for at the Cincinnati Hooverdrome for the final quarterdown of the semester as the Tampa Bay Beaver's new linebacker threw a twenty-two touchdown at the start of NFL's easy-over semi with fries. The offense sprang their wide-receiver on the Taco Bell Forty-niners, but the defense intercepted a whopper on rye with quarterbacks in the sin-bin hold the mayo looking heads up for the superbowl. It's okay we don't understand this either, but we daren't admit it or someone might say we're gay. Other news: London England. Prime Minister Blair apparently facing election. Many plan to vote against him 'to send message to Bush'. Oval Office responds: 'Whatever, I'm watching the game.'

Greenland Gazette: The entire Arctic ice cap melted this week and palm trees sprang up across the sweltering riviera of Northern Greenland as ocean levels look set to rise hundreds of feet leaving most of Western Europe under water. Meanwhile in Britain, the big issue in the election seemed to be National Insurance contributions.

Die Welt: Unemployment reached a post-war record of 12.7 per cent in Germany and 10.1 per cent in France last month. In Britain the number of claimants stands at 2.7 per cent despite predictions that Britain's minimum wage would massively increase jobless totals. 'This is all rather embarrassing,' said one English voter. 'We're doing our best to ignore it, but having the healthiest economy in the developed world goes against everything Britain has stood for, so most of us will vote against keeping Gordon Brown at the Treasury.' When asked whether this risked losing the minimum wage, sure-start and working families tax credit, the voter said he hadn't the faintest idea what we were talking about and ordered himself another bottle of wine.

Burkina Faso Newssheet: Give that Tony Blair a bloody nose! That was the verdict from the poverty-stricken villages of Africa watching the British election campaign.

Okay, so Labour have trebled aid to Africa after years of Tory cutbacks; sure they led the way on AIDS prevention and have cancelled 100 per cent of our debts – but the big issue here in sub-Saharan Africa is obviously the wording of legal advice given by Britain's attorney-general two years ago. Plus we don't like all that spin and sucking up to businessmen, so we say vote Lib Dem or Green or don't bother at all and see what happens. Because it won't be us who suffers if Labour lose power, the impoverished millions in the Third World, certainly not; it will be that Tony Blair, forced to eke out a living giving lecture tours in the United States. So come on, Britain, Africa urges you to vote for what's really important; an end to famine relief and debt cancellation to be curtailed. Ha! That'll teach Tony Blair.

Further overseas coverage of the British election is available on www.they-think-we-are-mad.com. We regret that coverage of genuine election issues is not available in British newspapers.

What I did in the election

6 May 2005

I was watching the Champions League semi-final when suddenly the phone rang. 'Who the hell is ringing me up in the middle of this?' I wondered. 'Hello,' said a recorded message. 'This is John O'Farrell,' continued my own voice. Oh, it was me. It was that appeal to Labour Party members I'd recorded earlier in the day. I hate those bloody things, especially when they ring again ten minutes later like this one did. 'I'm calling you because I believe this is important . . . ow, ow, I'm reading it, Alistair, let go of my arm . . .'

I have been involved in every general election since 1979 in some form or other. Since all my previous efforts had been so laughable, the Labour Party decided to head into the problem and this time asked me if I might be on hand for a few jokes during the campaign. But it's not always easy being humorous in support of the government of the day. You spend ages rewording gags that begin, 'Look, I was against the war and while we're on the subject there are quite a few other things that I'm not happy about but anyway, that Michael Howard . . .'

My first job was to write emails to the thousands of supporters (or otherwise) who in a moment of weakness had given their addresses to the Labour Party. I began by apologizing that they were getting another email asking for money but at least this one wasn't promising cut-price Viagra (at least, I think not, I hadn't read Labour's new pledge card). But my very first joke had to be cut. 'You can't put "Viagra", that word trips the spam filters!' Although these messages featured my signature at the end (just to assist any identity fraudsters out there), they were still official Labour Party communications so I was expecting lots of extended battles with the joke police. The first fundraising appeal began, 'Terrible news from the Labour Party accountants. George Galloway has finally remembered to cancel his direct debit.' Apparently this gag was touch and go for a while. 'Do we want to mention George Galloway? Won't that make our supporters immediately think of Iraq?' Then somebody at the top just went, 'Oh sod it! It makes me smile, leave it in.' And in the end pretty well everything I wrote was reproduced verbatim. And frankly I am appalled by the lack of control freakery in today's Labour Party! When the party's official magazine asked me to name a life-changing book, I emailed back:

'the book that changed my life was *Overcoming Tourette's Syndrome*, which I can tell you is a fucking corker.' And they went and published it! An email threatening to send round John Prescott to punch non-voters went out to thousands of computers across the land, including all the journalists and pundits. Visual proof that Labour's computer automatically crossed out the word 'socialism' was blithely distributed to a hundred thousand in-boxes around the country. But the wider message was, of course, we have a sense of humour about ourselves, we are not uptight, we are human. I think a few jokes just made people feel a little better about being in the Labour Party. The fundraising appeal raised over £50,000 in the first few hours, apparently rising to £110,000 within a couple of days. That was probably the most useful thing I have ever done as a political activist. And it certainly beats leafleting the Savona Estate.

Halfway through the campaign I was asked if I'd come and speak at a Labour Party rally focusing on world poverty. 'Who are the other speakers?' I asked casually. I had heard of several of them. One was the Prime Minister, one was the Chancellor and the name Bill Clinton definitely rang a bell. 'Best not argue about the running order,' I thought. And so in the spirit of World Poverty Day I went out onstage and did a load of jokes slagging off Michael Howard. Next up was Bill live from New York. Thankfully our speeches didn't overlap – in fact, he didn't have any Ann Widdecombe gags at all. He was nice about my speech though, which made me blush a little. Just before I went onstage the make-up lady had dabbed powder on my face. 'Hmm, you're a bit of both,' she said. I asked her what she meant and she pointed to the two shades of face powder she kept with her at all times. 'That one's Tony; that one's Gordon. You're a bit of both.'

I've never enjoyed an election so much, but now that it's all over I feel I should be going back to making jokes at their expense. It's important to maintain a certain amount of distance; after all, I wouldn't want to turn into some sort of court jester. Nice of Tony to send me a thank-you present though – I wonder why this floppy hat's got bells all over it . . .

Little Red Riding Hoodie

12 May 2005

What has happened to merrie England? Where once the sound of leather on willow echoed across the village green and rosy-faced English boys threw their grammar school caps in the air to celebrate their opponent's half-century, now the snarling gangs of hooded muggers stalk the graffitied concrete subways that have become jungle Britain. To read the papers this week, you would think that our society is on the brink of collapse from a chavalanche of scary teenagers. Tony Blair announced yesterday that one of the priorities of his third term would be to reverse the lack of respect in today's society, although it was hard to hear his exact words over all the shouts of 'Bugger Off!' coming from his backbenchers. Labour is set to tackle yob culture and anyone who disagrees with this idea will get a dead leg from John Prescott.

One of the surprisingly old-fashioned traits of this government has been its disciplinarian attitude to yobs, graffiti and anti-social behaviour. Who can forget the press conference when this was revealed?

'I really think the time has come to do something about nuisance neighbours,' said Tony Blair.

'Hmmm,' said all the political cartoonists, 'there must be an angle in there somewhere.'

'What I'm saying is that I, Tony Blair, who lives at 10 Downing Street, want to do something about having problem next-door neighbours.'

'Nope, beats me,' said all the humorists, scratching their heads and staring at a blank sketchpad.

'I mean, Gordon Brown, who lives at 11 Downing Street, will probably disagree with me again, but it's time for me to take him, I mean them, on.'

And the cartoonists gave up trying to find a satirical angle and went back to doing Mrs Thatcher as a mad cow again.

The issue has been forced to the top of the political agenda by the unlikeliest of social commentators. Bluewater shopping centre decided it was time to face the muzak. They have banned the wearing of hooded tops and baseball caps anywhere inside their private retail park. Can there be any greater punishment than being banned from one of Europe's largest shopping malls? What sort of existence is it when you are not allowed to go into Clinton Cards and browse through the Garfield fridge magnets? Of course, you'll still be able to buy base-ball caps and hooded tops in Bluewater, it's just if you say, 'No, I don't need a bag, I think I'll keep it on' you'll be wrestled to the ground by security guards the moment you walk out of the shop. Why hooded sweatshirts should be the most offensive item of clothing I don't understand. I'd ban those mustard-coloured corduroys that sloanes wear with stripy blue shirts and tweed jackets. And no business-man should be allowed to appear in public with a zany tie: 'Look at me, I'm a little bit unconventional. I've got a tie with brightly coloured Disney characters on it. And look, my cufflinks are miniature rugby balls! I'm mad, me!'

One attempted solution to our apparent yob culture has been the introduction of the ASBO. The hope was that once they had received an anti-social behaviour order, foul-mouthed drunken yobs would revert to wearing blazers and grey flannel shorts, as they knelt by the fire-place completing wooden jigsaws of the old English counties. Of course, middle-class communities do suffer from intimidating residents as well. The sort of people that tut at you for getting the wheelie-bins mixed up. However, the real victims of anti-social behaviour, of crime and intimidation, are the poor. And it's bad enough working long hours for no thanks and very little money without being slapped in the face and having the incident recorded on a video mobile for broadcast on Bravo's new reality TV show.

But while there is an issue out there that does need

tackling, I can't help wincing at the way a Labour government manages to sound so illiberal and right wing every time they talk about it. We've got the ASBO, now I'd like to see the introduction of a new legal power, the anti-*socialism* behaviour order. 'Anthony Lynton Blair,' declares the judge, 'you are accused of sounding offensively right wing in a manner likely to cause extreme distress to Labour Party members and everyone who resigned from it ages ago. You are hereby banned from talking about the wonders of private sector investment, the legal restraints facing our police force or what it means to be British within 500 metres of anybody carrying a copy of the *Guardian*. This anti-socialism behaviour order will remain in place until you put up the minimum wage again. Right, next case: call the Rt Hon. David Blunkett . . .'

The last farmer in England

20 May 2005

From special hide-outs constructed in the English countryside you can still occasionally spot them. Eager naturalists crouch for hours behind binoculars for a rare glimpse of the once common English farmer, before fleeing in terror as a rogue male suddenly starts stomping towards them bearing a double-barrelled shotgun and shouting, 'Oi! Get orf my land!'

This week it was declared the British family farm will soon be a thing of the past. Despite the billions that have been spent attempting to preserve their natural habitat, the last few breeding pairs may be about to disappear from our landscape. The writing has been on the wall ever since they knocked the second word off the title of *Emmerdale Farm*. It was simpler than calling the show

Emmerdale Farm and Holiday Lets and Heritage Centre Gift Shop and Off-Road Rally-Cross Track Available for Stag Parties and Executive Weekends.

In recent years British agriculture has been based on the same principle as cooking vegetables for the children. There is no demand for the cabbage, you know it will not be consumed, but you still have to go to all that trouble of optimistically putting it in front of them before scraping it into the bin. But now with reform of the Common Agricultural Policy, Brussels is seeking to shift the emphasis from food production to making the farmer 'the steward of wildflower meadows and cover for ground nesting birds'. That's a euphemism for 'unemployed bloke who lives next to abandoned overgrown field'. Nobody quite knows what to do with all this land. It doesn't pay to grow crops on it, it doesn't pay to graze sheep on it; even British wind farms are uneconomic – apparently it's cheaper to import our wind from Kenya. For years tourism has been a bigger earner than agriculture as people flock to visit the beautiful British countryside. Workers in the expanding tourist industry will need more homes of course, so most of the picturesque rural scenes will soon be covered in three-bedroom maisonettes, while ramblers walk alongside the dual carriageway clutching an old Ordnance Survey Map scratching their head.

Farming has always been a tough business. Who can forget that tragic scene in *Far from the Madding Crowd* when Gabriel Oak watches his entire flock of sheep plummet off the edge of the cliff as the man from Brussels explains the economic logic of this new policy. But the past decade has been harder than ever, with BSE, foot and mouth, and having to listen to Otis Ferry going on about the hunting ban. But the difference between agriculture and other threatened industries is that while the likes of miners and steelworkers tended to support a political philosophy that chimed with their demands for state intervention and subsidies, the only things farmers have been planting recently are great big 'Vote Conservative' placards at the edge of all their fields. While the farmers' greatest enemy was the greed of the supermarkets, the Countryside Alliance felt more comfortable marching against a Labour government carrying out its pledge to ban hunting. Where were the banners declaiming Asda and Sainsbury's? Why were they not storming into Tesco Metro to dump manure, paint slogans and get a pre-washed rocket salad for their tea while they were in there?

Of course, a true humanitarian would sympathize with any exploited workers on the basis of their plight, irrespective of their personal political views. Yeah, right, like any of us are going to stand shoulder to shoulder with someone wearing a Barbour and a tweed cap. Just as Amnesty International refuses to help prisoners who have committed violence, so socialists should refuse to support anyone in green wellingtons and an olive quilted gilet. Sorry, you might be ruthlessly exploited by the capitalist multinationals, but you have a Countryside Alliance sticker in the back of your 4x4, so you're on your own, pal. Frankly any more moaning from Tory front organizations and us city dwellers will have to begin some sort of co-ordinated fightback. We'll start going down to the countryside and deliberately leaving gates open. We'll speed up for horses.

So somebody needs to explain to the Conservative voting shires that it is simply no longer cost-effective to keep farmers on these huge tracts of land. The only way to make them economically viable is to intensively rear British farmers in huge barns where thousands of them can be kept in semi-darkness and fed mashed-up infected sheep pellets. The farmers always said there was no room for sentiment in agriculture so we'll take them at their word. Above the deafening noise of a thousand farmers all bleating about the hunting ban and the French, you'll occasionally hear the rumble of a few euros tumbling down the gulleys into each tiny stall, but it will be nothing like the ludicrous cost of the outmoded free-range farmer. Of course, some townies will say this all sounds rather cruel, but these people don't know anything about the ways of the countryside. At least, what we used to call the countryside, before it was all sold off for Barratt homes.

And now here isn't the news . . .

27 May 2005

It was a rude awakening for Britain on Monday morning when the radio alarm went off. Sarah Montague was sounding distinctly like Nicholas Parsons. 'That's odd . . . someone's been talking about dunking biscuits for ten seconds and hasn't been rudely interrupted by John Humphrys yet.' Replacing the *Today* programme with *Just a Minute* proved so popular with listeners that in future this approach will be used with politicians: 'Er, well, with respect I don't think that is the question you should be asking me. This government has brought down the rate of increase year on year . . .' at which point a buzzer goes off and the minister is challenged for deviation, repetition and hesitation.

With this week's BBC strike, the worst prophecies about

what life would be like under a Labour government became a chilling reality. Power cuts, rubbish piling up in the street and we couldn't even bury our dead. Well, it was nearly as bad; there was a new bloke presenting your local news update. In fact a whole cast of understudies were given their big break on Monday. This was their one chance. And, boy, did they blow it. 'And in Essex Vinnie Jones visited-ed a school at a school today. Er, today. (Glances nervously at notes – looks at wrong camera.) He was there to promote locally grown British food grown locally (turns to camera two just as new vision mixer switches to camera one) er, locally as part of a campagney, sorry "campaign" – you don't pronounce the "g", do you? Where was I?' she continued while the caption 'SCAB' flashed on and off at the bottom of the screen.

Strikes like these are deliberately engineered by the establishment to try and flush out subversives in the media. There is no third way with a picket line. If you cross it you are clearly Thatcherite, union-busting scab scum and will be cast as a baddy in the moving West End musical of the dispute in twenty years' time. If you refuse to cross you will be named and shamed by the *Daily Mail* as one of the Trotskyite infiltrators into the Bashing Britain Corporation who should never again be allowed to report on the Chelsea Flower Show. Experienced BBC presenters knew that the trick was to avoid having to reveal their personal politics; Andrew Marr, Natasha Kaplinski and Jeremy Paxman stayed away and shall be forever portrayed in Soviet-style banners beside Marx and

Lenin. Whereas Terry Wogan, like any emergency worker, felt compelled to turn up for duty, for without his Radio 2 show pensioners might have gone without light chat and the easy listening songs of yesteryear. Evan Davies failed the test but few lefties noticed because they never listen to the business report anyway.

John Humphrys was told not to come in. This was nothing to do with the strike, he was just told not to come in. Other TV celebrities will be judged for evermore for the way they responded to the call from their union. Smudge the *Blue Peter* cat showed complete contempt for the strikers by turning up for work as normal. You could always tell she was a closet Tory by the way she just lay about on the bean bag expecting everyone else to do everything. Meg, the *Blue Peter* border collie, was conflicted. The picketers told her to stay but then management told her to come, and the poor dog just barked desperately wanting both sides to love her.

It's not just the number of dismissals that angers the unions – it is the manner in which they are planned. BBC office managers will be lined up on stage and then Simon Cowell will tell them that they are a disgrace to the industry: 'That was the worst attempt to reload a photocopier paper feed tray I have ever seen in all my years in the business,' he'll spit, as they run to the wings in tears to be comforted by the other contestants. Now another strike is planned for Tuesday or Wednesday, depending on the long-range weather forecast for half-term week. The quarrel will escalate while Dr Tanya Byron talks to management through a radio mic about where they are going wrong. But celebrity presenters will not be able to keep making excuses for not being at work; now we want to see them joining the picket line with the lower-paid workers who have helped make them rich and famous. For I cannot think of a situation in which it is acceptable for a union member to cross an official picket line. All right, unless the strike was purely about saving the local weather after the main weather – in which case I think we would all have a duty to rush past the pickets chanting our support for management cuts. And now that same column all over again in your local area . . .

Every road a toll road

10 June 2005

Yesterday the transport secretary announced the introduction of road charging as the only way to avoid total gridlock by 2015. The speech would have got a rapturous reception but most of his audience were still stuck on the A406 Hangar Lane gyratory system. The big idea which will be piloted within the next five years is that cars will be charged for every mile that they drive, with their movements being constantly monitored by a satellite tracking system. 'It's just like Big Brother!' proclaimed one opponent while everyone else scratched their head wondering what this had to do with a bunch of twenty-something wannabes in their underwear locked in a house and talking about themselves. The satellites will have the technology to track every vehicle travelling down every single road. Digital messages will be beamed instantly from vehicle to space station and relayed immediately down to the Driving and Vehicle Licensing Authority in Swansea, where each docket will be processed in eight to twelve weeks.

Satellite tracking technology is already fitted to many new cars, whose drivers now have to put up with having a computer constantly nag them about which route they should take.

'Take the next left,' says the mellow electronic voice. 'NO, NOT THIS ONE!'

'You said left.'

'I meant first proper left – this is a drive-in McDonald's!'

'Why don't you bloody drive if you're so smart?'

'Because I'm a computer. Anyway, why do we always have to go and see your relations? You never take me back to Dixons . . .'*

Now the same basic technology can be used to track all British motorists so that instead of the flat annual road tax, we'll have to pay according to the distance travelled. Families will receive an itemized bill at the end of each quarter.

'Hang on, I never took the A22 to East Grinstead on the 23rd.'

'Oh, that must have been me. I have a secret lover I have been seeing while you're at work.'

---

* These machines now come with different settings according to what sort of driver you are. Switch it to 'Joyrider' mode and the voice says, 'Accelerate at speed, spin the vehicle round three times and then roll it down an embankment.'

'Oh that's all right then. I knew it wasn't me because I would have taken the A264.'

Different roads will be charged at different rates. The residents of tree-lined avenues in Surrey will probably start petitioning to have higher charges to keep up appearances. But every road in Britain will effectively become a toll road (except perhaps the drive out of north-east London to get to Stansted Airport – they should pay us to do that one). The scheme is bold and will be unpopular with all the Alan Partridge types who make up the motoring organizations, but we have to do something to reduce the use of cars. I have made it a point of political principle to only use my car for journeys that are absolutely essential and could not be made by any other mode of transport. So maybe once a week at the most I will use it to pop to the supermarket. Oh, and to take all those books to the Amnesty shop. And then there was the garden centre on Sunday and football, and running the kids to swimming and then down to my parents and that lovely drive through Richmond Park . . . but apart from that I barely use the car at all.

Having an on-board meter telling the driver how much each journey is costing is the surest way to discourage unnecessary journeys. Parents will be able to charge teenagers for twenty minutes' waiting time. The only downside is that with all these extra satellites up in the sky, there will be a serious problem of space congestion, which may necessitate the introduction of satellite charging. Owners of satellites will have to pay a small charge calculated by special tracking devices fitted to cars going round and round the M25. The government has said that the scheme will not be used for general tax raising, but this seems to be a wasted opportunity. The combustion engine is a major cause of global warming; it doesn't seem unreasonable that motorists should pay a bit more towards the cost of half the country being submerged by water. The motor car was the great success story of the twentieth century, but now we have to be persuaded to return to walking and cycling. With car-tracking satellites and on-board computers, we've come a long way since every car had to be preceded by a man on foot waving a flag. Except that now the man with the flag would have to keep stopping and waiting for the traffic to catch up . . .

What about a little five-card pension?

17 June 2005

Our twenty-first-century civilization may not produce the drama of the Tudors or the paintings of the Renaissance, but when it comes to playing poker on the Internet, we are living through a Golden Age. It seems that after a hard day in the office staring at a computer to earn a few quid, people like nothing better than sitting in front of their home computers and losing it all again. Playing poker online is just like the real thing. You are dealt a few cards, you bet, you raise the stakes and finally you reveal your fantastic hand.

'Ta-da! I win.'

'No, a straight flush beats a four of a kind, doesn't it?' asks the computer.

'Er, not sure, I thought that two pairs beat a flush?' comes another message.

'Not a royal flush, surely?'

'Well, I think the kids have been mixing the cards up because I've got a Top Trumps stegosaurus.'

Later this month will see the biggest share flotation for years as the company behind the highly profitable online gambling site PartyPoker is listed on the Stock Exchange. PartyGaming is valued at £4.73 billion, which is co-incidentally the same amount I've lost attempting to play online poker. The current turnover is huge, with up to 80,000 people playing at any one time, which is why thousands of investors are apparently so eager to invest their hard-earned cash in latest-craze.com.

People are attracted to online poker because it gives you the chance to try your hand at being a cool, card-sharp hustler, while sitting at home in your dressing gown and slippers. There are no people to see you blush and no-one to witness what an idiot you were to bet your last few quid on a pair of nines. The secret to gambling of course is if you lose some money, then bet a whole load more so that you can win it all back. That always works.

The old adage that the only way to make any money on the horses is to open a bookie's is equally true for the digital age. In ten days' time the four owners of PartyGaming will come into fortunes of around a billion pounds each as they sell a company which they set up less than a decade ago. Of course, it's all very well, these entrepreneurs putting years of their working life into a gambling website, but there's no spiritual fulfilment in a job like that. I mean, if you're a teacher or a health worker, you may not get a huge salary, but you go home feeling that you have improved the world a tiny bit each day. What do the owners of PartyGaming think last thing at night? 'What am I going to spend my billion pounds on?' Pah, where's the job satisfaction in that? Mind you, it's hard to begrudge these tycoons their massive windfalls when you look at all the worthy causes they have supported in the past; setting up sex chat lines, graduating into online pornography, before finally cashing in on a craze that has seen an increase in gambling addiction. No-one deserves a billion pounds each more than them. It's comforting to know that there is some natural justice in this world.

The only cloud on the horizon for the richest yet dot.com billionaires is that they could face jail in the United States. Although the Internet may know no borders, their company's wealth has been built on accepting credit card payments from a country where they knew this sort of gambling was illegal. We could yet see a high-profile gambling trial with lawyers trying to outdo each other on the poker puns. 'My client may have kept his cards close to his chest, but I can assure you that his company is no busted flush . . .'

Whether the internet billionaires appreciate the seriousness of their situation is not known.

'So this is like a virtual prison you are sending us to? In cyberspace, as it were?'

'No, it's a very real prison, with big metal bars and locks on all the doors.'

But this might be worth bearing in mind if you were thinking of investing in the safest bet since Shergar had to outrun those two Irish blokes with the lasso and the motorbike.

Thankfully most of us are far too sensible to get sucked into any sort of serious betting. Except, of course, your pension fund will probably be invested in PartyGaming shares. Strange that Washington doesn't have any problems with that sort of gambling. Still, it's only a bit of fun, isn't it? It's just a little flutter.

'Excuse me, what happened to all that money that I put aside for my retirement?'

'Oh, well I don't know if you remember way back in 2005, there was that brief online poker craze, and they floated the company and, well, we invested the pension fund in that and, well, who'd have thought it: the bubble went and burst! We lost it all on a gambling company! Isn't that ironic! Er, sorry.'

The Wiki-column

24 June 2005

Following last week's 'Wiki-torial' experiment by the Los Angeles Times *allowing readers to rewrite its editorials on the Internet, this week's comment piece has been communally created by readers in an exciting online search for impartial and well-judged analysis.*

So, Bush and Blair, your oil turns to blood for you, the Satan God-heads let Armenia earthquake be your warning (Leviticus 11.3) you will reap on the day of your blood-ness judgement and twin towers (zion money?) for AIDS you have created with your so-called 'scientists', your blood-dollars will be paid you in HELL.

   Sorry, can we start this Wiki-column again, this time without the nutter? And try to make sure the piece is pertinent and well-judged, with no axes to grind and no personal agendas. Come to the Kohi Noor Tandoori in Twyford. Try our delicious chicken patia and pilau rice. 'My favourite curry house!' says TV's Carol Vorderman. Oh and no advertising either! The piece is supposed to be about the concept of the 'Wiki-torial'.

This week the *Los Angeles Times* attempted to allow readers to rewrite its editorial over the Internet. The notion comes from the online encyclopaedia Wikipedia, which can be written by whoever wishes to contribute articles or amendments (this is more like it). However the newspaper's courageous idea was fundamentally flawed, not because democratic debate can never produce universal consensus (this is good stuff) but because the hell-born Prince Charles who murder Lady Di for oil will face Lucifer as Prophets foretold when flood and fire consume Zionist assassins of Bhopal (Isaiah 12.4) for USA death-heads knew but kill when Bush father CIA tell them for their blood-dollars. Oh no, he's back, look can't we block certain bloggers from accessing the computer or something? Okay, so the 'Wiki' concept of constantly evolving prose may sound democratic in principle, but can often mean that what appears to be an authoritative consensus is simply the mindset of the last person to have accessed the article. Furthermore, the BBC really ought to get that Noel Edmonds back on the screen, he was great with his Mr Blobby and his brightly coloured sweaters, that was proper family entertainment not like all this reality TV rubbish you get nowadays and I'm sure he'd be willing to renegotiate a lower fee, so come on, BBC, bring back Noel! *Furthermore*, the value of the evolving online encyclopaedia is obvious when it is providing incontrovertible facts, but opinion and comment must always be subjective and so comment pieces such as this one will never have the freedom to advocate provocative opinions without another contributor deleting or contradicting it. Yes they will. No they won't. Yes they will. They won't. RU up 4 sx? DP & 69 pics and vids click here. Is there really no way of controlling this? Our tandoori curries are cooked in the traditional style, we have Indian lager and Carlsberg and also English dishes available. Is this the Destiny's Child web-log? No, it is a communally written comment piece on the concept of Wiki-torials. Is it true they're splitting up? Who? Destiny's Child. I got a text from my mate.

Let's start again. Last week's experiment by the *Los Angeles Times* was abandoned after the quality of the editorial content rapidly descended. At 9 a.m. on the Saturday a carefully considered 1,000-word analysis entitled 'War and Consequences' was wiped and simply replaced with a more concise analysis: 'The Bush administration should be publicly charged for war crimes and crimes against humanity.' A few hours later the editorial simply said 'Fuck USA' and the final self-appointed leader writer did away with words altogether and replaced them with explicit images. So can there be a future for mature and considered 'Wiki' comment? Well, I reckon Beyoncé will be bigger than ever. *Noel's Houseparty* or *Multi-coloured*

Swapshop, they could bring back either of them. Or both, I've got time. Why not try our tandoori buffet? Look, my point is, there are quite enough narcissistic diarists, paranoid schizophrenics and tiresome conspiracy theorists on the web without lending them the unearned authority of a world-class newspaper. The purpose of leader writers is to lead opinion not to relay the point of view of the last person to shout the loudest. Let that be the final word on the subject. But Pentagon bloodheads you will not conquer (Deuteronomy 3.1); your weapons to drug dictators for mind-sleep suits Bush/Blair Satan-plot (Noriega) but Challenger disaster (foretold) prove judgement day now upon you the devilry of US computer mind-virus.

Actually, I have read nuttier stuff in the *Guardian*.

This Wiki-column experiment has now been terminated. With thanks to the thousands of registered users who attempted to contribute to an interesting column free of cliché. It's just a shame that a small minority had to spoil it for everyone else.

379

Blair guitar

1 July 2005

In the run-up to the G8 conference and Live8 Tony Blair has been saying all the right things about debt relief, Africa and European food subsidies. But still Bob Geldof hasn't invited him to come and play on the night.

'I mean, I only live down the road, Bob, and I've got my guitar here and everything . . .'

'I think we've got enough bands thanks, Prime Minister.'

'Oh, cos I can play the first bit of "Stairway to Heaven". And "Smoke on the Water" and the opening chord to "A Hard Day's Night" and then Paul McCartney could maybe take it from there?'

'This concert is to make you lot do something about global poverty.'

'Yes, of course. I just think it might help me understand

the issues more clearly if I could get to riff with Sting.'

In Paris, Jacques Chirac has been busy organizing a massive charity concert of his own to raise money for French farmers. 'Look, we need your money! Give us your f***ing money!' he implored. 'These cows are down to their last thousand euros, for God's sake.' Meanwhile George Bush is still struggling to put on his 'Make Poverty History' wristband without taking his knuckles off the ground.

The G8 leaders meet next week to discuss world poverty while spending ten times the global aid budget on subsidies that drive Third World farmers out of business. That's like a gang of burglars emptying every house in the street and then using their final victim's front room for a Neighbourhood Watch meeting. In Europe the inequities of our Common Agricultural Policy produce some shocking statistics. Did you know that the European Community actually pays for every Welsh sheep to have its own wide-screen plasma TV and DVD player? Twenty-pound notes are actually taken away from Oxfam and shredded to provide bedding for French battery chickens. Live8 tickets are in such short supply because under EU finance arrangements, two-thirds of the tickets have to go to Belgian dairy cows.

In fact the real statistics are not that much more ludicrous. For example, Britain's richest man, the Duke of Westminster, received £448,000 in CAP subsidies last year. Without this subsidy his pheasants would simply have to be taken out and shot. Or what about the fifteenth Duke of Bedford at Woburn Abbey? You can adopt an animal at his safari park for as little as £50 but the Duke himself is a little more expensive. He's already sponsored by the EU, who pay him over £1,000 a day. For that, the EU commissioners get a photo of the Duke, a car sticker and the chance to come and watch him at feeding time. The European Commission insists that the Common Agricultural Policy is there to help the smaller farmers. Small farmers like the Queen. Last year Her Majesty received £545,897 in CAP subsidies. An attempt to discuss this with the Palace was unsuccessful. 'Ooh-arr, my wife Liz can't talk to you right now,' said Farmer Phil, chewing on a piece of straw. 'Er, she's been up since 4.30 a.m. milking the cows! What's that, Liz? You've got to worm the heifers? Oh no, don't wear your white gloves when you're putting in bovine pessaries . . .'

It may suit Britain's political purpose to use this week's events to draw attention to the inequities of the Common Agricultural Policy, but Tony Blair and Gordon Brown are right to do it. With Britain's EU presidency starting today, and the political momentum built up by Live8 and the 'Make Poverty History' campaign, the hosts of the G8 summit are in their strongest position ever to confront the causes of global poverty. More importantly, it annoys the French. Wanting fair trade and an end to hunger and disease is all very well, but the commendable cause of annoying the French should never be underestimated. When Jacques Chirac insists he will allow no further changes to the CAP, Tony should say, 'I'm sorry, mate, I can't understand a bloody word you're saying. Can't you speak English?'

'Either the French delegation agree to the abolition of the Common Agricultural Policy,' threatens Gordon, 'or it's turkey twizzlers for lunch.'

We have to do something to make the rest of the world see sense. Tomorrow the rock stars will take one day out to pressurize British politicians to do something they have been working on for years. Britain has led the way in cancelling debt and campaigning for increased aid and fair trade. Maybe Tony Blair really should pick up his guitar to make other world leaders sit up and listen. 'Guess what, guys, I've re-formed my college band – I thought we might sing you "Feed the World". Obviously this would only be a final threat. There's enough suffering in this world already.

London wins Olympics – drugs test demanded

6 July 2005

It was an awkward moment as Jacques Chirac arrived at Gleneagles to shake the Queen's hand. The tension was not helped by her majesty putting her thumb and forefinger up to her head to make a letter 'L' and shouting 'Loser!' Tony Blair stepped in to avoid further humiliation for the French President, offering him a drink before dinner.

'London Pride, Jacques?'

'Quoi?'

'Are you a bitter man? Or do you feel like a good wine?' continued Tony as the other G8 leaders suppressed their giggles behind him. 'Do come through to dinner, we have some lovely British food tonight. Apart from the pudding, which is Finnish actually.'*

The winning of the London Olympics was the antithesis of the usual British sporting experience. Normally we allow ourselves to get swept along by our own optimism, telling each other 'I think we could really do it this time' and then we witness another humiliating penalty shoot-out and kick the TV screen in disgust, but, being English, miss the telly altogether and hurt our foot on the video. This time we doubted if we had a chance and then went and won it. A united Britain achieved something together and best of all there was no petty in-fighting or party political point scoring, so well done Tony Blair, Ken Livingstone, Tessa Jowell and apparently there was some Tory runner bloke involved as well.

Wednesday's events were dramatic and exciting. Seb Coe made it to the podium without being overtaken by Steve Ovett at the last minute. David Beckham was asked if he was taking part in the pole vault and explained that no, this was in fact his wife Victoria. Ken Livingstone and Princess Anne anxiously held hands under the table waiting for the result. IOC delegates were apparently attracted by the idea of an Olympic village in Stratford, which they vaguely remembered as a beautiful old place from that documentary on William Shakespeare. But the

* Jacques Chirac had recently rubbished British and Finnish food. Some suggested that the two lost Finnish votes cost France the Olympics, although it may just be that the Finns wanted the Olympics to be in London so they could sample our delicious microwave pepperami noodles.

masterstroke was getting thirty kids from the East End to make up part of the delegation which swung wavering voters who hadn't yet noticed that their mobile phones had gone missing. As the word 'London' was read out, astonished cheers went up from the British delegation and hundreds of cameramen realized they were pointing at the wrong part of the room. It didn't matter because photos of disappointed weeping Frenchmen were in huge demand from the British tabloids. 'Les Misérables,' screamed the *Sun* next morning, adding, 'Sacha Distel, Toulouse-Lautrec, Camembert, Astérix, Descartes . . . your boys took one hell of a beating!' If we can keep up that sort of Olympic spirit, it should be a wonderful games.

Meanwhile the television news was endlessly repeating the footage of cheering Brits jumping up and down in Singapore or waving flags in Trafalgar Square, and interviews with ecstatic British Olympic heroes like the Bronze medallist in the 1964 women's fencing. Schoolchildren cheered, unaware that they will be cynical teenagers in seven years' time and will think the whole thing is fascist. Frail pensioners in day centres were shown cheering the announcement until a care worker leaned in to whisper that this event would be taking place in 2012 and then the old people seemed to go rather quiet. Jets flew overhead trailing the red, white and blue of the national flag, although the stripes rather tactlessly produced the French tricolour.

The news was unequivocally good; this simply wasn't the right moment to play that footage of grumpy

Yorkshiremen moaning about paying all that money for 'bluddy Lundun'. A mass self-hypnosis descended on the country as we pretended that we'll be able to sustain being positive about something like this for more than a week or so. We may not hold that many world records, but Britain is about to pull off the fastest backlash ever. Team GB is tipped for a gold in the downhill whinge. It will be no time at all before the whole country is moaning about the cost, reminding each other that we may have won the Games but we're not going to win any medals and explaining that the stadium is never going to be ready in time. 'What a waste of money, not like the Dome, at least that was popular . . .' 'Blair for the high jump over Olympics,' the headlines will read; 'Red Ken red-faced over Olympic chaos'. That is why the Games are so important for this country. It will provide something to gripe about for seven whole years. But if we are really going to plan to think long-term, we should put in an immediate bid for the 2016 Olympic Games. Then when we don't win them we can all complain about our dismal failure. 'We never get anything like that, we're an international laughing stock, we really are.'

NB. This column was never actually published. London only felt like a great place to live for about twelve hours; the morning after the Olympic announcement bombers randomly killed over fifty people so comedy was not really the order of the day.

Harry Potter and the Cauldron of Clearasil

15 July 2005

Waterstones are opening at midnight tonight and I for one am determined to be there the moment the doors open and the crowds rush in. 'Hello, I wonder if you can help me. I'm looking for something on the Franco-Prussian war.'

'Er, well, we're mainly selling the new Harry Potter book tonight,' shouts the bookseller over the noise of the mob crushed against the tills clutching the new J. K. Rowling.

'Yes, I'm particularly interested in the siege of Paris and Gambetta's escape from the city – but there don't seem to be any shop assistants in your history department downstairs.'

'Er, well, there might be something about it in this

book here – *Harry Potter and the Half-Blood Prince*.'

The Harry Potter hype is now in full flow. I've just received an email from Amazon, telling me that 'extra owls have volunteered to help muggles get their copies of *Harry Potter and the Half-Blood Prince*'. This is clearly not going to work. What they need is a van. The publicity has been given a shot in the arm by the new pope, who it turns out condemned the Harry Potter books when he was a cardinal. 'You never know where these things are going to lead,' said the former Hitler Youth member. In the broadsheets social commentators will try once again to dissect the Potter phenomenon. 'In a way Harry Potter is an allegory for New Labour. The first book was published in 1997, yes, that's perfect, and while we were enchanted by the magic for a while, er, Harry Potter's cuts to lone parent benefit, no, hang on . . .'

Of course, with Harry Potter himself now reaching adolescence it's going to be much harder for us to like him. A mumbling zit-covered selfish fifteen-year-old thinking permanently about sex is a challenge to any author. In the new book, *Harry Potter and the Cauldron of Clearasil*, the teenage wizard doesn't actually appear before page 200 because he won't get out of bed until half past one in the afternoon, when he finally stomps down the stairs heading straight for the front door.

'Where are you going, Harry?'

'Out!' he grunts, slamming the door behind him. Occasionally he manages the odd conversation with an adult.

'I don't want a broomstick – Nimbus 2000s are poncy. I want a moped.'

'You're not having a moped, they're too dangerous.'

'You're ruining my life! I'm going to kill myself.'

'You can't kill yourself, Harry, you're immortal.'

In this sixth adventure there are also hints that Rowling is keen to give her stories a little more resonance with present-day Britain, such as the chapter when Hogwarts fails its Ofsted and is reopened as a City Academy specializing in Business Studies and Maths. There is also a pertinent scene in which none of the broomsticks will get off the ground because Hermione and Ron Weasley have grown so obese from eating nothing but crisps and burgers. Finally the pupils pass their exams but decide not to go to wizards' university because they don't want to be paying student debts till they're in their mid-forties.

But of course there is a dark side. Religious groups warned us of the dangers of dabbling with witchcraft and the dark arts but no-one could have predicted quite how much suffering would be inflicted upon publishers as a result of the Harry Potter phenomenon. Thousands of god-awful manuscripts have been sent in to agents and editors from members of the public who thought they might have a crack at this children's fiction lark. 'I could never write a proper book, so I thought I'd write a book for kids.'

The sheer scale of J. K. Rowling's sales has made it fashionable to deride the Harry Potter books, but their success in getting children to read should not be taken for granted. Never before have schoolboys hung around the cloakroom comparing the size of their hardbacks. Many young readers have raced through her books and then had the confidence to attempt more challenging titles, like the Quidditch World Cup PS2 game or the Lego Creator Hogwarts Express CD-Rom. Rowling herself has been quietly generous to various charities and has used her position to push for having her books published on ancient-forest-friendly paper following a campaign by Greenpeace. But her mistake of course was to sell too many books. There is nothing more vulgar in literary circles than selling too many books. Many authors are secretly jealous of her enormous success and would dearly love to attempt something similar. But the rest of us learnt long ago that artistic merit is what really counts and no-one ever became a great writer belatedly trying to cash in on the success of others.

John O'Farrell's new book, Barry Potter and the Su Doku Code, *is published tonight at midnight.*

Goodbye and thanks for the letter

23 July 2005

This will be my last column for the *Guardian*. No, really, after five years and hundreds of columns the point was fast approaching where I was going to have to write jokes about the Euro Constitution so I thought I'd better just get out while I could. Recent events have not made it easy to feel funny about what's going on around us, but that's not why I'm off. In fact, if anyone asks, I am leaving the *Guardian* in order to defy terrorism. That'll show them. In truth I just fancy a break from this sort of writing. There are only so many gags you can come up with about Alan Milburn. Anyway, I'm sure there are plenty of younger, leftier, funnier columnists waiting in the wings. Apparently that Michael Howard's going to have some time on his hands soon.

I realized that I have been writing topical jokes pretty well non-stop since the mid-1980s. Back then topical satire really stood for something, and Mrs Thatcher was eventually forced to resign after our mad-cap Radio 4 show suggested that she was perhaps a bit of a fascist.

'Oh no, Dennis,' she wept, 'they've compared me to Herr Hitler and he was, like, really, really right-wing.'

'I'll go and pack the bags, dear.'

In fact, I think I have come to the conclusion that most political jokes probably have the opposite effect to the one desired. You have a bit of a laugh about something and you don't feel so angry any more. What's more, the political leaders themselves are generally flattered by the attention.

'King Vlad – the satirists have come up with a nickname for you! They have dubbed you Vlad the Impaler.'

'Ha ha ha, oh yes, that's very good I like that! "Vlad the Impaler". They are clever, aren't they? I'd never noticed that about myself before . . .'

'Oh well, they always overemphasize one minor attribute. Now, erm, any chance of lifting me off this sharpened stake, Sire?'

Today in Indonesia and Iran political comics are arrested and tortured. In Britain they are invited to the Stakeholders and Satirists Buffet Breakfast at Downing Street. The received wisdom within the Guild of Satirists is that it is better never to meet your targets lest you become corrupted or bewitched by the *Führerkontakt*. I can think of no other branch of writing where knowing your subject matter is considered a bad thing. What this maxim really means is, 'You don't want to know the truth. It's boring. They're human.' The most important thing for any writer is honesty, as I always say to Martin Amis when he rings me up for advice. If you were writing a vicious caricature of a politician based on their brutal policies but found them to be charming and interesting on a personal level, then that apparent contradiction should make your exposé all the more fascinating. You take all that complexity into account and then the carefully considered three-dimensional portrayal becomes your magnum opus – a sketch in which the Maggie Thatcher puppet whacks the latex Geoffrey Howe over the head with a cricket bat. Anyway, no self-respecting humorist would ever allow a bit of familiarity or flattery to blunt their satirical scalpel. Though the other day I was at a Fabian Society event and Charles Clarke crossed the room to tell me how much he had enjoyed my new novel. And do you know, I was left thinking that Charles Clarke really is a man of exceptional judgement. I mean, putting my own shallow vanity aside, our Home Secretary really knows what he's talking about. Identity cards? Fine by me if he thinks they're needed. Remote-controlled electric-shock collars for disruptive pupils? Well, hear the guy out, he talks a lot of sense you know.

Can you be a cruel and 'hard-hitting' satirist after you have got to know some of the people in government as I have? Probably not. Can you still be a topical comedy writer? Certainly, and I would always much rather make a good joke than a good point (he said, making a rather dry and humourless point). It might suit my comic purposes to say that all politicians are corrupt and evil and mad, but it wouldn't be true. Many of them only fit two of those adjectives. There have been times when I've written a column and felt that I've not been completely honest because it was funnier to simply sneer than to be ambivalent or unsure. Was it fair of me to get laughs out of the suggestion that Jeffrey Archer was a dreadful, vulgar and lying egomaniac, who wrote crappy books and deserved to go to prison? OK, bad example, yes, it was. In fact most of my columns have not been about party politics at all but about all the other stupid and bizarre things that clutter up our news pages. And in the future, when something really funny happens in the news, when John Prescott punches Mark Thatcher and knocks over the cake at Charles and Camilla's coronation, I will think, 'I wish I still had my column.' I'll miss your postcards and emails and having my dad ring up and say 'This week's was your best column ever', as he has done every week. I will of course continue to pen those hilarious parodies of right-wing columnists that I've been doing in the *Mail* and *Express* under the guise of my fictitious creations like 'Quentin Letts' and 'Melanie Phillips', even though many people still believe my satirical spoofs to be serious pieces by real commentators. When I was asked to appear on *Question Time* as both myself and my ludicrous creation Janet Daley of the *Daily Telegraph*, it was the quick-change restaurant scene from *Mrs Doubtfire* all over again. But for now it's goodbye and thanks for the letter. As I said to that couple we met on holiday, we'll definitely keep in touch. If you see me cleaning your windscreen at Vauxhall Cross traffic lights, please give generously. I hate emotional goodbyes, so, er, I'll text you. It's been a privilege and a pleasure. But there are new challenges ahead, it is time to begin a whole new career – as 'That Bloke Who Used to Write in the *Guardian*.'

Bye-bye.

OTHER BOOKS BY JOHN O'FARRELL

Carrot – How One Root Vegetable Changed the World

In 1708, Sir Piers Mainwaring was despatched from the court of Queen Anne to the Himalayas to secure a trade agreement with the powerful Mongol empire that would outmanoeuvre the Dutch and corner the vital trade in balsa wood that was crucial to early-eighteenth-century English commerce. Instead he brought home a vegetable so exotic, peculiar and delicious when roasted with just a small knob of butter that it transformed the fortunes of the Royal Navy and precipitated the expansion of the British colonial territories into the greatest empire the world had ever seen. At once a travelogue, detective story and vegetarian cookery book, this thrilling account of Sir Peregrine's journey was nominated for the 2003 Kohl-Rabi Award for the best non-fiction book about a root vegetable.

Manners Maketh ~~Money~~ Man

How small does the last bit of poppadom have to be before you stop breaking it in two? Is it bad manners not to reply to a round-robin email that the sender has forwarded to everyone in their address book? What about getting off your face on Bacardi Breezers and vomiting undigested kebab on the back seat of the night bus? This modern-day Debrett's guides you through all the niceties of twenty-first-century etiquette, explaining how very rude it would be to rush out a book on manners when all the other publishers were already doing one.

Also available on audio, read by Gordon Fucking Ramsay.

To Chav and Chav Not!

A hilarious look at the dreadful working classes and how vulgar and amusing they are! Includes Wayne Rooney's *History of Western Philosophy*, the rules to 'Burberry Bingo' and a guide to getting your baby's ears pierced while they are still in the womb. Plus how you can get a dozen chunky gold rings for under a tenner (nick them).

'This book is even thinner than I am!'   Victoria Beckham

'I feel some vexation that there may exist a soupçon of snobbery, nay, even anthropophobia when one beholds the inimicality shown towards the ersatz sans-culottes.'   Jade Goody

Binary Sudoku

The ultimate in mathematical brain teasers. John O'Farrell takes the hugely popular Sudoku craze and reinvents the puzzles in binary form.

1	0
0	1

	1

0	

1	

Just as in conventional decimal sudoku, every row and every column must contain *all the digits*, with no number in any line being repeated. Only this time you can only use binary numbers! The first one is done for you.

'Minutes of entertaining filling in!'   Carol Vorderman

AN UTTERLY IMPARTIAL HISTORY OF BRITAIN (OR 2000 YEARS OF UPPER CLASS IDIOTS IN CHARGE)
John O'Farrell

Many of us were put off history by the dry and dreary way it was taught at school. Back then 'The Origins of the Industrial Revolution' somehow seemed less compelling than the chance to test the bold claim on Timothy Johnson's 'Shatterproof' ruler. But here at last is a chance to have a good laugh *and* learn all that stuff you feel you really ought to know by now . . .

In this 'Horrible History for Grown Ups' you can read how Anglo-Saxon liberals struggled to be positive about immigration; 'Look I think we have to try and respect the religious customs of our new Viking friends – oi, he's nicked my bloody ox!' Discover how England's peculiar class system was established by some snobby French nobles whose posh descendents still have wine cellars and second homes in the Dordogne today. And explore the complex socio-economic reasons why Britain's kings were the first in Europe to be brought to heel; (because the Stuarts were such a useless bunch of untalented, incompetent, arrogant, upper-class thickos that Parliament didn't have much choice).

A book about *then* that is also incisive and illuminating about *now*, '2000 Years of Upper Class Idiots in Charge', is an hilarious, informative and cantankerous journey through Britain's fascinating and bizarre history. As entertaining as a witch burning, and a lot more laughs.

9780385611985

NOW AVAILABLE FROM DOUBLEDAY

Doubleday

MAY CONTAIN NUTS
John O'Farrell

'O'FARRELL IS A CONSISTENTLY HUMOROUS WRITER WITH
AN ACUTE EAR FOR THE ABSURDITIES OF MIDDLE CLASS
PRETENSION. IT'S HARD TO FAULT HIS SATIRE ON
COMPETITIVE PARENTING OR HIS CONCLUSIONS
REGARDING SOCIAL INEQUALITIES'
Mail on Sunday

Alice never imagined that she would end up like this. Is she the
only mother who feels so permanently panic-stricken at the
terrors of the modern world – or is it normal to sit up in bed
all night popping bubble wrap? She worries that too much
gluten and dairy may be hindering her children's mental
arithmetic. She frets that there are too many cars on the road
to let them out of the 4×4. Finally she resolves to take control
and tackle her biggest worry of all: her daughter is definitely
not going to fail that crucial secondary school entrance exam.
Because Alice had decided to take the test in her place . . .

With his trademark comic eye for detail, John O'Farrell has
produced a funny and provocative book that will make you
laugh, cry and vow never to become that sort of parent. And
then you can pass it on to your seven-year-old, because she
really ought to be reading grown-up novels by now . . .

'O'FARRELL IS ONE OF THE BEST CONTEMPORARY SATIRISTS
IN THE BUSINESS AND HE HAS MIDDLE CLASS PUSHY
MOTHERS DOWN TO A TEE IN THIS LATEST TOE-CURLING,
HACKLE-RISING CHRONICLE OF HYPER-PARENTING . . . THE
ONE-LINERS ARE SUBLIME AND THE COMEDIC SITUATIONS
UTTERLY HILARIOUS. DON'T MISS THIS'
Daily Record

'O'FARRELL HAS SCORED A BULLSEYE WITH THIS
SATIRICAL SALVO . . . TAPS INTO MIDDLE ENGLAND'S
NEUROSES WITH TERRIFIC WIT'
The Herald

9780552771627

BLACK SWAN